The
BOVEY BOOK

The story of a Devonshire town in words and pictures

The BOVEY BOOK

The story of a Devonshire town in words and pictures

Compiled by Veronica Kennedy

for the Bovey Tracey Heritage Trust

Cottage Publishing

(In association with Forest Publishing)

First published in 2004 by COTTAGE PUBLISHING, Bovey Tracey, Devon TQ13 9AE (Tel: 01626 835757), in association with:–

Forest Publishing, Woodstock, Liverton, Newton Abbot, Devon TQ12 6JJ

British Library Cataloguing in Publication Data

A catalogue record for this book is available from the British Library.

ISBN 1–897785–11-9

COTTAGE PUBLISHING

Editorial by:

Veronica Kennedy

Design and layout by:

Mike Lang

Typeset by:

Carnaby Typesetting, Torquay, Devon TQ1 1EG

Printed and bound in Great Britain by:

The Latimer Trend Group, Plymouth, Devon PL6 7PY

Contents

Acknowledgements

Without the contributors, all busy people, this book would not have been possible. My thanks go to them and to all of the people who have helped in different ways with information, and for lending me precious family photographs. They are acknowledged individually in most instances. I have also tried to include as many stories as possible in the text.

On behalf of the Bovey Tracey Heritage Trust I should like to thank Mike Lang for undertaking to publish this book and for being such a pleasure to work with. It would be difficult to find a more helpful and supportive publisher.

It is almost unfair to single out people when eveyone has been so helpful, but I should particularly like to thank Dave Lewis who, when I undertook this task, compiled me a list of old Bovonians, most of whom I have talked to. Since then he has answered all my questions and allowed me the pleasure of going through his extraordinary collection of old postcards of Bovey Tracey when despair at the enormity of my task washed over me. Stephanie and Geoff Wills have put up with me turning up unexpectedly and asking yet more questions, while Pat Tregoning, Anthony Porter and Victor Coombes have been extremely patient in dealing with my queries. Mike Steer, by email from Australia, has regaled me with wonderful Bovey stories which have enormously increased my understanding of Bovey life. I have felt privileged to be able to make contact with so many delightful people and hear so many fascinating stories.

John Adey has taken the wonderful photographs of some of Bovey's 'characters'. It has been time-consuming and demanding work. John Parnell, by compiling the index, has drawn together the many threads that could have come untangled in a book like this.

Last of all, I want to thank my husband, John Porter, for his unfailing support, both practically in looking at text over and over again and emotionally for accepting that I would be eating, dreaming and talking Bovey for over a year.

Introduction

In the last 30 years Devon, and South Devon in particular, has changed enormously. The decline in traditional industries (most obviously in agriculture), near universal car ownership, the growth in second homes, the greater life expectancy and the aspirations of retirees have all contributed to these changes. Bovey Tracey has experienced all these changes, and many of the older residents are in a state of shock. The population has grown dramatically; in the 100 years between 1800 and 1900 it almost doubled from 1,431 to 2,658. It then increased to 3,501 in 1970, but has doubled again in the last 30 years. People have moved to Bovey because it is convenient for work in Plymouth or Exeter during the week, and provides good access to the leisure facilities of the coast and Dartmoor. Even more people have retired here. And the newcomers, although they like the town, do not, perhaps, appreciate its rich industrial, ecclesiastical and agricultural history.

Two books have been written on Bovey Tracey's history, one by Armitage Hargreaves, published in 1968, and no longer in print, and the other by Lance Tregoning, published in 1983. In some ways it seems impertinent to try and add to them, but any history book reflects its time, emphasising things that are important to it, and, in so doing, has its own limitations and strengths. In the spring of 2004 the Heritage Trust museum is being moved into the old railway station, now refurbished, and it seemed an appropriate moment to look at Bovey's story anew.

I am a Devonian but only came to Bovey $2^1/2$ years ago. I joined the Heritage Trust and found myself taking over the compilation of this book. It was a daunting task and someone less foolhardy than I am would have run a mile from it. Sherryl Healey provided a basic structure using the archives at the heritage centre, but it made sense to open the history up to a variety of 'voices' in order to capture the memories of people who actually made Bovey's history. Members of the Heritage Trust's research group have done much work on Bovey's history and many chapters are a result of this work.

This book is a compilation so inevitably there will be things left out that should have been included. Some of the omissions have been deliberate because the subjects are well-covered in Lance Tregoning's books but, in some cases, there will be oversights. There is also a real danger, in relying so much on people's stories, that there will be errors, either of fact or interpretation. Wherever possible things have been checked but, inevitably, there will be mistakes. I apologise in advance for these and hope people will take the opportunity of letting the Heritage Trust know so that the records can be changed. I hope that, for most people, the redeeming feature will be the self-evident affection all the contributors and storytellers have for Bovey.

Veronica Kennedy
March 2004

An aerial view of Bovey Tracey taken in the 1930s (Dave Lewis)

Origins

In ancient times the town took its name from the river - Boui or Bofa – and became South Bovey. The Romans are known to have been at Exeter, and a possible Roman presence in Bovey is indicated by coins found at Furzeley Common between 1837 and 1839. Furzeley would have been on a route from the Teign via Hennock and Trusham to Exeter. A.J. Wyatt suggests that Vagabond's Stoneborough on the Brimley Road may mark the site of a Roman villa, but this is unsubstantiated and his source unknown.

The heathfield was created by the Saxons who felled the primeval trees upon it. A track crossed the River Bovey by a ford and went up the hill into Hind Street, dividing near the present-day 79 Mary Street for the roads to Moretonhampstead and Hennock. Reminders of Saxon agriculture, the long narrow strips or parallel fields, can be seen in the lines on the fields and gardens above Mary Street.

Near Parke View another track followed Fore Street, East Street, Bradley and Little Bovey. This track to the east and the one from the river to Hennock were joined by one running north - now

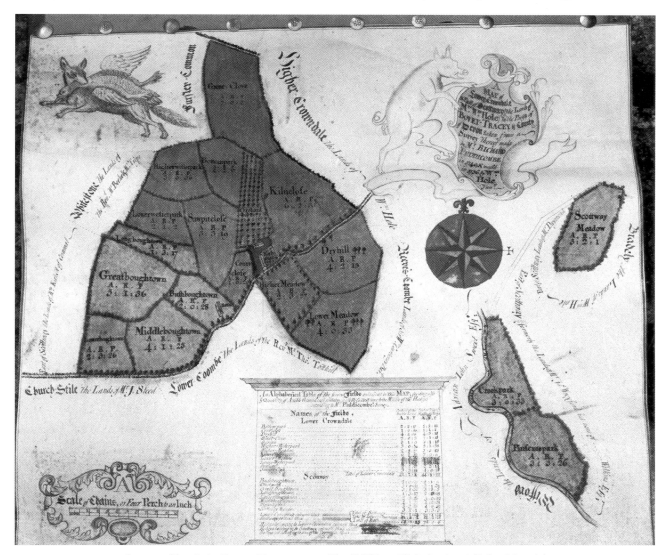

A map of lands in Bovey Tracey owned by William Hole in 1756 (John Morris)

Mary Street. The triangle thus formed enclosed the original houses of the village. At the north of the triangle was Forces orchard which may have been the site of the gallows of the Tracey family, who possessed the sovereign right of capital punishment.

An extract from the Domesday survey of 1086 describes Bovey:

Edric held it before 1066. It paid tax for 2 hides. Land for 10 ploughs. In lordship 3 ploughs; 8 slaves; half hide, 16 villages and 8 smallholders with 10 ploughs and one and a half hides. A mill which pays 10s; meadow, 5 acres; pasture, 50 acres; woodland, 60 acres. 1 cob; 30 cattle; 7 pigs; 85 sheep; 5 goats. It pays £10, less 30d...To this manor has been added the land of 15 thanes in [Little] Bovey, Warmhill, Scobitor, Brungarstone, Elsford, Woolleigh, Hawkmoor, Hatherleigh and Pullabrook. On these lands the 15 thanes have 2 hides and half virgate of land. Land for 8 ploughs; 7 ploughs there. They pay £4 4 0d to Bovey [Tracey] in dues. [This is] in addition to the above £10.

In the 11th century William the Conqueror gave the manor of Bovey to be part of the English barony of Geoffrey de Moubray, Bishop of Coutances, his lieutenant at the Battle of Hastings. Attached to the manor was the estate of fifteen theigns. After William's death the Bishop chose the losing side in the dispute over the succession to the Crown and lost his English barony. The Bovey manor then passed to Judhael of Totnes, whose daughter married a Tracey, and South Bovey became Bovey Tracey to distinguish it from North Bovey.

One of the earliest known photographs taken in Bovey Tracey, showing the road being resurfaced in 1895. Henry (Harry) Godfrey, seen with his horse, supplied the road stone (Eric Godfrey)

Charter

On 28th July 1260 (the 43rd year of Henry III's reign) Henry de Tracy, lord of the manor, obtained a charter allowing a weekly market on Thursdays and an annual fair on 7th July at 'his mana of Bovey on the Vigil, Feast and the Morrow of the Translation of St Thomas the Martyr'.

The fairs and markets were held regularly for many centuries. In 1799 the fair was mainly for the sale of wool. By 1822 there were four annual fairs, on the 7th July, Ascension Day, Easter Monday and the first Thursday in November. The annual fair was similar to fairs today except for the drinks - men drank ale called huffle cup, the mad dog, angel's food and dragon's milk. One could buy and sell just about anything. Traders might have a workshop where goods would be made to order, but nothing was kept in stock. Cattle fairs were held three times a year but gradually declined. The charter included the grant of Free Warren (hunting) in all the manor lands. The quarry was the fox, wolf, hare, cat, coney and squirrel.

In 1960 Lt. Col. B. St J. Storrs, a resident and former parish councillor, suggested a 'Charter Celebration' for the 700th anniversary of the granting of the charter. The parish council called a public meeting and a committee was set up. Their aim was to link the celebrations with the past and produce a programme of events which would give the greatest pleasure to all, both young and old. This account of the celebrations has been taken from Stephanie Wills' scrapbook.

Before the charter celebrations began, there was 'Beating the Bounds' on 25th June. The beaters walked 11 miles, starting at Heathfield station, being cheered on their way by workmen at Candy's, then to Drumbridges and halfway up Bovey Straight. They then had to cut across country to where Farmer Upham took them across Langaller Farm to Thorns Cross, where refreshing drinks were served. They continued to Green-lane End, where a lunch of pies, sandwiches, beer and squash was served. After lunch they walked to the Lustleigh boundary and then turned back. The town band met them as they reached Bovey. Then the procession marched round to all the inns in town and demanded that the licensee should produce his best ale for sampling. At the end of the evening it was announced that 'there is no bad ale supplied in this ancient borough'.

The proper programme began on 7th July with a procession in costume, led by the town crier and Bovey Tracey band. The Earl of Devon then opened the fair. Over the next three days there was an

Charter celebrations in 1960 (Stephanie Wills)

archery demonstration, the pageant, a performance of West Country songs by a male voice choir and a performance by the Bovey Tracey handbell ringers. Bovey's schoolchildren danced round the maypole and performed English folk dances. On the last evening there was a ram-roasting barbecue arranged by Bovey Tracey Young Farmers Club. An exhibition was held picturing the past life of Bovey Tracey. The farmhouse kitchen was designed by Helen Mann and the Victorian drawing room by Mrs W.H. Tregoning, with local people lending furniture and artefacts.

The pageant was written and produced by Marie Goss: it included nearly 100 performers and compressed over 1,000 years of history into 70 minutes. It ranged from showing Bovey dwellers in ancient times right up to events which took place in Victorian Bovey. The granting of the charter starred Joe Weeks as Henry III, Reg Hodge as the Earl of Pembroke, Bill Daymond as a knight, Claude Steer as a Tracy squire, and Michael Steer, his son, as a choirboy.

The Upham, Boyce and Heale families, and others from the Methodist Church Sunday School, depicted springtime and harvest in 1260.

The civil war scene showed Parson Forbes (Rev. Duxbury) and his wife (Stephanie Wills), who hid the church's brass eagle lectern under her shawl, while passing through the parliamentary lines. The Cavaliers were played by Barry Baty, Billy Fisher, Robert Pickford, Peter Bond, David Kelly, Anthony Oliver, James Gate and Joe Coombes. In opposition as Roundheads were John Ayres, Raymond Pickford, Robert Carpenter, Peter Mann, Roger Powesland and Brian Short.

The firefighters, as in real life, were Roy, Leonard and Geoffrey Coombes, Geoff Wills, Les Harris, Frank Phillips and Harold Heale. They used the ancient handpump appliance from the old pottery, with water pumped from the River Bovey.

The Women's Institute provided the traditional closing dance and included Helen Mann, Jean

Mountford, Mrs Harris, Mrs C. Brealey, Mrs Hydon, Mrs Turner, Mrs H. Kendall, Doris Mallett, Margaret Cornish and Misses Leaman, Rogers and Johnson. The pageant had a rousing finale with every member of the cast singing 'Land of Hope and Glory'.

The charter celebrations were a tremendous success, involving an enormous number of people. For three days thunderstorms raged all around Bovey, but the rain kept off in Bovey Tracey itself. Many of the families mentioned here still live in the town.

The cast of the pageant (Graham Newstead, courtesy of Stephanie Wills)

The Court Leet

This was a form of civic government (for the freeholders) and under the ultimate control of the lord of the manor. It was administered by elected officers at a Court Leet held annually. These officers were the portreeve and his assistants, specifically the surveyors of the assizes of bread and beer, of the Ways and collector of taxes on the woollen serge sold at the fair, the scavenger, town crier and two constables. Bovey's Court Leet was held in a large room, like a servants' hall, behind what is now the Riverside (then the residence of Miss Divett). There were large double doors opening from the road onto a cobbled yard and the room was entered by a short flight of steps.

The Bovey Tracey Town Trust is a remaining link of the old Court Leet which controlled the affairs of the town until the parish and rural district councils were formed in 1883.

In 1984 the town council purchased the 'Lordship of the Manor of Bovey Tracey' for the town. Each year it is awarded to a citizen of the town who has made a significant contribution over the years, allowing that person to be the lord of the manor of Bovey Tracey for twelve months.

The de Tracy connection

There is very little actual record of the origins of the de Tracy family available and, as Armitage Hargreaves said, 'the de Tracy family tree can hardly be relied upon as accurate'. It is further complicated by illegitimate births and the overuse of the names William and Henry.

It appears that the manor of Bovey first came to the de Tracy family through the marriage of Henry de Tracy to the daughter of Judhael of Totnes. The de Tracys held the living of Bovey Tracey until Henry III's reign, when the manor passed to Nicholas Martin, of Dartington, on his marriage to the daughter of the last Henry de Tracy.

The family maintained the old manor house, which stood just behind the Park Barton house. Miss Tracey, who lived in East Street until the 1930s, had an old deed in her possession which stated that:

on September 12th 1577 William Gilberte of North Tawton, Gentleman, son of Edward Gilberte sold to Thomas Barkeley for £230 his interest in that capital mansion house called 'Henstreate' in Bovietracie including all the messuages which were the inheritance of Edward Gilberte.

This may substantiate the assertion that the manor house was opposite what is now the Cromwell Arms, on the site of the present Lloyds chemist.

Traditionally it is believed that Sir William de Tracy, the chief assassin of Archbishop Thomas à Becket in 1170, stayed at Parke. The head of the de Tracy family, another Sir William, lived at Toddington and founded a chapel in honour of the martyr at Tewkesbury, so he may also have founded a chapel at Bovey, particularly if the murderer, his namesake, lived here. It seems unlikely that the assassin built the parish church as it dates from earlier than this.

A Snapshot of Bovey Tracey in 1841
by Walter Mountford

In 1841 the first real census was held and, coupled with the tithe maps of 1840, with their apportionments (schedules), this produced the most accurate record in the country since the Domesday Book.

The Tithe Commutations Act of 1836-60, Bovey Tracey 1840, substituted a money rent in lieu of goods. Maps were produced for almost 12,000 parishes, accounting for three-quarters of the country's land. Three maps were made, one for the Tithe Commissioners, now with the Ministry of Agriculture, one for the Diocesan Registrar, and one for the parish. These large-scale maps vary from six chains to the mile (26 inches to the mile) to two chains to the mile: the size of the Bovey Tracey map is about six feet by nine feet. Messrs Sawdye and Tappernal tendered for the parish of Bovey Tracey, were successful and completed it in 1840. The Parish Tithe Map is now at the Devon Record Office.

The Tithe Apportionment book/schedules lists all the landowners and occupiers (tenants) with full details of acreage, field names, value and the nature of land they held. Every common, garden, orchard and yard are clearly noted. The total amounts of 10 per cent of the tithes are given. These amounted to £671 in 1841, of which £451 was paid to the vicar. When the agricultural wage was around 15 shillings a week, this clearly represented a considerable sum. One copy of this apportionment, which measures about 24 inches by 24 inches, is at the town council offices.

The Tithe Map reveals that the majority of the inhabitants lived in Main Street, now part of Fore Street, St Mary Street (now known as Mary Street), East Street, Hind Street, College and the surrounding farms. Six buildings were unoccupied and two were under construction.

Most of the buildings were then under thatched roofs. Those still under thatch are part of Pludda, The Old Thatched Inn, 65 Fore Street, Atway and Church Steps. The Duke of Somerset, who had recently acquired them from the Templer family, owned most of the cottage dwellings.

The waterwheel and the Devon Guild buildings replace Noah's Ark. This building was occupied by Mr Flood and, according to the late Emmanuel Hamlin, was well named as the building was often surrounded by water during the winter months. The Duck Pond at the top end of St Paul's Close, south of College, has long disappeared and the town hall replaces the five cottages at the north side of the village green.

A framed copy showing the village and surrounding area is on display at the heritage centre. This map lists approximately 80 field names in and around the village. It is interesting to find that three fields in the new estate around Churchfields Drive were named Waterleak, Outer Waterleak and Inner Waterleak. These spring to life after torrential rains about every 30 years or more, so we must hope that these springs have been diverted into the streams which run through the estate.

On 12th June 1841 four enumerators undertook the first real census for the parish of Bovey Tracey and recorded a population numbering 1,823. John Beer, a wheelwright living at Townsend, was allocated schedule Number 9, which covered the west side of Bovey River; George Harris, a

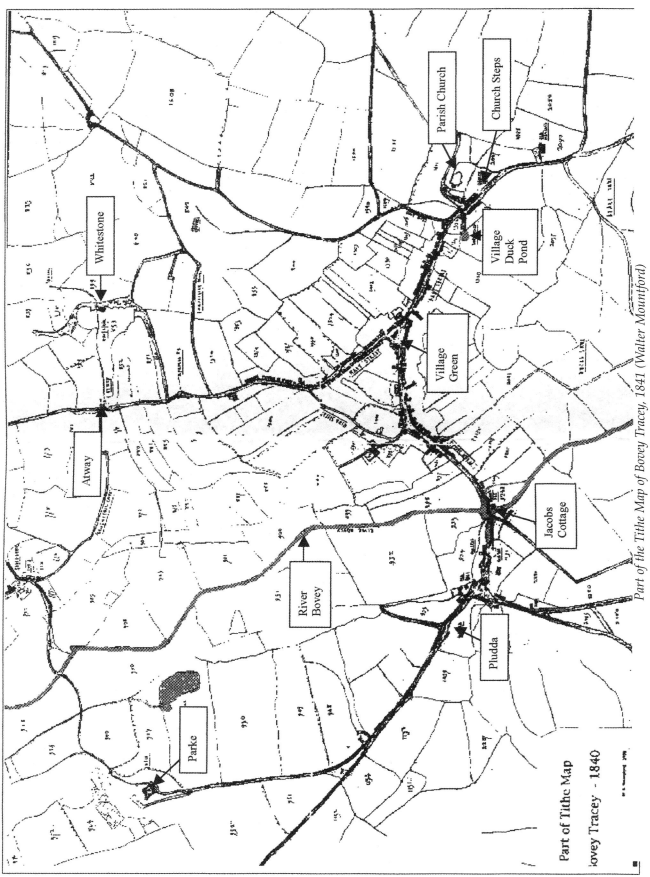

Part of the Tithe Map of Bovey Tracey, 1841 (Walter Mountford)

Part of Tithe Map
Bovey Tracey - 1840

retired farmer, undertook schedule Number 10, which covered the outlying farms and dwellings north of East Street and St Mary Street; Mr Chudleigh, a schoolmaster, undertook two schedules, Numbers 11 and 12, covering the whole of the village; and Mr Loveys, publican at the Union Inn (Cromwell Arms), undertook schedule Number 13, which covered the south side of East Street, Main Street, Pludda and Townsend.

Family names which dominated the census were Steer, Dymond, Ellis, Gale, Harris and Heath, all names we recognise in Bovey today. Only five people reached the age of 80 and these were William Adair of Colehayes (85), Ann Croker of St Mary Street (80), Mary Lamacroft of Main Street (80), all described as having independent means, Grace Edmonds of Main Street (80), a seamstress, and Joseph Widdor of St Mary Street (80), a carpenter.

As recorded in the parish register of 1841, twenty-two children were baptised, nine couples were married and eighteen people died.

In 1841 the predominant occupation was agricultural labourer, with 300 listed. There were 45 farmers, 18 female and 19 male servants, 57 people of independent means, 8 tailors, 4 shopkeepers and 1 physician and 1 surgeon.

This information gives us a much clearer and more accurate picture of Bovey Tracey than had been available previously, and the outline of the village from the Tithe Map of 1840 helps us to imagine just how Bovey looked then.

The maps that appear on the following five pages have been included to illustrate the growth of Bovey over the last 125 years and are reproduced courtesy of Roy Wills:–

Map 1 shows that in the latter part of the 19th century the town was primarily ribbon development, with most properties built adjacent to the through roads. The notable exceptions were the established country houses such as Parke, Whit(e)stone and Indio, and Devon House.

Map 2 reveals that few changes have taken place except for the construction of some properties in Brimley Road, two terraces of houses in Pottery Road (built by The Bovey Pottery Co. for their employees) and a terrace of private houses – South View – to the east of Fore Street.

Map 3 illustrates that there has been a period of rapid expansion. Council houses have been built off Brimley Road (comprising Brimley Park and Moor View) and at Priory, and private housing provided in the Wallfield Road/Brimley Road areas as well as off Newton Road and Bradley Road. Homes built in two areas of the town were named after famous battles – Blenheim Terrace and Marlborough Terrace, off Haytor Road – and, in recognition of the Boer War, a road off Mary Street was named Spion Kop and the housing off this road named Eureka Terrace and White Heather Terrace. On the railway Brimley Halt, which was opened in 1928, can be seen.

Map 4 shows that further housebuilding has taken place: the council stock now includes Cromwells Way and Brimley Vale, and additional private housing has been provided off Bradley Road and the Moretonhampstead road.

Map 5 illustrates the large-scale developments that have taken place over more recent years and the changes brought about by the construction of the bypass (completed in 1987) and Le Molay-Littry Way, which was opened in the mid-1990s prior to the start of a large housebuilding scheme to the south of Fore Street and East Street. As indicated on the map, other areas where housing has also mushroomed since the 1950s are to the north-west of the town (this includes the Crokers Meadow estate, where development commenced in the 1960s) and around the southern outskirts in the vicinity of Wallfield Road, Pottery Road, Indio Road and Newton Road. Additionally, the mobile home site at New Park, off the road to Liverton, can be seen to have expanded considerably, and more houses are evident off Station Road as a result of the development of the former railway station yard and corn mill in 2001.

© Crown copyright.

Map 5 is reproduced from Ordnance Survey mapping on behalf of The Controller of Her Majesty's Stationery Office © Crown Copyright 100042123.

The Bovey Book

The **Bovey Book: Map 1 – 1880**

BOVEY TRACEY

Scale 1:8000

0   300m.

The Bovey Book: Map 2 – 1905

The Bovey Book: Map 3 – 1930

BOVEY TRACEY

The **Bovey Book: Map 4 – 1950**

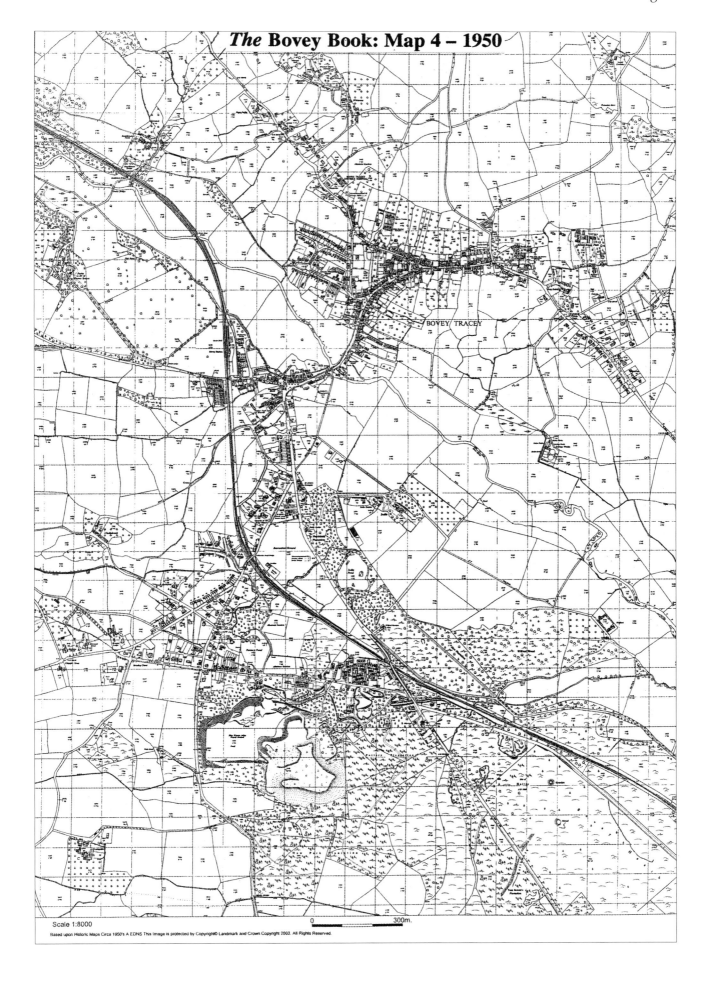

BOVEY TRACEY

Scale 1:8000

0   300m.

The Bovey Book

The **Bovey Book: Map 5 – 2003**

The Ancient Stone Crosses
by Mike Lang

The subject of the stone crosses to be found on and around Dartmoor is somewhat complex, for not only do they fall into a variety of different categories, but they are also of varying age. For this reason an account of their history, even in the broadest of terms, is well outside the scope of this book and, instead, any reader interested in learning more about this fascinating topic is referred to the list of books included in the bibliography at the end of this chapter.

Generally speaking most of the crosses are constructed of granite, date from between the late Saxon period to the mid-20th century and may be categorised as follows:-

1. **Wayside Crosses** - these were erected for the purpose of marking the various tracks and to serve as guideposts, both on the open moorland and elsewhere. It has been suggested that the arms of each cross would point in the direction of the track that it marked, but so many of the crosses have been re-erected it is impossible to validate this theory.

2. **Village Crosses** - usually erected upon the village green, these provided the focal point for various activities such as preaching, collecting dues and making proclamations.

3. **Churchyard Crosses** - these were normally erected to act as a symbol of sanctity for the church and its grounds, and also to serve as a preaching point. At the coming of Christianity, many of the churches were built on former pagan sites and it is possible that the crosses replaced original pagan stones.

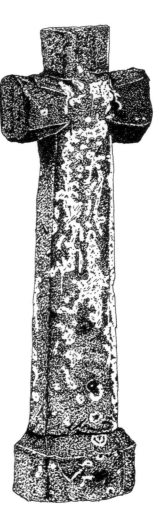

4. **Boundary Crosses** - these were erected to mark the boundaries of manorial and ecclesiastical land. At one time the removal of, or interference with, such crosses was punishable by death.

5. **Market Crosses** - these were erected in the market place and provided the focal point for fairs, preaching, proclamations and the collection of various dues.

6. **Memorial Crosses** - these tend to be of later origin and usually carry inscriptions or plaques in memory of various people. Some modern-day memorial crosses can also be found, in miniature form, erected on boulders, or rocks, near the favourite locations of people who have died.

In Bovey all six of these categories are represented, even though there are only four crosses - still more than most towns or villages can boast! They are as follows:-

Bovey Churchyard Cross

Location: In the churchyard of the Church of St Peter, St Paul and St Thomas of Canterbury.

In the early part of the 19th century the then Lord Courtenay (later the 10th Earl of Devon) found fragments of the original cross - the lower portion of the shaft and an arm - being used as a step at the churchyard gate. He then arranged for them to be removed and for

Bovey Churchyard Cross

the cross to be re-erected near the east end of the church. However, possibly because of a conflict troubling the Church of England at that time, it was thrown down and, eventually, following a repetition of events, the fragments were removed to Powderham for safekeeping. Here, the cross was properly restored and set up on a pedestal of three octagonal steps resting on a large octagonal platform with a chamfered top edge.

In 1849 the Reverend Honourable (later Canon) Charles Leslie Courtenay became vicar of Bovey and, when the Earl of Devon told him about the cross, it was agreed that it should be brought back to its rightful home; it was then re-erected at its present location in the churchyard. Later, following the death of Canon Courtenay, an inscription was added to the pedestal, which reads: In memoriam - Charles Leslie Courtenay. Priest. - 45 years vicar of this parish. - Obiit October 29th, 1894.

As an aside, it is worth mentioning that on each side of the south porch of the church is a flat slab of granite, about six feet long and a little over two feet wide. These are of interest because they both have a large incised cross on them, and other ornamental lines cut in relief. It has been suggested by one writer that they are early sepulchral slabs, and stated by another that the pattern of these lines bears a resemblance to the stripes on the national flag of the Royal Navy. He adds that the pattern is also similar to the lower half of the monogram usually known as the cross of Constantine.

Bovey Market Cross

Location: The War Memorial, adjacent to the town hall.

This cross falls effectively into three of the above categories – market, village (or town) and memorial – and originally stood on the site of the town hall, a short distance away from its present location. In fact, it was to make way for the town hall in 1865 that the cross was removed. When it was re-erected the original socket-stone and tapered shaft were mounted on a pedestal of two octagonal steps, both with projecting top edges, and a large base of cut granite, square at the bottom, but with the corners steeply sloped so that its top is octagonal.

Bovey Market Cross

Unfortunately, the original head and arms of the cross went missing sometime before it was resited. However, when it was re-erected Canon Courtenay paid for a new head and arms to be cut by Mr Treleaven, a local stonemason, and these were linked to the shaft by a stone circlet.

The base now bears the war memorial inscriptions.

The Bovey Stone

Location: The roadside wall of Cross Cottage, almost opposite the hospital.

The remains of this wayside/boundary cross - a roughly octagonal socket-stone bearing a short stump of a shaft with chamfered edges - originally stood at the junction of the nearby lane leading to Higher Atway Farm, but was removed to its present location by Dr Croker in 1815 so as to allow for the road to be widened. On the face of the shaft is a small incised cross, which is said to have been cut in that same year.

In former times, up until the late 19th century, the day on which

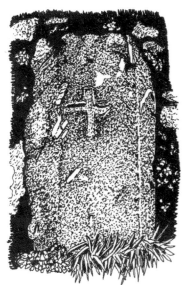

The Bovey Stone

the portreeve of Bovey was chosen was observed as a holiday. Traditionally, this was always on the first Monday after 3rd May and was known as 'Mayor's Monday'. This not only featured the beating of the bounds on horseback, but also a ceremony whereby the newly-appointed Mayor of Bovey would ride three times round the cross (before it was resited) and then strike it with a staff. This, apparently, was to symbolise his authority.

Challabrook Cross

Location: To the west of the bypass, alongside the footpath to Challabrook.

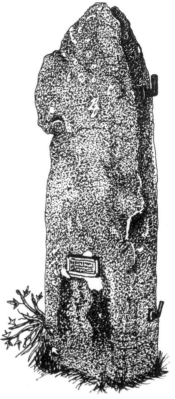

This cross is sometimes referred to as the Longstone (or Langstone), but this is almost certainly the name given to the cross in its original, and much taller, state rather than the name of the officer that it now commemorates. It is of rough rectangular section and has an incised cross on the south-eastern face of its shaft, but, unfortunately, having been used as a gatepost at the nearby farm for many years before being re-erected at its present location, it is badly mutilated and has only one, short, arm remaining.

The original site of the cross, whilst likely to have been somewhere on Bovey Heath, is unknown, but it was restored in 1923 by a local historian, Mr A.J. Wyatt, who attached a brass plaque to the shaft with the following inscription:-

This old cross once marked the grave of a Royalist officer who fell near here 1645 when Cromwell's troops defeated the Royalists -A.J.W. 1923.

N.B. The battle on Bovey Heath took place on 9th January 1646, but prior to Chesterfield's Act in 1751 the English year started on 25th March (Lady Day) and not on 1st January. Consequently, contemporaries would have reckoned the year to be still 1645.

Challabrook Cross

Bibliography

Sandles, Tim. *A Pilgrimage to Dartmoor's Crosses.* Forest Publishing, 1997
Starkey, F.H. (Harry). *Dartmoor Crosses and Some Ancient Tracks.* Published privately, 1989
Harrison, Bill. *Dartmoor Stone Crosses.* Devon Books/Halsgrove, 2001
Crossing, William. *The Ancient Stone Crosses of Dartmoor and its Borderland.* J.G. Commin, 1902

Drawings reproduced by kind permission of Tim Sandles.

❊ ❊ ❊ ❊ ❊

The Battle of Bovey Heath, 1646

by Robert Hesketh

Two Regiments of foot and one of horse marched from Crediton to Bovy-Tracy about fourteen miles, and about six at night fell on three Regiments of the Enemies horse at Bovy-Tracy, took near four hundred horse and five Colours, some prisoners, many escaping in the dark; The Rendezvous for the rest of the army this morning near Bovy-Tracy, from whence they march on a further Design, of which shortly you will hear more...

In these words William Lenthall, Speaker of the House of Commons, was appraised of Parliament's victory at Bovey Heath. The battle was won on 9th January 1646, as Thomas Fairfax and his Lieutenant General, Oliver Cromwell, swept westwards through Devon in the concluding stages of the First Civil War.

Marston Moor (1644) and Naseby (1645), which were signal victories, had been won before the Battle of Bovey Heath. Although the King's flag still flew over the cities of Oxford, Worcester and Winchester, there could be little doubt about Parliament's ultimate success. Scattered Royalist outposts, such as Exeter and Dartmouth, still held out in Devon, and Royalist troops were besieging Plymouth. Bringing these centres of resistance to heel and subduing traditionally Royalist Cornwall was the 'further design' referred to in the letter to Speaker Lenthall.

Bovey Heath was thus one of the smaller actions of the Civil War, but it was on such engagements that complete mastery of the country depended. The route to Bovey involved several smaller fights, such as that at Canonteign on 6th January 1646, when Roundhead dragoons took a Royalist captain, nine men and twenty horse.

This said, the Battle of Bovey Heath was a major event for local people. If the town is mentioned at all in national histories, 1646 is the year attached to it.

Not surprisingly, several enduring local stories emerged from Bovey's brief encounter with the tide of national events. Each brings the Civil War into sharp focus in a different way.

On the evening before the battle, 8th January, a stranger entered the Presbyterian Chapel in Hind Street, Bovey Tracey - the site of the present Baptist Chapel. After the service he presented a letter of introduction to the elders from the Presbyterian Church in Moretonhampstead.

The elders spoke to this stranger privately, giving him all the information he desired on the state of the Royalist forces under Lord Wentworth. They kept his identity secret from their flock - he was none other than Cromwell.

Cromwell slept at the chapel, but sent his information by letter to Lower Atway, about a mile away on the Moretonhampstead road. A resident there, Coniam, whose descendants still live in Bovey Tracey, was sheltering several of Cromwell's troopers and acted as their guide. They took Cromwell's letter back to Sir Thomas Fairfax, who followed Cromwell's suggestion that part of 'Fairfax's Command' should enter Bovey at dusk the next evening and thus surprise Wentworth.

Fairfax's men moved so rapidly and secretly that they did surprise Wentworth's officers, who were playing cards in Bovey. They would all have been captured but for the quick wits of one officer. A letter to Edmund Prideaux, MP sent from Ashburton on 11th January 1646 describes the incident:

We lost but one man, divers of the Enemy sore wounded, some slain; some of their chief officers, being in a house, shut the door, and threw out of the window about ten pounds in silver, which the foot soldiers were so busy about getting their shares, that the officers escaped in the mean time over the River, through the darkness of the night...

Front House Lodge, now a guest house opposite Bovey's town hall, may have been the scene of this escape. The sign outside illustrates the story. William Ellis, however, sets the action at the Old

Manor House.

After the battle many fugitives took refuge in Ilsington Church, but fled on Cromwell's approach. Meanwhile, part of his army slept at Bovey and the next day they buried the dead of both sides.

Tradition has it that one of the dead was a Royalist officer called Langstone, much respected by both sides. He was buried on Bovey Heath and, until early this century, a long stone and a high granite cross marked the spot. The stone, restored with a small plaque in 1923 by A.J. Wyatt, can be found in a field leading to Challabrook Farm, near Bovey Tracey.

William Ellis, born in Bovey in 1804, but who emigrated to the United States, was given the following poem written by an American woman, E.A.C., to commemorate the battle:

It is no sacred ground
Which marks the soldier's tomb, but far around
The dreary moorland stretches…One sign alone
Where the uncoffined dead reposes low,
An old grey stone its broken form uprears…

The last story connected with the battle comes from Baring-Gould and concerns John Cann, a Royalist in charge of the troops' pay, who hid with the money at Bottor Rock, near Hennock. Here he was tracked down by bloodhounds, taken to Exeter and hanged. His treasure, said still to be hidden at Bottor, has never been recovered. More than one Hennock resident will tell you he has searched for it.

Exploring the area today, the most noticeable evidence of the Battle of Bovey Heath is the traces of the earthworks, behind which Lord Wentworth's Royalist troops entrenched themselves just south of the town. Roads recently built on Heathfield Industrial Estate, which covers much of the battle site, bear names like Musket and Battle - an odd tribute to the past.

This first appeared in *Dartmoor Magazine* (No. 41, Winter 1995) and is reprinted by permission of the editor.

The First World War

by Tim Dunce

Albert Coombes of the Royal Engineers (Victor Coombes)

As the nations of Europe moved inexorably towards war in the summer of 1914 even the *Mid Devon Advertiser* was expressing the hope that England might escape becoming involved. On 1st August it reported that 'last evening there was still hope that the international situation will not develop into a general war'. Sadly, it was a forlorn hope, and on 4th August 1914 Great Britain declared war on Germany. The next issue of the weekly paper, on 8th August, had the headline 'All Europe Fighting', followed by an analysis of the military situation. It then moved on to examine the immediate impact of the war in the locality. It must be remembered that, without radio, newspapers were the only source of information for the population, and as the war progressed everyone would come to depend on the local press for news of their men at the front, and of what was happening on the home front, too.

Even at this early stage in the conflict there were many locally who seemed aware that this would be a war unlike any other. That men would be required was obvious; Lord Kitchener, now Secretary of State for War, wanted an additional 100,000 men for the regular army, and his famous appeal appeared in the paper. Those who could not join the armed forces nevertheless wanted to help, and many appeals were set up. The Devon Patriotic Fund sought subscriptions to be used for the benefit of the wives and families of the regulars and territorials for the county of Devon, and for the benefit of the sick and wounded.

On 15th August the *Mid Devon Advertiser* reported on 'Bovey's Preparations'. A 'largely attended' meeting in support of the Devon Patriotic Fund was held at the town hall, with local worthies present, including Mr H.A. Bentinck, lord of the manor, and his wife, of Indio. An executive committee had been formed to meet any emergency, and Albion House was at their disposal as a temporary hospital. Mr and Mrs Bentinck offered Indio for the same purpose, and Major and Mrs St Maur did the same with Stover House. Drs Goodwyn and Dallas undertook to conduct classes in ambulance work and bandaging for men and women. Mr Park-Smith offered his residence for use as a hospital, and Mr Alfred Aggett was arranging a fleet of cars to convey the wounded to hospital. In that same meeting Lieutenant Colonel Mawson asked old soldiers and sailors to give in their names and join the National Reserves. Mr Evans raised the question of forming a class for men who desired to know how to shoot; such men as could not join the territorials, or serve in any other way. Reverend Hythe mentioned that he had been preparing a list of the names of those serving from Bovey. Although the list was not complete, it numbered 63. A 'Civilian League' was being 'rapidly formed' in the town for men who wished to be trained in the use of the rifle. Thus, less than two weeks into the war, Bovey had begun an impressive list of preparations.

As the process of mobilisation began, it became clear that the army required many more horses than during peacetime, and the impact on Bovey Tracey was immediate. A large number of horses was requisitioned, and, although the army paid good prices, the local farmers and deliverymen found it very difficult to cope with the sudden loss of their motive power. Bovey Potteries were immediately affected by the war, due to difficulties with the transportation of clay and, probably, because of employees joining up. However, the firm elected to remain in business, although working half time only. Mr and Mrs Bentinck made a 'striking appeal' to all young men and boys of the town to join the colours, and nearly £500 was subscribed to the Devon Patriotic Fund. The Bentincks entertained to tea 49 wives and mothers of Bovey soldiers, sailors and territorials who were already serving in the war; the first of several such gatherings.

As the initial wave of enthusiasm began to fade, so a degree of common sense prevailed. The *Mid Devon Advertiser* reported that the idea of a civilian league or rifle club had apparently 'fizzled out', the general opinion being that Lord Kitchener's recruiting scheme superseded it. Bovey St John's Football Club decided to withdraw from some of its fixtures as several players were serving with the territorials. Hoping to get recruits for Lord Kitchener's army, the Bovey national reservists held a parade one Saturday. There was apparently a good muster, and the men, headed by the local brass band, marched through the streets. Despite this, however, only two men came forward to enlist. Some support remained for teaching youngsters how to handle a rifle. An idea prevailed locally that money paid out of the Patriotic Fund to wives and children of men on service was only in the nature of a loan and had to be repaid, but the newspaper commented that this impression was entirely misleading.

The *Mid Devon Advertiser* then moved on to a rumour which had been heard nationwide in September 1914; namely that Russian troops had been seen on trains headed through Britain for the front line. Stating that people in Bovey believed this to be true, the paper declared that 'the trains that carried them through our stations have been trains of dreamland'. Returning to the real war, it transpired that out of the local detachment of 'G' Company, 5th Devon Territorials, no less than 22 had signed on for foreign service and were in camp on Salisbury Plain. A series of pictures of the war was given in the Temperance Hall (now Ashley Dawes' premises in Fore Street), the proceeds being handed to the War Fund. In the same issue a roll of honour listed the men of Bovey currently serving in the forces; sadly, some of those names would be found on the war memorial after the war.

Britain had joined the war because Germany had invaded neutral Belgium; with that unfortunate country now almost completely overrun, many Belgian refugees had arrived in Allied territory. Several were expected to arrive in Bovey, to be accommodated at the Devon House of Mercy. Girls of Bovey National School contributed seven shillings as a first instalment to the Devon Patriotic Fund, and were also busily engaged in making garments for destitute Belgians. As time went on 'several' Belgian refugees arrived, and were 'well treated' at the House of Mercy. The council school held a variety bazaar for the Belgian Fund, and raised £20 18s. 8d. The refugees were entertained to

Three Steer brothers in India. Lou Steer is at the back, with Cecil and Ronald at the front (Victor Coombes)

tea by Mr and Mrs Bentinck; some wounded soldiers from Stover Hospital were also invited.

A good number of people travelled from Bovey to Newton Abbot to see a contingent of Canadian troops arrive, amongst whom were two men from Bovey who had emigrated to Canada in the past and were now returning to fight. The first Bovey tradesman's son to join up was Willie Mann, son of Mr and Mrs John Mann of Fore Street (still in the same family ownership). The second was Reginald Mardon, whose parents ran The Beehive Stores (the premises currently occupied by the Mare and Foal Charity Shop). Three sons of Edwin Steer, of Abbey Road, were to sail for India with the territorials, whilst a son-in-law was attached to the Royal Marines.

At this time it was not uncommon for families receiving letters from relatives serving in the forces to forward them to the local press for publication. Thus we learn that Private Frank Burnett of the Scots Guards wrote to his brother, John, of Lower Bowden, Furzeleigh Lane, to tell of the heavy losses the Guards had experienced. Sergeant Edward Nicholls, of 'G' Company, 5th Battalion The Devonshire Regiment, wrote to his mother in East Street from Port Said, Egypt, saying it was 'very interesting and very hot' there. After serving in India and the Middle East, Sergeant Nicholls was posted to France, where he was killed on 14th September 1918. Fred Northcott and Charles Holland wrote of their time aboard HMS *Cumberland* which, whilst off the Cameroon River in West Africa, had captured ten German vessels.

As 1914 drew to a close it became clear that the war would not be 'over by Christmas'. The people of Bovey had seen 190 of their menfolk join the forces and six had died. The local tradesmen, especially Manns and Bovey Tracey Stores (where the Spar supermarket is now), were advertising their Christmas bargains with the added suggestion that 'if you cannot send your sons to the front to fight for their King and country, you can at least send some Tommy of your acquaintance some little reminder from Bovey'. This advice was followed; many people sent parcels to men in the forces or subscribed to the various war funds. Others continued supporting the war effort; Mr and Mrs Pets placed Albion House (now an antique shop in Fore Street) at the disposal of the local committee for any immediate emergency, rent-free. A party of wounded soldiers from Torbay Hospital visited Bovey, stopping briefly in Union Square: they were given a 'kindly reception', and a collection was taken for them. A few days before Christmas Mrs Smith, of Southbrook, heard from the War Office that her husband, Gilbert, had been killed in action at the front.

As the new year of 1915 opened there was little cause for optimism. The price of bread rose from 6d. to 7d. per loaf and the weather was dire, causing flooding in parts of the town. The initial enthusiastic rush to join the army had now largely disappeared; men were aware that it would be a long war and there was little chance of glory. There were whispers of a new recruiting scheme; a precursor to conscription, and a Captain Cuthbert Bearne had visited the town to drum up support. Nevertheless, men were still enlisting voluntarily; Mr W. Scagell, who had, for many years, worked at the Dolphin Hotel, joined the Army Medical Corps, whilst another well-known Bovonian,

Charles Abbott of the Yew Tree Dairy, enlisted in the Devonshire Regiment. Mr Arthur Stokes, of 11 Blenheim Terrace, fourth son of J.S. Stokes, builder, joined the Sportsmen's Battalion of the Royal Fusiliers. He had been a clerk at Michelmore's, the Newton Abbot solicitors, for six years and the firm presented him with a cheque on enlisting. He would be killed in action on 30th July 1916 at the Battle of the Somme. His body was never found.

Mr and Mrs Whitworth of Parke, having made their house available as a hospital, saw the first six patients arrive. The men expressed themselves delighted with the splendid house and the manner in which they were cared for by the matron and civilians. The Horticultural Society decided to hold their summer show as usual, but with all profits going to war funds. A football match in aid of Stover Red Cross Hospital between the 5th Devonshire (Territorial Force) and Bovey 1st Team raised 10 shillings gate money. An analysis of recruiting in local parishes showed Bovey, at 8.2%, to be amongst the highest. Miss C. Mann, eldest daughter of Mr and Mrs John Mann of Fore Street, had volunteered to assist at the Stover Red Cross Hospital. The local paper reported that the sinking of the Cunard liner *Lusitania* caused great consternation when it became known in Bovey. It was spoken of in sermons with the keenest regret that 'so noble a vessel and so many hundreds of souls should thus be wantonly destroyed' by a German submarine.

The sinking of HMS *Goliath* on 13th May by a Turkish submarine was causing more direct anxiety in Bovey; three local men were known to be aboard her. Walter Aggett, of 79 Mary Street, and William Boyce, of 28 Mary Street, both lost their lives in the disaster, whilst Frederick Hyssett survived. His brother, Ernest, would not be so fortunate; he was aboard HMS *Triumph* when she was torpedoed and sunk at Gallipoli. He survived the sinking but died of blood poisoning at the Royal Naval Hospital in Devonport in August. Private Horace Setters, of 12 Mary Street, had been invalided home in December 1914, suffering from frostbitten feet; he rejoined his regiment in June, but was killed in France on 21st August 1915.

Back in Bovey, Mr Bentinck proudly wrote to the paper that the local branch of the Vegetable Products Committee had supplied far more than the national average of vegetables for the fleet, Bovey giving more than ten hundredweight of fresh vegetables per week. Almost 250 men from the town had now joined up. The employees at Bovey Tracey Potteries were granted a $7^1/2\%$ war bonus on their wages.

Driver Arthur Weeks of the Royal Field Artillery was back home with his parents, William and Jane Weeks of Virginia Cottage, East Street. He was on sick leave, having been thrown from his horse whilst dispatch riding. He would return to the front, only to be killed in action in April 1918 on the Somme. The *Mid Devon Advertiser* reported that persistent rumours swept Bovey to the effect that Achi Baba, a Turkish stronghold in Gallipoli, had been stormed and occupied by the Allies. The report, said the paper sarcastically, was, of course, founded on 'good authority'. The Allies never captured Achi Baba; this was an interesting example of the wartime rumour. More Bovey men enlisted in August, including Felix Nankeville, potman at The King of Prussia in Fore Street. Details of his service record are unclear, but he died on 20th October 1918 and is buried in South Wales.

In August a detachment of the 4th Wessex Royal Field Artillery visited Bovey. After they had paraded through the town a recruiting meeting was held, with a large crowd present, but there were only three responses. Only one of these subsequently passed his medical. The local paper commented that Bovey had contributed a large number of young men to the army and navy, which probably accounted for the small response. The working party of ladies, under the direction of Mrs H.B. Hyde, had, by early September, completed 888 sandbags for the use of troops at the front; by 18th September the total was 1,212. The 'Vegetables for the Fleet' campaign continued, with Bovey once again doing well above average in terms of both quality and quantity.

In late September the Chancellor of the Exchequer's Budget hit every household hard. Some of the major changes included an income tax increase of 40%, with reduced exemptions, an increase on sugar, tea, coffee and tobacco tax, a rise in petrol duty and increased postal charges.

The newspaper reported that, owing to the war, life in Bovey Tracey 'is pretty quiet just now'. A travelling cinema show had just visited the town and done very fair business. The paper also referred again to rumours, including one that 'a well-known young man hailing from here had had both legs blown away by a shell in France'. This turned out, however, to be untrue.

By this stage in the war it was becoming clear that the principle of purely voluntary enlistment could not provide sufficient manpower for the forces. Lord Derby had devised a complex and unpopular scheme whereby potential recruits would be personally interviewed and encouraged to join up. By the end of December the paper reported that a very large number of Bovonians had 'grouped' under the Derby scheme, very few eligibles having been left out. It hoped that the voluntary system would be sufficient. This, however, would prove not to be the case, and, in January 1916, the first Military Service Act was passed, and conscription became a reality for unmarried men between 18 and 41. A second Act, in May 1916, was passed and included all men regardless of marital status, with military tribunals set up to examine claims for exemption.

By mid-November 2,210 sandbags had been sent to the Devonshire Regiment in France; the ladies responsible were planning to knit woollen mufflers and mittens during the winter months. Five young men from Heathfield enlisted in November 1915; one, Wilfred Bowden, would be killed in action in France on 2nd July 1918. The vicar gave an illustrated lecture in the town hall on 'The War on the Eastern Front'. There was a good attendance and a collection for the Devonshire Regiment was taken. The schoolchildren sent over two dozen Christmas parcels, including socks, cigarettes and sweets, to soldiers and sailors.

The second Christmas of the war was gloomy; 15 Bovey men had died on war service during the year. 1916 began with a sad reminder that not all deaths occurred at the front. Mrs Eva Coniam, of Mary Street, died on 27th January. Her husband was on active service with the Army Service Corps, leaving their two young children to a very uncertain future. The price of bread rose to 8d. a loaf.

In the spring the authorities decided it was time to put Bovey on a war footing in case of air attack. Arrangements were made with the police that, in the event of a Zeppelin raid warning being received, the pottery hooter would be blown for two minutes, and the gas and electricity supplies would be shut off at the works. All lights in private houses had to be extinguished, and the inhabitants were advised to remain under cover during the raid. There were, in fact, no air raids in the South West during the war.

The military tribunals had begun and their effect was being felt in the community. The local paper reported the results of one such tribunal as it affected Bovey in May 1916. Archibald Frederick Rowe, a Bovey draper, claimed exemption on the grounds that he was indispensable to his business. He had stock, which would be left on his hands if he went, valued at £1,000. He was granted an exemption until 15th July. On the grounds that he would have to give up some of his bread round, William Leaker, a Bovey baker (whose premises are now those of Thomas's, near the Dolphin Hotel), asked for the exemption of an employee, Walter Stoneman, who was married. He was exempted until 1st August. An exemption for Richard Dayment, horseman and ploughman in the employment of his father at Frost Farm, Bovey, was sought. This was allowed until 1st January 1917. A similar exemption was granted to Sydney Fry, a 19-year-old horseman working for Mr Diamond at Luscombe Farm, Bovey Tracey. The Bovey Tracey Co-operative Society applied for the renewal of exemption certificates held by two of their employees, Samuel Heath and William Bennett. A representative of the society appeared in support of the claim and stated that, as the society supplied 3,000 persons, it was considered that both men were advantageously employed in the interests of the public. Both were exempted until 1st July.

The Bovey Pottery Company applied for the exemption of 17 employees, all married. Mr Robinson, for the company, said that the men formed the chief producers of the business and if they were conscripted it would prejudice and jeopardise the industry to a very serious extent. Prior to the war 128 men had been employed, 35 of whom had joined the services, leaving 93. Of these, 45 were over military age, and, of the remainder, 31 were married and 17 single. Dependent on the remaining men were 61 women and 24 boys, and if the men for whom the applications had been made were taken it would displace many employees. The firm was overburdened with orders and government work was being done. The company's export trade was also very considerable. All the men were exempted until 1st January 1917.

Another change imposed by the government in 1916 was the imposition of Daylight Saving Time (now British Summer Time). This had a particular impact on communities such as Bovey, which were largely agricultural in nature. This, along with the imposition of restricted licensing hours later in the war, is one of the few effects of the war that are still felt today.

Bovey Tracey Temperance Hall was the scene in June of a 'smoking concert' for a contingent of Canadian Forestry Battalion troops encamped near Stover. About 100 soldiers were present, plus a large number of townsfolk. It was apparently a very successful concert with much singing by all concerned. That war was a dangerous business was brought home to Bovey when Private Heath, of the territorials, was home on leave from India at this time: he was displaying an Indian revolver to some friends when it went off, and the bullet hit Alfred Steer in the leg. An operation was necessary to remove it. Apparently some children standing nearby had a narrow escape. One of the more unusual wartime activities taking place in the district was the collection of sphagnum moss for use in the treatment of wounds. A total of 105 sacks had been collected. Another memorial was erected at this time; a tablet was placed on the exterior of the western end of St John's Church in memory of Captain Beaufort. Although partly weathered, this may still be clearly seen.

In mid-July the Battle of the Somme was raging in France. A Bovey man, Private H.P. Underdown, of Blenheim House (now the Blenheim Hotel, Brimley), serving in Queen Victoria's Rifles, was seriously wounded and brought to the military hospital in Shaftesbury Avenue, London. His parents were asked to visit him immediately, but on reaching the hospital they found him slightly better. He had to undergo the amputation of an arm. Another Bovey man wounded at the Somme was Private Arthur Bowden. Two Bovonians were killed on the first day of the Somme battle (1st July 1916). One was Private Fred Mountford, only child of Mr and Mrs George Mountford of 4 Victoria Terrace (off Fore Street), the other being Private Fred French (19), who had worked for Candy and Co. before the war. Their bodies were never found. The casualty lists in the paper showed two more local men wounded in the Somme fighting – Lance Corporal J. Phillips and Private S. Shillabeer. The Bovey Tracey Parish Church Choir passed a vote of condolence to their chairman, Mr Stookes, and his family on the loss of their son, Herbert, fighting in France.

The war now fully involved the whole nation. Even a small South Devon town like Bovey was experiencing casualties in increasing numbers. The authorities were becoming desperate for men to fill gaps in the ranks, and military tribunals were examining closely all requests for exemption from conscription. For some reason the tribunal heard the claim of James Voysey, a 29-year-old married gardener of Plumley Cottage, on the Moretonhampstead road, Bovey, in private, but he was only given a short exemption.

At a parish council meeting Mrs Bentinck said that she had just learnt of the death of another Bovey man, making a total of 16. This had inspired her to suggest some kind of memorial, perhaps on the existing Market Cross, or similar. She felt that those who had lost their dear ones should at least have the pleasure of their names being perpetuated and held in honoured memory. A Mr Pascoe agreed, saying that a memorial of some kind should be erected for their children's children to look at in the future. More men enlisted; Ralph Mardon, second son of Mr and Mrs George Mardon of The Beehive Stores in Fore Street, was posted to the Royal Field Artillery. The war was also having an unexpected effect on the education of Bovey's youth. During the summer holidays Mr Pickford, headmaster of the National School, had moved to North Devon; Mr Lamacraft, headmaster of the council school, had been called to the colours; and four other teachers had left.

Fund-raising continued. Between 1,500 and 3,000 people attended a fete at Indio, home of the Bentincks. Canadian Forestry Battalion troops attended in force and participated in a range of activities, raising the sum of £50 for war charities. Torbay Electric Theatre was showing the 'Official War Film' on the Battle of the Somme, thus giving astounded audiences a glimpse of modern warfare. Not every soldier's death occurred on the battlefield; Mr May, of Southbrook, lost his son, Ernest, a sapper in the Royal Engineers, when he was run over by a truck and killed. More men came before the tribunals; William Sharp, 35, an insurance agent of 77 Mary Street, was said by his manager to be 'utterly unfit' for service - he was sent for an official medical examination. So, too, was Harold Hooper, a 21-year-old single man who worked as a horseman at Stickwick Farm. Lewis Shobbrook, 30, married, of Station Road, Bovey, applied for exemption on the grounds that if he had to join the army he would suffer serious financial and domestic hardship. He was given until 1st March 1917 to sell his business and enlist. Percy Prescott, 'Dibby' to his chums, of East Street, had been killed in France at the age of 19. His body was never found.

Bovey shops continued to be affected by wartime regulations. The government had decreed that the Whitsun Bank Holiday should not be granted in 1916, so in October a meeting of Bovey traders took place to discuss the possibility of a closure at this stage. It was agreed to close for the day on 30th October and, in addition, adopt the new guidelines for earlier closing times. Henceforth, Bovey shops would close at 7 p.m. on Mondays, Tuesdays, Thursdays and Fridays, 1 p.m. on Wednesdays and 9 p.m. on Saturdays. Military tribunals rarely agreed exemptions, but Lewis Snell, 29, who lived at South View and worked as a pottery warehouseman, was allowed one on account of his wife's ill-health and having four children under eight. The parish council had agreed that Mrs Bentinck could erect a roll of honour at the Town Cross. This was done in early December 1916; there were 22 names inscribed on the tablet. The latest name on the list was that of Private Samuel Hawkes, son of George and Caroline Hawkes of Mount Pleasant, Mary Street, who had died on the Somme. Christmas 1916 was marked in Bovey by a whist drive and dance at the Constitutional Club (now the Conservative Club). Mrs Underdown distributed the prizes, and members remarked on how pleased they were to see her wounded son home again.

The new year of 1917 began with tribunals pushing harder for men, but they were willing to grant conditional exemption to William Bowden, 24, single, an agricultural smith at Broadmead Works. Bowden claimed that the troublesome ground around Bovey damaged machinery more than in other places, and members of the tribunal confirmed that this was so. Men of the Canadian Forestry Battalion were cutting at Furzeleigh Copse (at the top of Furzeleigh Lane, which leads uphill from Bovey Tracey Hospital) with their tractor and trailer, making a mess of the roads. The men were billeted at the town hall whilst doing this work, and this was also the venue for a concert and tea to about 80 wounded soldiers, arranged largely by Mr and Mrs Bentinck. The prices of basic foodstuffs had risen again; bread from 9d. to 10d. a loaf, and milk from 4d. to 5d. a pint. In January 1917 Miss Bessie Wright of Bovey married Mr S. Rochon of the Canadian Forestry Battalion.

A reminder that this war raged worldwide came in the form of a report that Sergeant Slee, of the Devonshire Territorial Force, had been wounded in the right arm at Armara, just north of Baghdad. He was the third son of Mr and Mrs Slee of South View. The town hall was the scene of another concert, this time supported by the band of the London Rifles. Proceeds went towards providing comforts for the men of that regiment serving at the front. Mr E. Wyatt, dairyman and miller of Bovey, applied to the tribunal for exemption of his cowman, Richard Cornish, 37, married, of 20 South View. Although his staff in the dairy business had already dropped from 17 to 12, with another due to go very soon, he was only granted an exemption until June.

The government was, at this time, introducing a voluntary 'National Service' scheme. This was an attempt to keep up drafts of properly-trained men for the front, while keeping men in mines, on transport and in agriculture, and in other essential services. Farmers were anxious that they would lose labourers, but were assured this would not happen. The parish council urged the people of Bovey to economise, and thus cut back on imports, to conform to the voluntary regulations laid down by the government (4lbs of bread, 2$\frac{1}{2}$lbs of meat and $\frac{3}{4}$lb of sugar per week) and to enrol as national service volunteers. Such volunteers would be directed to jobs where their skills would be of maximum benefit to the war effort.

The gallantry of a Bovey soldier was reported in the press. Private Walter Clatworthy was congratulated by his divisional commanding officer for helping to bring in wounded under heavy shellfire. Mr Clatworthy formerly resided at Thorns Cross and worked for Mr Phillpotts at Bridge House. Sadly he was to be captured by the Germans later in the war, and he died in a PoW camp in Germany in August 1918. Mr and Mrs C. Bowden, of Blenheim Terrace, received the sad news in March of the death of their son, Henry, who had been wounded and sent to hospital in Mesopotamia (now Iran/Iraq). Mr Bentinck had applied for exemption for his married gardener, Francis Topps (35). Perhaps surprisingly, this was granted, but Mr Topps was sent for another military medical.

From 30th April 1917 licensing hours were to change; in populous areas closing time would now be 10.00 p.m. and in non-populous places it would be 9.00 p.m. Drinkers would not suffer alone; a new Order came into force 'prohibiting entirely the making for sale of any muffin, crumpet, teacake or fancy bread, or any light or fancy pastries'. Anyone disobeying these severe restrictions would be liable to prosecution.

Back in 1916 Archibald Rowe, a Bovey draper, had sought exemption from military service. Up before the tribunal again, he claimed he had been unable to sell his business, and also produced a medical certificate stating his elderly father's health to be poor. He was denied leave to appeal, but the military were asked not to call him up for two more weeks. Mr Mann, of Fore Street, applied to keep his slaughterman, Arthur John Mitchell (who would set up in business as a butcher after the war in what is now Pedricks, Station Road). Mr Mann's application was turned down, but he was allowed to keep Mr Mitchell until 15th May. Mr Parr, of Bullaton Farm, near Trenchford Reservoir, asked for the exemption of his brother, Ernest, 37, single, a horseman. He was granted three months. The owner of Five Wyches Farm (near the Edgemoor Hotel) did not get any exemption for his horseman, William Bolt, 18, single. The newspaper reported several Bovey soldiers as being wounded at this time, the case of Private William Wyatt being particularly sad. No definite news had been heard for some time, and it would eventually be confirmed that he had been killed in action on 9th April. The waiting period for his parents, William and Mary, of 1 South View, must have been agonising. Mrs Hull heard that her husband, Arthur, a private in the Devonshires, who had worked as a gamekeeper for Mr Lee on Yarner Estate, had been killed in Salonika in northern Greece.

The 'King of Prussia' in Fore Street found itself in the news in June 1917. An application to transfer the licence to a new landlord led to an exchange of words in the courtroom. The new landlord, Mr Pinsent, was asked to consider changing the name, as it was inappropriate. The 'King of Bovey' was suggested. The news of a Bovey man winning the Military Medal came through in June. Private F.G. Jones of the Machine Gun Section of the Seaforth Highlanders was granted the award for digging out his gun, which had been buried by a shell-burst, and turning it on the enemy. Jones had lived at Southbrook and attended the National School.

The Bovey Pottery Company was struggling to comply with regulations, stating that no more than 50 per cent of its pre-war staff level could be allowed to remain employed. The call-up of two men was dismissed, and thus the firm was able to continue. Another big employer, Candy and Co., similarly applied for the exemption of three Heathfield men on the same grounds, but exemption was only granted until 1st January 1918, thus leaving the company in a precarious position. Alfred Aggett, 38 and married, was a Bovey garage proprietor. He told the tribunal that his was a single-handed business and that he was also secretary to the Dartmoor Electricity Supply Company. He also produced a letter from a local doctor in support of his exemption claim, but the military representative said he would be better employed driving in the army, and his application was refused.

The local paper carried an advertisement on 28th July 1917 stating that labour for harvesting would be available during August and September from 'Public Schools Camps' at Chudleigh and at Elsford, just north of Bovey Tracey near the reservoirs. These camps were to be run on 'Military Lines and under Military Discipline'. The scale of pay would be 4d. per hour for work done by the boys, and 6d. per hour for that done by the masters. The tribunals continued to hear cases; Mr Tapper, of Pool Mill Cottages, Tottiford, applied for his son, John James Tapper, 19, single, a rabbit trapper, on the grounds of indispensability. They both worked for Torquay Corporation, and rabbits were damaging the crops. An exemption of two months was granted. Mrs Hellier, at the Moorland Hotel, Haytor, employed William Husband, 28, married, of 41 Mary Street, as chauffeur. Although the recruiting officer said 'chauffeurs of all medical classifications are wanted in the army', he was granted an exemption until 1st January 1918.

In France the casualties continued to mount; Mr and Mrs Mountford, of Mary Street, learnt that their son, Private Alfred Mountford, had just been wounded. A piece of shrapnel had entered his left elbow and exited through his forearm, whilst another piece had caused a scalp wound. Captain Harold Vaughan Watts died of wounds in August 1917. He had been a partner in the Newton Abbot solicitors Watts Woollcombe and Watts (now Woollcombe, Beer and Watts, who still have an office in Union Square, Bovey), and had lived at Edgemoor and Heathcot, East Street. Before the war he had been a well-known cricketer, playing for South Devon.

Baron de Bouck, of Parke, asked for the exemption from military service of Henry Kent, a 41-year-old widower of Southbrook Cottages, whom he employed as a pigman and poultryman. The baron explained that in peacetime he would be employed as a gamekeeper, but as there was now no shooting he was engaged in rabbit trapping. Kent also had two dependent children. He was granted exemption until the end of the year.

It was common practice for commanding officers of men who had been killed to write to the man's spouse. On rare occasions these letters would be published in the press, and one such occurred in September 1917. Under the headline 'Bovey Hero's Death', the newspaper stated that 'widespread regret was expressed at Bovey Tracey when the news was received of the death on the field of battle of Staff-Sergeant V.W. Cox, MM, of 26 Pottery Road'. The major of his unit wrote the following letter:

Dear Mrs Cox, I find it extremely difficult to know how to write a letter which I so deeply regret to have to write, as it conveys such sad news. Your husband was most unfortunately killed by a shell on the night of the 23rd of August. It is some small comfort perhaps to know that he was killed instantaneously, and nothing possible could have been done for him. He was going from one dugout to another on duty when he was killed. He was buried in the British cemetery in the sand dunes near a place named Coxyd, and I am glad to say a large number of his comrades were able to pay him a last respect. I shall not only personally miss him, for his work, which was of the very best, - and I can honestly say I never want to find a better and more willing man at his work - but I shall miss him as a friend. All of his officers used to enjoy a chat with him, and we had grown to like him very much. He will be deeply missed by the whole battery, and we are all very sorry to have lost him. Please accept our deepest sympathy in your great loss; his memory will help us to 'carry on' with that cheerful and willing spirit with which he always did, in this cruel struggle for the great cause for which he so nobly laid down his life.

Staff Sergeant Cox had lived in Bovey most of his life; his parents were from Pottery Road. He had been chief engineer at the potteries, where an invention of his for stamping patterns on pottery had been of great benefit to the industry. On enlisting in the Royal Garrison Artillery he had been rapidly promoted due to his technical expertise. He had recently been awarded the Military Medal for 'showing presence of mind and valour when his battery was being hard pressed'. This story illustrates the tragedy of the war; a popular and talented local lad made good – a promising career cut short by his enlisting – a splendid career in the Artillery ended one night by a shell-burst. His death left behind a grieving mother and widow.

At a wider level the war was not going well for the Allies, casualty lists were lengthening and German U-boats were sinking Allied shipping at an horrendous rate. This, in turn, raised the spectre of food rationing, and in mid-September 1917 post offices received 'sugar cards' for everyone. This was a concept completely alien to the population and, indeed to the government, and there would be many problems in the months to come as rationing became more widespread. Deaths in action continued; Private Stanley Daymond, of the Somerset Light Infantry, was killed in September. He was the son of Mr and Mrs Daymond of Fore Street, and prior to joining up had worked for Mr Pring, the tailor. Next to die was Private Charles Tremlett, of the Devonshire Regiment. He was the son of Mr and Mrs Tremlett of Slade, and was aged 20 when he died of wounds. In one of war's appalling coincidences his brother, Private Thomas Tremlett, was killed on the same day whilst serving in the East Surrey Regiment at the Battle of Passchendaele. His wife and child lived at White Heather Terrace. Second Lieutenant Leslie Parnell, son of Major Parnell, a well-known Bovey man, also died at Passchendaele, on 9th October. The local newspaper reported on 17th November that 'Bovey is being hard hit just now by casualties'. Apparently much anxiety was being felt regarding the welfare of Private F. Waldron of Pottery Cottages, Private Hext having written to say that he believed 'poor Freddie' had 'gone West'. Further concern centred on his brother, Gunner William Waldron, who was in Keighley Hospital, Yorkshire, suffering from gunshot wounds in the head and arm received whilst in France. The position of Private Walter Cox, of Atway, Bovey, had given rise to great anxiety. His foot had been amputated, and Mrs Cox had been granted a pass to go and see him. It was to no avail; he died on 16th November.

On the home front the government had fixed the price of milk at 2/- per gallon and prohibited the sale or use of cream between 8th December 1917 and 30th April 1918 except for making butter, or for consumption by invalids, young children or others 'on the orders of a doctor'.

Mr and Mrs Prescott, of East Street, had just returned from France, where they had visited their son, Sergeant William Prescott, who had lost a leg in the fighting. He would not survive, and was the second son they would lose in the war. Freddie Waldron's name continued to appear in the list of 'Missing'. Driver A.A. Skipper, a Bovonian serving in the Honourable Artillery Company, had been wounded. The Palestine campaign was causing casualties in the ranks of Bovey men fighting there. Mr and Mrs C. Staddon, of Heathfield Terrace, on the Old Newton Road, were officially notified of the death of their only son, Sergeant Frank Staddon, who was killed in Palestine. He was aged 22 at the time of his death and was described as a 'very popular young fellow'. Private E. Holmes, of East Street, had been wounded in the fighting there, as had Private E. Endacott. Trooper Reginald Mardon, son of Mr and Mrs George Mardon of 27 Fore Street,

Fred ('Nipper') Waldron. Before the war he worked at Indio as a gardener and after the war at Bovey Pottery (Andy Waldron)

was wounded in the advance on Jerusalem on 3rd December. He received a bullet wound in the thigh, and for seven hours was unable to get back to the dressing station. Trooper Willie Mann, of Mann and Son, had also been wounded in Palestine, suffering an injury to his wrist.

Thus 1917 ended on a gloomy note for the town; the war was causing more deaths as increasing numbers of men were conscripted, and, although not threatened directly by air raids, the civilian population was beginning to feel the effect of food shortages caused by the U-boat campaign. The new year opened with the news that Second Lieutenant G.W. Ferguson, MC, of the Royal Flying Corps, had been wounded in the thigh. Ferguson was a Bovey man who had won his MC in 1917 whilst a pilot in an artillery squadron, having forced down two enemy aircraft and strafed enemy infantry. The news of Private Waldron was better; feared 'missing, believed killed', it transpired he was a prisoner of war in Germany.

The Newton Abbot Urban Food Control Committee announced a one-week 'Food Hoarding Amnesty' from 12th February 1918. Householders now keeping in excess of a three-week supply of any food (other than home-made) could be prosecuted. Ration cards for meat, butter and margarine were to be delivered to all householders who applied for them. This was done at very short notice, which indicated the scale of the food-supply problem and somewhat alarmed the population. The numbers of servicemen discharged from the forces was rising, and an organisation called 'Comrades of the Great War' was formed. This would eventually become the Royal British Legion. Bovey council agreed to allow them the use of the town hall free of charge for their meetings. At the end of March two more 'war weddings' took place in Bovey; between Miss Emily Paddon and Private Brown of the Canadian Forestry Battalion, and Miss Eva Wills and Private Cook, also of the

Canadians. Light and power restrictions were imposed; no person was permitted to consume more than five-sixths of the amount of gas or electricity used in the previous year.

As Bovey householders received their ration cards, the situation on the Western Front was causing the politicians and the military men great concern. With Russia out of the war due to the revolution, Germany had been able to transfer troops to France and was thus able to launch a major offensive, which was now pushing back the Allied armies. The prime minister, Mr Lloyd George, warned Parliament that everything necessary must and would be done to stave off defeat. Essentially this meant more men for the army. The military tribunals acknowledged this; Samuel Tolley, 36, a butcher, of 11 Fore Street, applied for exemption, saying he had 2,000 persons registered with him. The tribunal reluctantly sent him for another medical, as they did in the case of Francis Topps, the gardener for Mr Bentinck. In his defence it was stated that Topps managed five acres solely for the 'Vegetables for the Fleet' scheme. William Brealey, 37, widower, of 4 South View, and employed as a quarryman, was granted a three-month exemption.

Meanwhile, the casualties mounted inexorably. Mr and Mrs Weeks, of East Street, received official notification that 'a bomb exploding in France' had killed their son, Private Arthur Weeks. (In the Great War a hand grenade was known as a 'bomb'.) News reached Mr C. Snow that his brother, Driver/Wheeler Fred Snow, had been killed in action in France. Major Hubert Symonds, of the Royal Field Artillery, had been wounded and captured in the German offensive. On 11th May it was confirmed that he had died in enemy hands. He had married Mary Ferguson of Little Wooleigh, on the Moretonhampstead road, Bovey, in 1912, and had already been wounded twice in the war before his final, fatal wound. A bomb killed Private Basil Larkin, only son of Mr and Mrs E. Larkin of Bridge Cottages, off the Pottery Road roundabout, at the age of 19.

The tribunals examined the cases of agricultural workers; they had to balance the needs of a country desperate for home-produced foodstuffs with an army desperate for all the men it could get. Cyril Dadd, of Wilmead and Hatherleigh farms, near Slade Cross, Bovey, was granted conditional exemption to 30th November; Leslie Derges, of Woodhouse Farm, was given six months, Richard Dayment, of Frost Farm, was ordered to join the army, and the case of Sydney Fry, of Luscombe Farm, was deferred. Mrs Mary Prescott, of East Street, pleaded with the tribunal to be allowed to keep her youngest boy, John, 18, from having to join the army. She had already lost two sons in the war, and her third was on active service in Mesopotamia. 'I beg you to let me keep my last boy,' she appealed. The tribunal decided the lad must join up on 15th July, although the chairman expressed his sympathy with Mrs Prescott. William Parsons, a dairyman of Fore Street, who was aged 45, married, and had already served ten years in the army (until 1914), was given a final exemption until 1st August. The Ministry of National Service announced that the shortage of agricultural labourers, coupled with the vital importance that the harvest be successfully completed, meant that public and secondary schoolboys must do useful work on the land. The Ministry were, therefore, 'reluctantly compelled' to appeal to schools to release suitable boys during term-time during this period of national crisis. Paper supplies were becoming scarce; the *Mid Devon Advertiser* was no longer allowed to print on a 'sale or return' basis.

Until this point in the conflict there had been no conscientious objector in Bovey. In July 1918 John Tapper, a 45-year-old married carpenter from Pool Mill Cottage, Tottiford, claimed exemption. He had refused to be medically examined and contended that he could not take any part in the war because if he did he would not be obedient to the Word of God. By growing eight acres of potatoes, he considered that he was doing something for the country in which his lot was cast. Tapper also quoted many passages of Scripture to support his claim, but Mr McGregor of the tribunal observed that by using detached portions of the Scriptures even the devil or the Kaiser could find something to justify his actions or suit his purpose. After some further debate the tribunal granted Tapper exemption from combatant service only, but Tapper told the chairman that he could not accept their decision.

The Food Control Committee complained that many people had incorrectly completed their application forms for ration cards, and reminded everyone that 'no card, no rations'. The committee went on to announce that there might be an allotment of sugar for the purpose of making blackberry jam. It would, however, only be made to working-class families who undertook to gather the fruit themselves, and who would not use the sugar for any other purpose. Mrs Heath, of Station Road, Bovey, was informed of the death of her son, Sergeant Thomas Heath, in the recent heavy fighting in France. This fighting was the beginning of the Allied offensive on the Western Front that would end the war. As it became clear that the victories achieved by the British army were the real thing people began to hope that the end of the war might be in sight.

The tribunal heard the case of Francis Topps, Mr Bentinck's gardener, after his recent medical. Mr Topps was granted permission to remain a civilian until 15th November. Mr Bentinck's application to keep his valet and butler, John Irving, on the basis that he needed such a man whilst High Sherriff of the county, was partially successful, exemption being granted until 1st January 1919. Bovey men continued to fall victim to the war; Sergeant Edward Nicholls, son of Jane and the late James Nicholls of Vicarage Cottages, was killed on 14th September, and Sergeant Sydney Maddicott, son of Mr and Mrs H. Maddicott of 5 Heathfield Cottages (near the railway bridge by the Heathfield Industrial Estate), was killed in action that same week. Prior to the war Maddicott had captained the Chudleigh Knighton Ramblers football team. He and his brother, Cecil, enlisted with two horses belonging to Mr Reddacliffe of Whisselwell Farm, near the Edgemoor Hotel.

On a more cheerful note another war wedding took place in Bovey; in September Miss Radford, daughter of Mr and Mrs Radford of Fore Street, married Private Cogan of the Army Medical Corps, who was home on leave from France. In October 1918 the local paper carried, under the Defence of the Realm Regulations, a 'Public Warning against interference with Carrier Pigeons'. Following cases of carrier pigeons being shot whilst carrying military communications, a new regulation threatened six months imprisonment with or without hard labour for anyone found guilty of such an offence. A reward of £5 was offered for information about such crimes. Through the war the

government had appealed for the population to lend money by purchasing War Bonds at 5/- each, and in early 1918 had asked communities to 'buy' a weapon, such as a tank or an aircraft. In the autumn Wireless Operator H.S. Abbot, RAF, of Bovey, wrote home to say that, whilst passing an aerodrome in France, he noticed an aeroplane marked 'Bovey Tracey'.

Mr and Mrs J. Gilley, of Brimley Farm, Bovey, were notified that their youngest son, John, had been killed in action on 27th September in France. William and Jane Weeks of Virginia Cottage, Mary Street, learnt that their son, Sydney, had died in India on 22nd September. Prior to enlisting he had worked for Mr Pring, the East Street tailor. He was the second son of this family to die in the war. Mrs Ernest Holmes was told that her husband had been seriously wounded, and the same intelligence reached Mr and Mrs Hydon about their son, Alfred. Both these men would, however, survive. By this stage in the war it was becoming clear that the Allied armies would now prove victorious. Just as the picture in March and April had seemed so desperate, so it now seemed rosy. For the first time the newspaper carried a pictorial supplement with scenes of the enemy in full flight. The army was not disposed to cease their demand for men, and the tribunals still operated. Charles Wills, 19, of 3 South View, had his exemption certificate withdrawn, whilst Sydney Payne, of the Bovey electricity

The war memorial after the First World War, with the original rolls of honour (Pat Tregoning)

works, and Mark Nicholls, a builder, of 3 Orchard Terrace, off Fore Street, were both deferred until 1919.

And then, suddenly, the war was over. The armistice came into force at 11.00 a.m. on Monday, 11th November 1918, and everyone could begin to hope once more. The newspaper reported 'great rejoicing all day' in Bovey; shops closed at midday and work was generally suspended. A thanksgiving service was held at the church, and in the evening the bells rang out.

This chapter has examined how the war affected the town in 'concrete' ways – the price of bread, conscription, casualties and so on. But the town and its people were also affected in many other ways, most impossible to measure but nevertheless real enough. The loss of her fighting men who never returned from the battlefields is obvious; some had a grave for relatives to visit, but some bodies were never found, with the consequent anguish for those denied a focal point for their grief. The whole concept of mourning was dramatically altered during what was known at the time as the Great War; for many there would be no grave on home soil, which is why the Tomb of the Unknown Soldier in Westminster Abbey became of such importance.

But what of those men who returned, wounded in mind or body? The experiences of war and the horrors they had seen stayed with them for the rest of their lives. They were changed men, and no-one who had not gone through the miseries of the trenches could understand how they felt. They returned to a world quite different from that which they had left. The women left behind had suffered, too; they had watched as their menfolk went away to war with the anguish of not knowing whether they would ever see them again.

Today, in the early years of the 21st century, the Great War has almost receded from memory into history. The acres of trees removed by the Canadians have been replanted and are now fully grown. There are few tangible reminders of that conflict to be seen in the town. The war memorial outside the town hall, the stained-glass window and memorial tablets in the parish church, the memorials in the Church of St John the Evangelist, and the Church School roll of honour held in the heritage centre are all that remain. But every year on Remembrance Sunday the town honours its dead with a church service and parade, and older members of a few long-established Bovey families may recall grandfathers and great-uncles who wore their Great War medals with pride.

Using information provided by Mark Bailey, and with thanks to Dave Lewis and Anthony Porter for identifying locations in the text.

An early remembrance parade led by Ted Endacott, J. Fogwill and Arthur Jeffery, who all fought in the Great War (Dave Lewis)

The Landscape and its Industrial Use

The Granite and Clay Industries around Bovey Tracey
by Sheila Perigal

Dartmoor granite and its derivative, clay, provided considerable employment for many people in Bovey Tracey during the 18th and 19th centuries. Since Bronze Age times granite has been extensively used for building and many other purposes for which wood was used in more fertile areas with good trees. Haytor granite was the first to be demanded for well-known buildings in London (including the former London Bridge and the British Museum), and production grew to a peak at the beginning of the 19th century.

Clay is formed from feldspar (one of the three constituents of granite) when the granite breaks down. Two different forms of clay result, according to the surrounding conditions. 'Ball clay', or 'pipe clay', derives from kaolin (from feldspar) which has been washed into streams and become mixed with sand and gravel impurities before settling in lower land - such as the valley between Chudleigh Knighton and Kingsteignton. 'China clay' is formed underground when the feldspar is hydrolysed by superheated steam and carbon dioxide under pressure. There are large areas of china clay at Lee Moor on Dartmoor. Ball clay was given its name because of the method of extracting it from the ground with special spades, which cut the clay into cubes, or balls. It was also known as pipe clay because it was used for making pipes for tobacco smoking. Over the years a variety of uses for ball clay was found, while in the 1960s a new mining technique was employed, using boring machines working into inclined adits: nowadays, clay is mined to a depth of 400 feet. Ball clay has a plasticity, which makes it ideal for porcelain and chinaware. In the early 18th century the clay was sent to Staffordshire for firing because of the coal available there. From 1765 Josiah Wedgwood developed 'Queensware' and he ordered tons of Devon clay for this purpose; this demand diminished when Wedgwood became more interested in Purbeck clay. Nowadays, there is still a thriving industry in the Chudleigh Knighton area, with different quality clays being extracted at different levels for particular requirements.

Both the ball clay and granite industries of Bovey Tracey are associated with the Templer family of Stover. James Templer was born in 1722 to a poor family in Exeter. He ran away to sea and later made a fortune building the Madras Docks in India. He then returned to Devon, where he was active in the construction of Plymouth Docks and, having acquired considerable wealth, bought the run-down Stover estate. Here he settled, building a new Stover House (using granite from Haytor) and improving the grounds. His son, James, inherited the estate in 1782, continued to develop the area and endowed a new church in Teigngrace, where his son, John, became vicar. At this time the ball clay industry was increasing at Chudleigh Knighton, and James built the Stover Canal to facilitate the transport of clay to the Teign estuary and thence to Teignmouth. A loading bay was constructed at Ventiford, with the two-mile canal leading to a quay at Jetty Marsh. Clay was loaded on to barges and transferred to sea-going ships at Teignmouth. The canal proved a profitable venture and James died a wealthy man. His son, George, further developed the quarries at Haytor and built the famous 8-mile long Haytor granite tramway to Ventiford in order to connect up with the Stover Canal. At Teignmouth he built the New Quay, where granite was transferred from the barges to seaworthy ships and sent to its destination.

Unfortunately, the name of the engineer of the granite tramway is not known, but it was remarkable for many reasons. The rails were made of granite, which was chosen, firstly, because there were masses of rock on site so there was no need to import other materials; secondly, because the stone track could carry the heavy weight of wagons loaded with granite blocks; and thirdly, because the iron used for railways elsewhere at that time (early 1800s) did not behave satisfactorily in changeable weather and buckled in the heat. There are only two other, very much shorter, stone-

The number 3 milestone of the Haytor granite tramway in Bovey Tracey, photographed in 1991 (John Adey)

built railways in England – one at Doncaster and another near Towcester.

The Haytor track, single all the way with two sidings, gently descends more than 1,300 feet, and there is only one cutting. The stones average four feet in length and were each cut with a flange along one side. These blocks were laid end to end in two parallel rows, forming a 4-feet gauge track. The blocks were not joined as their weight was sufficient to hold them in place. On curves, shorter blocks with carefully cut flanges were laid (on straight passages the depth of the flange varied more). Where two tracks from two different quarries merged, the wagons were directed to the single track by metal cheek-pieces rotated on pegs fitted into the junction stones.

The wagons for carrying the stones were adapted from open, flat road wagons, with wheels fitting into the flanges on the rails (not on top of the rails as in conventional railways). These wagons were drawn up to the quarries by horses, 18 of which were stabled at Ventiford. The return journey of the loaded wagons was accomplished simply by gravity down the carefully graduated slope of the track. The only

braking system was by means of a 10 to 12 feet pole applied to the rim of the wheels. Rather surprisingly this seems to have been sufficient.

The tramway was opened with a grand fete day on 6th September 1820, with large crowds from Bovey Tracey. During the period of peak production that followed some workers were housed in cottages alongside the main quarry and near the Rock Inn in Haytor Vale. Among the famous buildings built mainly or partly with Haytor granite were the former London Bridge (now in Arizona, at Lake Havasu City, where it was reassembled after being dismantled and shipped there in 1970), the British Museum, Goldsmiths' Hall, Fishmongers' Hall, Christ's Hospital and Buckingham Palace.

Sadly, the Templer relationship with clay and granite was not to last. In 1829 George Templer sold the canal, the tramway and the Stover estate to Seymour, Duke of Somerset. By 1858 the Haytor quarries were deserted: competition from cheaper Cornish granite

The remains of part of the granite tramway (John Adey)

had grown and, on Dartmoor, finer-grained and better quality granite was being exploited in quarries at King Tor, Foggintor and Swell Tor, and the pink-coloured granite favoured for monuments and plinths at Trowlesworthy. Merrivale was the last to supply granite. At the end of the 19th century the quarries at Haytor briefly opened again, but the granite tramway was no longer used. Instead, the granite was transported by tractor to Bovey. The last time Haytor granite was used was in 1919, when stone for the Exeter war memorial was cut.

The granite tramway was an extraordinary enterprise, but it was badly costed and badly thought through in terms of its long-term potential. George Templer had many positive qualities. He was very popular, a tremendous huntsman, was artistic, wrote poetry and was warm-hearted and generous, but he was no businessman and by 1843 he was impoverished, having lost a vast fortune in about 20 years. A fascinating revelation has been that he had six children with one of his tenant farmer's daughters and, although these children were 'base born', he sent them all to good schools.

The Templer Way is a walk which can be followed for most of the way from Haytor to Jetty Marsh, Newton Abbot. From Haytor the tramway can be seen clearly on the moor, and where it enters Yarner Wood it runs through a beautiful avenue of beech trees. From there onwards the track disappears for long stretches where it has been built over, but at Lower Down the track runs alongside the road, and at Chapple the rails run over the only bridge which crosses the Bovey Pottery Leat. In Bovey Tracey, on a path behind houses fronting on Pottery Road, the number 3 milestone can still be seen.

Bibliography
Ewans, M.C. *The Haytor Granite Tramway and Stover Canal.* David and Charles, 1964
Harris, Helen. *The Industrial Archaeology of Dartmoor.* David and Charles, 1968

Mining in Bovey Tracey Parish
by Nick Walter

The history of mining around Bovey Tracey goes back several hundred years, although very little documentary evidence survives, and the earliest mining features are now obscured by later activity, such as farming, industry and housing. Extraction of minerals ranges from probable tin workings in medieval times, through to clay, lignite and iron within living memory.

The parish of Bovey lies on the eastern edge of the Dartmoor granite, which was formed about 300 million years ago. The molten granite was forced up from deep underground, distorting and heating the surrounding earlier rocks. At the time of formation the granite did not reach the surface, probably remaining about one to two kilometres under it. Most of the useful minerals found in the area are generally believed to have been formed when superheated liquids circulated within cracks in the cooling granite. As this liquid cooled it deposited minerals in narrow veins within the granite and in a narrow band of the surrounding rock (the 'metamorphic aureole').

Millions of years of erosion have stripped off the surface, exposing the granite. More importantly, the eroded material was eventually carried down the river systems. This led to the formation of the large clay and lignite beds of the Bovey Basin, and the deposition of tin-rich gravels in most of the riverbeds on and around Dartmoor. The alluvial deposits of tin, clay and lignite have all been worked in the parish. Underground working for copper took place at Yarner, and in the northern part of the parish there were several mines producing micaceous haematite, sometimes known as 'Bovey silver'.

Tin has been obtained from Dartmoor for hundreds of years, though the main periods of production were in medieval times and the 16th century. Around Bovey the activity would have centred on 'blowing houses' that smelted the tin-bearing gravels deposited beside the River Bovey, and in the clay beds of the Bovey Basin. No blowing house sites have yet been identified in the parish, though there was one just outside, at Drakeford Bridge, and the distinctive stream side ridges resulting from tin 'streaming' have been noted at the northern end of Bovey Heath. In 1797 Richard Polwhele wrote in his *History of Devonshire* the following:

In the parishes of Manaton, Kingsteignton, and Teigngrace, are many old tin-works of this kind, which the inhabitants attribute to that period, when wolves and winged serpents were no strangers to the hills or valleys...and indeed all the valleys from the Heathfield to Dartmoor, bear the traces of shoding and streaming.

Later farming and industrial activity has destroyed most of the tinning traces in the fertile lands around the river.

In the western part of the parish is the Yarner nature reserve. Hidden in the depths of the wood are the remains of Yarner (or Yarrow) Copper Mine. The recorded history of the mine starts in 1858, though it is thought to have been worked earlier. The high price of copper in the mid-19th century resulted in many mines being developed, Yarner being a moderately successful one. By 1862 a pumping engine was in use, 50 workers were employed, and the mine was working down to 50 fathoms (c 100 metres). The copper ore obtained would have been roughly crushed and sorted on site, then sent to one of the major copper-smelting works, probably Swansea. In 1864 a parliamentary commission investigated miners' working conditions, and one of the miners interviewed was from Yarner. He stated:

Many of the men have to walk two miles to the mine over an exposed road. They then go underground for eight hours, come up fatigued and freely perspiring and have to put on their wet clothes in which to go home.

Miners of this period were prone to all kinds of lung diseases, typically tuberculosis, silicosis and pneumonia. It is thought that this parliamentary report resulted in the introduction of the 'miners dry', where the miners' clothes could be dried when not in use.

Most of the Yarner workforce would probably have been local men, only a small proportion of professional miners being brought in from elsewhere. By 1865 the copper boom was over, and Yarner Mine was closed down and advertised for sale. Although only worked for a short period, Yarner produced over 2,000 tons of copper ore, valued at about £6,000 (several million pounds at today's values). In 1866 the site was sold to a concern called Devon Wheal Frances. This is thought to have carried out extensive development work in the extreme west of the parish, near Black Hill, where several old workings can still be seen on the open hillside. Despite employing 30 men, and working until 1870, no copper seems to have been produced by Wheal Frances.

In the northern part of the parish, iron mining has been carried on since the 18th century. The iron obtained was a rare form of iron oxide, technically called micaceous haematite, but more usually known as 'shining ore'. This material was found in narrow, almost vertical, veins in the granite, usually worked by tunnels ('adits') running into the steep hillsides above the Bovey and Wray valleys. The 'shining ore' was first used as a blotting sand for ink, as a substitute for black lead for stoves and, as Richard Polwhele in his 1797 *History of Devonshire* said, 'the remainder is disposed to the color-grinders, who work it up with their paints to add to the weight of them'. In later years it was used in welding rods, in tile and pottery manufacture, and, most importantly, as the base of a corrosion-resistant paint.

The micaceous haematite mines in Bovey parish are those at Kelly, Hawkmoor, Plumley, Slade and Shaptor, with possibly another at Hatherleigh. The earliest reference to these mines is in 1797, when Polwhele mentions the production of micaceous haematite, and from Cecil Torr's *Wrayland Documents* we learn that John Pinsent leased for 21 years 'a certain mine of black lead or some other substance' at South Kelly. By the late 19th century 'shining ore' was in great demand, resulting in a major expansion of Kelly, Hawkmoor, Plumley and Shaptor mines, though all remained small affairs compared to the great tin and copper mines of West Devon and Cornwall. Typically all the mines carried out ore processing on site, usually with waterwheel-powered machinery and drying furnaces to produce a pure, dry metallic sand as the finished product. The ore was usually despatched from either Bovey or Lustleigh railway stations, packed into hogshead barrels.

By the First World War only Kelly remained active of the Bovey mines, and continued operating until 1944, being worked in conjunction with the larger mine at Great Rock, near Hennock. After a short closure, the processing site at Kelly was reopened by a company operating a nearby small underground working known as Slade. However, this closed in 1951 when blasting caused a collapse into unrecorded older workings; one miner remembered 'you could look right down; the "old men" had been there before us'. Thus ended over 150 years of 'shining ore' production in the parish.

These miners were normally local men who learned their trade 'on the job'. In the early 20th century a boy would join the workforce at 14 or 15 and be put on the job of ore washing (the dirtiest and coldest task). He would work on that until a younger lad

Francis Heath at the entrance to Kelly Mine, 1951 (B.T. Heritage Trust)

joined, when he would move up the ladder or, perhaps, start working underground. Mining the ore was fairly easy, as the material was quite soft and could normally be extracted with pick, bar and shovel. Drilling and blasting were used to remove the harder rock surrounding the narrow veins. In later years the introduction of powered rock drills caused major health problems; the constant breathing in of quartz-laden dust resulted in many miners dying of silicosis in the 1930s. It is known that the Stancombe family of Bovey was prominent in mining, 'Old Jimmy' Stancombe being the mine foreman at Kelly for several years.

It should be noted that access to most of these sites is very difficult, and there is often very little left to see. Of the mines, the best preserved is Kelly, where access is possible, but only by prior arrangement. The little that remains of Yarner Mine is visible from the nature trail through the reserve. The other mine sites are potentially dangerous, as the ground above is prone to collapse and the underground workings themselves are very hazardous. Very little has been published on this subject, and most relevant books are now long out of print. Useful publications are listed below and should be available from the local library.

Bibliography

Polwhele, Richard. *History of Devonshire.* 1797

Richardson, P.H.G. *Mines of Dartmoor and the Tamar Valley.* 1992

Hamilton-Jenkin, A.K. *Mines of Devon Vol 2*

Torr, Cecil. *Wrayland Documents*

Lignite

The story of Bovey's lignite is one of great optimism followed by failure, and it is interesting to imagine how very different Bovey would be today if any of the schemes had worked out. Lignite is a substance halfway between wood and coal. It is usually brown in colour and, although it is inferior to coal as a fuel, having a lower carbon content, it is mined and has been widely used, particularly in Eastern Europe. The Bovey Basin contains the only significant lignite deposit in

Britain. William Pengelly (1812-94), the geologist, wrote on the fossil plants and trees found in the Bovey deposit and dated their growth to the Tertiary Miocene Period, when Britain was not an island but part of a great European continent. Lignite was dug from a number of small pits in the Bovey Basin, but the main excavation came from Bluewaters, called that because of the spring of clear, blue water which came from its strata. It is believed that local lignite, or 'Bovey Coal', was used for lime burning in the 17th century. In *Billings' Directory* of 1857 'Bovey Coal' is described as being divided into two species,

> *distinguished as stone coal and wood coal, but the unpleasant smell which it emits being found to be very injurious to health, it is seldom used, except by the poorer inhabitants.*

But then, in the mid–19th century, there began to be great excitement about the potential for expanding the exploitation of lignite. The potteries were established, local Dartmoor mines producing tin, copper, iron and lead required a cheap fuel for smelting, and the lime burning industry was expanding. Excavation of lignite was fairly extensive, reaching a depth of 100 feet and covering about 7 acres. The *Mining Journal* of 1862 stated that the deposit formed 'an inexhaustible supply of a cheap and excellent fuel for all manufacturing purposes'. However, the coming of the railway to Devon brought cheap coal from South Wales, and lignite was no longer needed.

At the beginning of the 20th century German scientists discovered that certain lignites contain a valuable mineral, Montan wax. This had various uses, such as for insulating cables, in polishes, in the gramophone industry, and in making waxed and high gloss papers. In 1913 German scientists came to Bovey Tracey with the intention of exploiting the lignite and exporting the wax back to Germany. Several boreholes were sunk and a small power station was built. This experimental unit ran on gas, from lignite burnt in a producer, and enough electricity was generated to light Liverton. The outbreak of the First World War in 1914, however, saw the Germans rapidly depart from Bovey!

Little interest was then shown in the lignite deposit until after the Second World War. In 1920 a geological survey on mineral resources in Great Britain declared that 'British lignite as a fuel is of little value'. During the general strike of 1926, when no coal was available, certain clay companies in the area tried to fire their boilers on local lignite, but the product was of such poor quality that, as soon as the strike was over, the companies returned to coal, and lignite was allowed to languish again.

Some Bovey residents used it as a fuel. Christine Holmes remembers how, as a child, she would go with her family on picnics to Bluewaters, where they would go digging for lignite. They put it in a bag and drove it home in an old pram. She describes the 'pong' it made when burning, but said it kept them warm.

The desperate shortage of coal after the war led to a renewed interest in the lignite deposits. J.H. Wilson, who had studied the deposit for many years, pioneered an enterprise to satisfy the demand for fuel. There was also a shortage of Montan wax which, it was hoped, could be supplied as well. Finance was obtained from the El Oro Mining and Exploration Company of Mexico, who formed a subsidiary for the purpose called British Lignite Products. Interest in the venture was enthusiastic and the 300,000 ordinary shares of 3/6d. each were over-subscribed. The mining rights were obtained for over 3,000 acres and operations began. The Bluewaters pit was drained by pumping out 870,000 gallons of water every day for ten weeks. Drainage disturbed some of the extant mine shafts, and at least one of the pottery kilns vanished down the old shafts.

In 1947 C.W. Parish wrote a pamphlet dedicated to Stafford Cripps, who was President of the Board of Trade, in which he made a very strong case for the development of the lignite at Bluewaters. He talks of the terrible fuel problem and then says, 'let us see what Bovey Tracey can do about it'. The plan was to produce briquettes using lignite residues after the extraction of the Montan wax. Parish believed that cities the size of Exeter and Plymouth could be rebuilt using lignite as district heating. He even imagined trains running to London on pulverised lignite produced in Bovey. His final claim for lignite was that it was clean and healthy, and he quotes a miner as saying 'You could mine this stuff in a white suit'. He then described a Welsh miner suffering from incipient lung trouble who, after three months mining Bovey lignite, was restored to health.

In 1947, with day and night shifts, output reached 15,000 tons a month. A wax extraction laboratory was set up on site, although it never came into operation. A briquetting machine was also set up and some briquettes were made and sold under the name of 'Lignuts'. Devon House was bought and converted into flats for the expected influx of miners, many from South Wales. The boiler house was designed to burn off lignite in spite of it giving off an awful, sulphuric smell, which many Bovey residents remember. By 1949 1,820 tons of 'Lignuts' had been sold, but operations had resulted in a loss of £26,950. However, the extraction of Montan wax was expected to ease the situation and eventually lead to huge profits. Then I.C.I. developed a Montan wax substitute which was four times cheaper than the wax produced from lignite. As a result, British Lignite Products went into liquidation, their assets were sold off and Bluewaters filled with water again. Surrounded by trees, it then became a popular beauty spot in the town, but when people began dumping rubbish there, causing problems, it was eventually sealed off.

Lignite mining in 1946 (Pat Tregoning)

Bibliography
Scott, P.H.W. *The Geology and Mining of the Lignite in the Bovey Basin, Devonshire.* Camborne School of Mines, 1979
Lignite Mining in Devon. Mining magazine, Dec 1974
Parish, C.W. *The Creation of an Industry,* 1947

✳ ✳ ✳ ✳ ✳

Work

The Potteries
by Brian Adams

Pre-Victorian Potteries

The significance of Bovey Tracey in the history of the British pottery industry is primarily in the geology of the area. The Bovey Basin is renowned for its deposits of ball clay, now exported worldwide and which have been a primary source of raw material for the Staffordshire potteries since their beginnings in the early 18th century.

In 1750 Lord Courtenay, the Earl of Devon, opened a clay and lignite pit (known later as Bluewaters) on his land at Bovey Heathfield. With the assistance of 'adventurers' from Cornwall, he exploited the local raw materials by setting up new manufactories making just the kind of pottery then being made in Staffordshire. This association with the centre of the industry was something that was to distinguish Bovey Tracey from Devon's traditional country and craft-based potteries for over 200 years.

The early potters soon experienced difficulties. Jeremiah Milles, the Dean of Exeter, wrote:

... they succeeded tolerably well, but it soon miscarried, either as the Proprietors said, because the workmen (from Staffordshire) were bribed to destroy it, or as the workmen said, because the Bovey coal (lignite), which they made use of in burning it, was not of a heat intense enough to answer the purpose.

At about the same time a Mr Hammersley and his sons from Staffordshire opened another pottery in the town. Remains of what could have been their kiln survived undisturbed until they were discovered during building works at Pixies Holt in 1934. Whoever this kiln belonged to, recent research shows that it is the most complete example of an 18th century rectangular industrial potkiln surviving anywhere in Britain and is a major historical asset to the town.

Mr Hammersley is said to have moved his pottery to Pond Garden next to Indeo Pond and then to Indeo House, where, in 1766, a new enterprise making delftware, saltglazed pottery, creamware and porcelain was started by Nicholas Crisp, who had previously been a partner in a pottery at Vauxhall in London. This new venture suffered financial difficulties, alleviated for a short time when Nicholas Crisp and his employees assisted William Cookworthy of Plymouth with his experiments in porcelain production. Both men are now well known as key figures in the establishment of 18th century porcelain production in the United Kingdom.

These faltering early attempts to establish the industry at Bovey Tracey were given a boost when, in about 1772, several businessmen invested in the Indeo Pottery, then under the management of William Ellis. This enterprise went on for a further 65 years employing up to 40 workers. They mainly made tableware, some of it very fine, and are renowned for producing pottery inscribed with local people's names, particularly tea canisters now valued at four figure prices in the antiques trade.

Josiah Wedgwood visited Indeo in 1774 and commented:

it is a poor trifling concern, and conducted in a wretched slovenly manner... having the clay within 5 or 6 miles of them, from the same pitts which furnish our potteries in Staffordshire...The coals are only 2/6 per ton, at the pit, and so near the works,...Notwithstanding all which advantages, We can carry their clay and flints from Devonshire into Staffordshire, there manufacture them into ware, and send it back to their own doors better and cheaper than they can make it...

These comments have, until recently, been the basis of a belief by collectors and researchers that the Bovey Tracey potteries should be dismissed as unimportant and poor relations of their Staffordshire counterparts. As new discoveries are made it is becoming apparent that they not only made pottery to rival at least the average Staffordshire product, but also experimented with the rich diversity of locally available raw materials, pioneering several new kinds of pottery and porcelain.

In 1800 there was a fragmentation of the potteries when William Mead, a woolcomber, and Samuel Lamble, a blacksmith, built new works at Bovey Heathfield in competition with Indeo. This new enterprise soon came under the ownership of the Honeychurch family and, by 1812, was known as 'The Folly Pottery', according to one writer, 'so called because of the failure of different speculators'. The Folly Pottery was also plagued with difficulties, but survived until around 1836 when, together with the Indeo Pottery, it closed down. Lack of factory marks meant that no pottery from The Folly was identified until the discovery of distinctive potsherds on the site in the 1990s.

The Victorian Pottery
In 1843 Captain Thomas Wentworth Buller (R.N.) of Strete Raleigh and his brother-in-law, John Divett, set up a new business at the Folly Pottery site, trading as The Bovey Tracey Pottery Company, and expanded it to include many more buildings and kilns, still within the customs of Staffordshire. The poor quality of Bovey lignite meant that it had to be supplemented with good quality coal brought by sail to Teignmouth, up the Stover Canal and then by horse and cart to the pottery. The introduction of a railway system to Devon offered a way of alleviating the high transport costs involved, so John Divett asked the people of Bovey Tracey to contribute to the cost of a new railway line, explaining that the alternative might be to close the pottery. The Moretonhampstead & South Devon Railway, branching to Bovey Tracey from the main London to Plymouth line at Newton Abbot, was opened in 1866, part of it running along the course of the old granite tramway. There were two sidings at the pottery, one for loading granite brought down from Haytor and the other for pottery use. The new railway extended to Lustleigh and Moretonhampstead and brought an influx of tourists in the summer months, made welcome at the pottery with conducted tours.

A leat from Becky Falls was dug to feed new watermills for mixing clay bodies and grinding raw materials. A new, narrow-gauge tramway system, thought to be unique in the English pottery industry, carried the clay and other raw materials and pots between the various workshops at the pottery. Bricks were made on Bovey Heathfield and fired in 'clams' - kiln chambers built below ground level. Walter Steer, last of the clam firers, worked alone cutting and firing bricks up until 1938.

The Bovey Tracey Pottery Company, isolated from the centre of the industry, had to be self-reliant. Raw materials were prepared on site, and every pottery and ancillary trade was employed within the enterprise. Patents for easier manufacturing techniques were taken out by T. W. Buller, who also used his naval connections to establish trade with the colonies. His son, Wentworth William Buller, inherited his father's part of the business in 1852 and went into partnership with the Bovey Tracey businessman Jabez Mugford, marketing patent kiln furniture at Hanley, Staffordshire. This enterprise eventually became Bullers Limited of Stoke-on-Trent, one of the world's foremost producers of ceramic electrical insulators.

In June 1891 the Bovey potters went on strike after their wages were cut by 20 per cent. The pottery manager, Mr Clay, tried in vain to break the strike by importing workers from his native Staffordshire. There were about 250 workers at that time. By 1894 the pottery was bankrupt, yet again, and lay empty for 18 months.

The Bovey Pottery Company Limited
Debts to the local ball clay supplier, Charles Davey Blake, meant that it was in his interests to rescue the Bovey Tracey pottery, so in 1895 a limited company was formed with directors of The Bristol Pottery (another Blake interest) taking on responsibility for the new company. There was considerable new investment in buildings, equipment and new designs, and the workforce expanded to about 350. This was the first pottery in the South West of England to have its own electricity supply. There were government contracts, particularly for the supply of earthenware to the armed forces during the World Wars.

The Bovey Pottery as it appeared before the First World War (B.T. Heritage Trust)

The general strike of 1926 was, perhaps, the start of a decline in the fortunes of the Bovey Pottery. Many workers were on short time during the 1930s, a situation alleviated to some extent by war work making undecorated utility ware.

A departure into the art pottery market was made with the introduction of hand-painted Dartmoor Ware and Fruit Ware in about 1916. Prestigious Wemyss Ware was made between 1930 and 1957, the famous pottery artist Joseph Nekola applying his talents to hand-painted art ware, including flowery pigs and a large service for United States president, F. D. Roosevelt. This was one of a variety of products offered by the Bovey Pottery agent Wallace Findlay of Hatton Garden, London, and by agents in Australia and New Zealand. Wemyss Ware is now eagerly collected

Remains of the kiln found in 1934, photographed at the Candy Tile works in 1994 (Brian Adams)

Above left: A Wemyss Ware pig, freehand painted by Joseph Nekola. It is 16¹/₂ inches long (Brian Adams, courtesy of Brenda & Martin Hicks)

Above right: A figure of Winston Churchill illustrated in the Bovey Pottery catalogue of 1940. This was the first of the 'Our Gang' series and inscribed underneath 'The Boss' (Bovey Tracey Pottery Museum Archive)

worldwide, as are the Wemyss-like animals made for the London wholesaler Jan Plichta. Although Plichta was never appointed as an agent, he sold a large proportion of the decorative 'fancies' made by the Bovey Pottery after 1940, but all with his own backstamp.

The modern craze for collecting decorative 20th century pottery has, in recent years, made these items as sought after as any, but they are, in fact, much rarer than most of the highly regarded pottery on offer in the collectables and antiques trade. Just as uncommon is a series of wartime figures known as 'Our Gang', which was introduced to wartime Britain in 1940.

A group of pots and figures made at the Indeo Pottery (Brian Adams – access to the pots was by courtesy of Anthony Thomas, David Thorn, Peter Wadham, The Bovey Tracey Pottery Museum and The Royal Albert Memorial Museum, Exeter)

Attempts to inject new impetus to the Bovey Pottery by updating pottery designs in the 1950s came to little as economic pressures and the need for rebuilding put a strain on the business. In an attempt to keep their jobs the workers accepted a one and sixpence in the pound pay reduction, but the deal was rejected by The National Society of Pottery Workers, based in Stoke-on-Trent, who called the potters out on strike. The management closed the business and the industrial whiteware potteries, Bovey Tracey's largest employers, were brought to an end in 1957. The expected economic disaster for Bovey Tracey never came about, most of the potters finding new employment within a year or two.

Most of the large bottle kilns were demolished, but three of them still survive and are preserved as ancient monuments.

Other Potteries

Several small potteries operated near the Bovey Pottery for a time.

The Bovey Tracey Art Pottery made red clay art ware and small animals, much of it slip decorated in the tradition of the Torquay potters, between 1920 and 1942. Devonshire Potteries Limited was established in about 1947 in the same buildings. They were well known for pottery animals and Trentham Art Ware, mainly produced in a white clay body. They finally closed in 1982.

William and Frank Bond opened the Devon Tors Art Pottery in 1921 making slip-decorated novelty and art pottery with clay carted from pits in Torquay. They closed in 1967.

A larger concern was The Candy Pottery at Heathfield, established as a limited company by 1882. The pottery was initially made from clay extracted from a large deposit adjoining the site. Early wares were of vitrified stoneware, mostly bricks, and ornamental architectural ceramics. In the 1880s a small amount of art pottery resembling the products of Doulton of Lambeth and known as 'Chudleigh Ware' was made. An art ware department was re-established in 1916, and a new range of Wescontree Art Ware was made from1922 to 1957.

The Fox family directed the business from the 1920s and built many of the houses close to the factory for the workers. Potters from Staffordshire were seconded to the works during the Second World War. At one time there were up to 600 employees, a large part of the business being the production of tiled fireplaces: these were popular in the 1920s but went out of fashion in the late 1950s, which meant that the business then declined. Candy Tiles Limited was established as a new company, operating from 1964 to 1992. The site is still in use as a tile works.

Bovey Tracey - a continuing centre for pottery

The Bovey Tracey Pottery Museum at the House of Marbles and the Ball Clay Heritage Society are just two manifestations of recent local enthusiasm and awareness of the importance of the Bovey Tracey area in the history of the development of British ceramics. Although the fortunes of the industry at Bovey Tracey have varied considerably since 1750, pottery has been made here continuously for over 250 years. This town, sitting within its rich resource of good clay, continues as a significant centre of interest in pottery making.

Bibliography

Adams, B., Thorn, D., Weeks, E. *Wemyss Ware Pottery The Devonshire Years*. B. & T. Thorn and Son, Budleigh Salterton, 1990. Out of print.

Adams, B. *A Bovey Tracey Saltglaze Kiln*. D.Thorn, Budleigh Salterton, 1994

Adams, B. and Thomas, A. *A Potwork in Devonshire*. Sayce Publishing, Bovey Tracey, 1996. Out of print.

Brisco, V. *Devon Tors a Family Pottery*. V. & B. Brisco, St. Albans, 1998

Turner, Ian. *Candy Art Pottery*. Hillian Press, 2000

Brian Adams is honorary curator of the Bovey Tracey Pottery Museum at the House of Marbles, Bovey Tracey.

Farming
by Veronica Kennedy

I grew up on a typical Devonian mixed farm in the years after the Second World War. When I was a child, milking was still done by hand and carthorses were used for ploughing; there was no electricity or telephone on the farm and the farming methods would have been recognisable by anyone who had wandered in from the 19th century. By the time I went to school an electricity generator and a telephone had been installed, the carthorses had been replaced by an Allis-Chalmers tractor and milking was done by machine. Since then, of course, the changes in farming have made it unrecognisable. It is now part of agribusiness with all that that entails.

The history of the farms around Bovey Tracey gives us a snapshot of all the changes that have taken place and, for those who are interested in an old way of life, it is still possible to get glimpses of it. Chris Chapman's beautiful and elegiac book, *Wild Goose and Riddon*, shows what we are losing and as he says,

> *Like it or not rural England, in a post-industrial backlash, is now set upon a path of urbanisation, challenging the countryside and all its traditions.*

Farming has always been a cyclical industry. Obviously, the weather plays an important part: extreme conditions can affect a whole season; the onset of disease such as foot and mouth can have terrible consequences, but it has been politics, particularly war, which has affected farming most. In times of war, farmers have been needed; more corn is grown and prices are good, but these times are often followed by a severe downturn. The Napoleonic Wars and their aftermath, which included the Corn Laws, led to immense changes in farming. From the 1841 census of Bovey Tracey we can see that there were 45 farmers and 300 agricultural labourers out of a population of 1,823. The 57 people of independent means probably received rents from the lands, and the occupations such as farriers, saddlers, millers, wheelwrights would have been dependent on the land for their work. In addition, many of the people who had other occupations would have worked on the land casually in times of need.

In the late 1870s and 1880s came the great agricultural depression. A series of bad seasons aggravated its initial stages, but the main cause was the development of the American prairies as grain lands, combined with the development of railways and steamships and the lowering of freight charges. Frozen meat started arriving from Australia, New Zealand and South America, which led to a fall in the prices of sheep and cattle. The importation of butter from Denmark and Holland affected dairy farming. The belief in free trade meant there was no attempt by the governments of the day to make any effort to save the rural way of life. Least of all did the late Victorians see any need to grow food in their own country to provide for the necessities of future wars. Farming was very hard and the lot of the farm labourer particularly wretched. Tied cottages meant they were trapped into living in dark, damp cottages and crippled with rheumatism at an early age. Farmers often paid their workers in kind, perhaps with free cider, which made their condition even worse. It was only the sheer hard work, noted by many commentators as characteristic of Devon farmers and their men, which saved numerous farms from going under.

The arrival of the railway in Bovey Tracey in 1866, which opened up access to manufacturing towns and the colonies, as well as alternative employment such as the pottery, meant that many labourers were able to leave the land. From the censuses of 1881 and 1891 we see that there was a rapid decline of people involved in working on farms. The First World War improved matters for farming, but by the 1930s it was, for many, a depressed industry. The government, which had been grateful for the farmers' contribution to the nation's food in the dark years of the war, did nothing to intervene against foreign competition. It was during these years that farmers first learnt to diversify, with their wives taking in visitors during the summer months to keep going. J.H.C. Harvey of Langaller Farm was advertising board residence with their own farm and dairy produce and their celebrated Devonshire cider in Bovey Tracey guides of this period.

By 1939 British farming had declined so much that less than half the food the country needed was being produced. When war came and it was not possible to move food around in the same way, rationing was severe. After the war the government realised that this should not be allowed to happen again, and in 1947 an Act of Parliament was passed which formed the basis for rebuilding British agriculture. Its aim was to guarantee to farmers reasonable prices and a market for such food that could be produced economically. To this end various marketing boards were set up. For two or three decades farmers experienced real prosperity. Many changes took place; farming became more and more mechanised, so less labour was needed. It made economic sense for farms to be bigger, so small farms were swallowed up by bigger ones. Intensive farming has changed the traditional landscape; hedges have been destroyed to make fields larger, and animals have been reared inside on a large scale, so the traditional sight of a few pigs roaming an orchard is no more. Machinery has become so expensive that farmers can no longer afford to buy their own machines, so contracting has become more common. DEFRA have set up stewardship schemes which encourage farmers not to grow crops but to turn their fields into wildlife habitats and create 'more biodiversity in the countryside'.

In latter years farming has become very hard again, particularly for small farmers, who are in the majority around Bovey. And yet, in spite of the difficulties, the farms around Bovey do show evidence of continuity with son often taking over from father. John Gilley was the bailiff of the Divett estate and lived at Langaller, but came to Brimley Farm as a tenant in 1888 and farmed it with his son, William, who, in turn, farmed it with his son, Cyril. When the Divett estate was broken up William was able to buy the farm. John Gilley had bought Hillside Farm in 1900 but sold it again in 1920. Cyril's daughter, Glenda, married Maurice Mortimore from Chagford and they came to live on the farm. When their daughter, Anne, was born there were four generations living at the farm. William died in 1964 at the age of 90. A major indication of the changes in farming is that the farm used to keep three families with a full-time worker plus casual labour at harvest-time and now it is run by two pensioners with contractors brought in for the bailing, hedge trimming and shearing.

The Gilley family and helpers making hay at Brimley Farm (Glenda Mortimore)

Above left: Maurice Mortimore and Alan Brealey stopping for a drink of cider at Brimley Farm (Glenda Mortimore)
Above right: A delivery at Five Whyches Farm (Keith Bruce)

Robert Dadd's family acquired Whisselwell Farm in 1966, buying it from Mr and Mrs Paxton who retired to Manaton. The Paxtons had previously been farming in Africa and they kept cattle and sheep, employing one man. John Dadd continued dairy farming, as on his previous farm in Newton Abbot, employing one person until 1970, when the herd of about 100 cows was sold. He then farmed single-handedly, growing barley and selling hay. Robert returned to full-time agriculture in 1980 and has been at Whisselwell ever since, keeping sheep and growing a small area of cereals. The farm has gradually expanded over this time and now incorporates part of Five Whyches and Hillside farms.

Five Whyches was a small farm which was run as a dairy farm by a family called Hubbard, then by Kingsley Spencer. It was broken up 15 to 20 years ago and now consists of pony paddocks under about five different owners, a block of land remaining with the farmhouse and a converted building, and a block farmed by Robert Dadd.

Hillside was a small farm at Higher Brimley. It now consists of pony paddocks, barn conversions and the more inaccessible fields farmed by Robert Dadd.

Tom Wedden came to Lower Bradley in 1936. The previous tenant had not been able to pay his debts when farming was particularly depressed, so had been forced to give up. It has never been an easy farm to manage as it has four different landlords, and the Weddens had a very hard time when Tom was seriously injured by a carthorse in 1942. Paying guests were taken in to help finances. During the war they had 12 evacuees living with them. Peter took over from his father, Tom. It was a mixed farm from the start but finally went completely dairy in 1982, when Peter's son, Robert, left school and came to work on the farm. One of their landlords is the clay company and, although the Weddens say the clay company has always been very fair, four or five years ago it started boring holes in the fields and then, extensively, in 2002. This has created a lot of insecurity so, now that Peter has reached retirement age, his son, Robert, has decided to start again near Crediton.

The Weddens talked about the changes that have affected them. One of the unexpected ones has been the impact of the huge increase in traffic. It is too dangerous to walk the cows across the road to get to the farm from the fields, so they now have to take them on a circuitous route around the farm. There were lots of orchards at Bradley but they were all ripped out when the price for apples fell. Farmers no longer grow mangolds; they needed too much labour. Peter remembers taking time off from school to help with them and, with unerring instinct, Mr Hoskins, the school attendance

Above left: Lower Bradley farmhouse (Dave Wedden)
Above right: Harvesting with a horse-drawn binder at Lower Bradley. Tom Wedden is in the centre and Alan Hill is sitting on the binder (Dave Wedden)

officer, always seeing him. Now farmers can't even get the seed for mangolds. So the cave of orange-coloured globes covered with ferns from the common and then layered over with brambles is no more.

Hugh Mann was born in Bovey, his father being a tenant farmer at Brimley. Hugh milked the cows by hand before going off to Newton Abbot Grammar School and then, when he came home, spent another couple of hours working on the farm. Hugh took over the tenancy of Challabrooke, a farm of 100 acres, in 1969. Since then he has been able to add another 100 acres and buy the farm, and he now farms with his two sons. They milk 120 cows twice a day.

The outbreak of foot-and-mouth disease in 2000 was an enormous strain for a livestock farmer. Although there was no outbreak on this side of the moor, there was a constant sense of fear. Hugh Mann said he watched the news three or four times a day wondering where the disease would strike next. Rumours abounded. A lorry delivering cattle cake came one day and it was found that it had been, the day before, to a farm where an outbreak was confirmed, so Challabrooke was put on schedule D. His herd of cattle was pure, so to lose them was almost unthinkable. Nothing could be sold, so the cattle were eating up the next year's supply of fodder. One of Hugh's sons, who lives near Holsworthy, phoned one day to say he could see three different pyres burning at once. The Mortimores of Higher Brimley said it was a terrible time as they couldn't sell anything for nearly a year and then, once the restrictions had been lifted, they had almost to give away animals as they couldn't afford to feed them any longer.

Hugh talked of how farming has become so isolated. When he was a young man Bovey Tracey had its own young farmers' club and it was the mainstay of his social life. Now even Newton Abbot can barely support such a club. Farms have been sold off and now there are only three farms in the Bovey area doing milk. At one time all the pottery workers had worked on the farm and, even when they started working at the potteries, still came and helped at the farms at harvest-time, thus maintaining the links between country and town life.

Hedley Upham came to Langaller Farm in 1951, when his father borrowed £6,000 to buy it. Hedley was able to expand it to 310 acres. It was originally a mixed farm but became predominantly dairy. One son has developed a stud farm of stallions and the other son grows cereal.

Atway is an example of a farm which was once able to provide a living for a family, but no longer exists as such. Lewis Hext from Widecombe bought it in 1926. His only child, Edith, who married Thomas (Ned) Hern, moved there to live in 1942 with her two daughters. A third daughter was born in 1945. Atway was 23 acres and had two arable fields, six pigs, eight South Devon cows and poultry. Their first tractor was a Ferguson T20, bought at a sale and cherished like a baby by Ned Hern. After the day's work was over, Ned put it in the shed, waited until it had cooled down and

Three generations at Atway Farm in 1950. Standing, left to right: Louie Lavis, Ned Hern, Edith Hern and Annie Chudley. Seated, left to right: Lewis Hext, Eileen Small and Lizzie Hext (Annie Chudley)

Above: Francis Heath with Darling winning 1st prize in 1944 (Francis Heath)

Right: Francis Heath making the transition to a tractor and winning a ploughing competition in the 1950s (H.R. Rivers, courtesy of Francis Heath)

then wrapped it in bags for the night. Edith and Ned never had a car but went off to visit relations at Widecombe by tractor, with Edith on the back – a not very comfortable journey of at least 16 miles there and back. Ned died in 1980 and the grass was let, but the Hern's son-in-law, Francis Chudley, and Edith continued to look after all the hedges until 1989, when Atway was sold and broken up.

Francis Heath, born in 1914, has worked on farms all his life and is very aware of the changes. He drove a team of horses, often winning competitions with them, from the age of 14 when he left school. In 1948 he had to switch to tractors. 'Driving horses is company. You can talk to them but you can't talk to a tractor.' Every day he walked miles and miles behind the horses and earned 12 shillings a week. He was also able to thatch a rick and shear sheep.

Jim Ayres, who is 84, is still working on the same farm, Bottor Rock, Hennock, that he started work on at the age of 14, in 1933. Then he earned 10 shillings a week, with an extra shilling if he worked on Sunday as well. He looked after five carthorses and would plough an acre a day, walking ten miles to do so. He joined the Royal Horse Artillery in the Second World War and, when he came back, returned at once to his old farm. He and his wife, Bet, had nine children and, to help their finances, he set rabbit traps every night, making 3d. a rabbit. To feed his family, he grew enough vegetables in his garden and was always allowed a patch of potatoes on the farm. These lasted his family most of the winter. Jim says he has thoroughly enjoyed his life and wishes he could do it all over again. He would change nothing; being out in all wind and weather in the wide open spaces is all he ever wanted.

Yet everyone can see that irreversible changes are taking place. Farmhouses are being sold off, farm buildings converted, often to make second homes for city dwellers, and globalisation has made it impossible for British farmers to make a proper living. The countryside is seen as an amenity, something for tourists. Nevertheless, in spite of all the difficulties, most farmers love what they do. Hughie Mann said, 'farming gets in your blood'. Hedley Upham echoed this sentiment. 'No-one would invest in farming if he wanted to make money, but it's a way of life.'

Bibliography
Chapman, C. *Wild Goose and Riddon*. Devon Books, 2000
Hicks, Norman. *Farming in the West Country*. David Rendel, 1968
Hoskins, W.G. *Devon and its People*. Wheaton, 1959

The Farmers' Market

One of the ways to encourage consumers to buy more locally is to set up farmers' markets. In 1999 the people of Bovey, when questioned about what they wanted for the town, asked for a market. The Bovey Tracey Community Forum has now set up a farmers' market which is run on behalf of the people of the town. Tina Richardson, who was one of the people strongly believing that Bovey needed a market, phoned farmers working within a 30-mile radius and found 15 who were prepared to come to Bovey and so, on 15th September 2001, the market opened. Bovey Council and Teignbridge have been very supportive, and sponsorship has come from, amongst others, the House of Marbles, Mann Jenkins, the Riverside Inn, Ashby's and Woollcombe Beer Watts. Every other Saturday Tina Richardson and Louise Pawson are up at 5 a.m. to put up the stalls and then hope that the farmers and the customers will turn up. Members of local band, the Blue Lagoon, provide the music and help to create a cheerful atmosphere.

Agricultural Engineers

Farmers would not be able to function without the support of agricultural engineers. They need someone to provide their machinery and they need someone to repair it once the time-honoured remedy of a piece of binder twine has failed. **E. Bowden and Sons** have provided this service for the farmers of Bovey Tracey for over 140 years. Their story began in the early 1800s, when Emmanuel Bowden started up a small repair and manufacturing business in North Devon.

Jim Ayres with a Standard Fordson tractor on Bottor Rock Farm (Jim Ayres)

Bovey Tracey Young Farmers' Club outing in 1950. Back row, left to right: Dick Wills, ?, Mr Skedgell (coach driver), Hugh Mann, David Brealey, Arthur Mann, Bert Bowden, John Dadd and Bill Amery. Middle row, left to right: two BOCM staff, Dennis Martin, Andrew Ellis, Donald Harvey, Heath Dadd, Derek Tooze, Bill Holding, Godfrey Langford, Henry Raisey and two BOCM staff. Front row, left to right: Nancy Winsor (now Cleave), Sarah Bowden (now Harvey), Helen Bath (now Mann), Silvia Stephens (now Singleton), Mr Barker (BOCM rep), Betty Glanville (now Bowden), Kitty Amery (now Daw), Jose Amery (now Dadd) and Gwen Webber (now Mortimore) (Bert & Betty Bowden)

The farmers' market in 2001 (Tina Richardson)

Emmanuel was a blacksmith and, like most blacksmiths of that time, made the implements such as the ploughs the farmers needed. He was responsible for making a one-wheel reaper and a tyre-bending machine. His wife's brother had established a foundry and engineering business in Liverton and, in 1863, Emmanuel, with his wife, three sons and a daughter, moved to Bovey Tracey, where he set up a business in Town Hall Place.

When Emmanuel retired, his son, Edwin, took over. Their farm machinery proved to be very popular and was well known for its durability. In 1929 the firm was awarded a gold medal at the Devon County Show for the most improved farm implement. This was a new type of hay rake, designed to move quickly and easily, which could expand when in full use or contract to pass through any gateway or through narrow lanes. This was patented and advertised as the most up-to-date rake and described as a perfect implement.

In due course Edwin's two sons, William and Herbert, took over from him and their two sons, Bert and Henry, joined the firm. When Bert, William's son, left school at the age of 14 and joined the firm in 1940, he worked in the blacksmith's shop, where there were three forges. The work then included repairing horse-drawn implements such as harrows and cultivators, as well as making new ones. By the time Henry, Bert's cousin and Herbert's son, joined the firm at the age of 16 in 1950 most of the work was on tractors and converting horse implements so they could be used by tractors. Bert married Betty Glanville, whose uncle had a rival company in Bovey Tracey (see below); her aunt told her she was 'marrying into the opposition'. In 1964 Bert and Henry moved the firm, with its 20 employees, to a site next to the Dartmoor Hotel.

Every year Bowdens had a stand for the three days of the Devon County Show, where they were able to display their latest range of machinery. William and Herbert's wives, Louie and Flossie, and later Betty and Yvonne, Bert and Henry's wives, did the catering, providing food, tea, coffee and beer for all the farmers. Betty says she bought the milk from Mann's and the bread from Thomas', and catered for over 100 people each day.

In 2002 Bowdens moved to a new site on the Old Newton Road, where they still sell and service the latest farm equipment but now also provide a large horticultural service. Henry now works with his son, Derek, who started work as an apprentice in 1979 and is the fifth generation of Bowden to work with the firm.

Randolph Glanville was born in Newton Ferrers and went to work in Canada as a young man. When he returned to England in 1895 he bought Ellinmore Farm in Lustleigh. Two years later he

E. Bowden & Sons in Town Hall Place (Bert & Betty Bowden)

Above left: Bert Bowden with his two grandfathers, Edwin Bowden and William Brooks (fishmonger), in Town Hall Place in about 1938 (Bert & Betty Bowden)
Above right: An advertisement for Bowden's expanding horse rake in 1930 (Bert & Betty Bowden)

R.E. Glanville at the Devon County Show (Betty Bowden)

started selling agricultural machinery. In 1910 he moved to Station Works in Bovey Tracey and traded there until 1960 under the name of **R.E. Glanville and Sons, Blacksmiths and Agricultural Engineers.** During that time two of Randolph's sons joined the business.

Milling in Bovey Tracey
by Keith Bruce

We know that there was a mill built in 1670, probably on the site of an older mill. The wheel was turned by water from a leat taken off the River Bovey at Parke weir and which flowed back into the river under the bridge. In 1870 Albert Wyatt bought the watermill, which was on the site of the present Dartmoor Garage. Later, his son, A.J. Wyatt, inherited it and built a flour mill alongside the railway. This, however, was subsequently destroyed by a fire, as was a replacement building, and when a third building was constructed it was designed for use as a provender mill, buying and selling to farmers - a farmers' grocer, the equivalent of today's agricultural merchant.

A.J. Wyatt (or Bertie, as he was known) decided to retire in 1938 and James Scott Bruce began negotiations to buy it. A company was then formed incorporating the old and new names, which marked the beginning of Wyatt and Bruce Limited.

The Bruces were hard working and progressive, and during the Second World War the business earned a well-deserved reputation for quality, integrity and fair dealing. In those days of limited and slow transport facilities to farms, trade was relatively parochial and was mainly with local farmers and merchants selling processed grain and factored feeds manufactured by the large national firms at the large ports such as Avonmouth and Plymouth, and also buying and merchanting farmers' grain, especially wheat for flour and barley for malt for beer or for distilling for whisky.

After the war James Bruce's son, Keith, joined the firm after service in the army. He brought with him the drive and enthusiasm of youth as well as the characteristic of the family for hard work. It was not long before plant was installed for the manufacture of compound animal feeds to replace those previously factored from national manufacturers. In due course these were sold throughout the West Country under the trade name of Abbot Brand.

A youthful staff, who took great pride in being part of an enthusiastic and successful team, grew up within the business. Many worked for the company for 30 or 40 years; one for over 50 years.

Wyatt & Bruce's stand at the Devon County Show in the 1960s. From left to right: ?, Dennis Martin, Bob Bruce, James Bruce, Keith Bruce, Eddie Carnell and Malcolm Bruce (Keith Bruce)

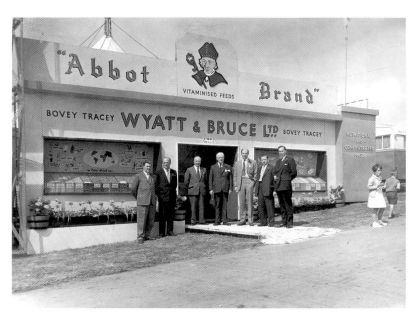

Wyatt & Bruce drivers competing for lorry driver of the year in the early 1960s. From left to right: Bill Stoneman, Francis Chudley, Peter Hinds, Gilbert Hookway, Ray Cose, Dennis Battershaw and Ian Rowe (Francis Chudley)

Bulk outloading plant at Wyatt & Bruce. Francis Chudley checks the order before he loads the lorry (Francis Chudley)

Sometimes several members of the same family did so at the same time. In one case as many as five of the Hutchings family were employed contemporaneously. The business grew to become one of the foremost family animal feed firms in the South West, built upon quality, reliability and service.

To be able to compete with large national companies it was necessary to provide the same level of technical expertise, and this was done by means of in-house specialists with access to the advisory and technical department of feed additive manufacturers, Beecham, with their international research facilities.

W&B was one of the first in the country to make use of computer least-cost feed formulating technology which gave a valuable head start in the accuracy and cost of producing feeds for all classes of farm livestock, including specialist feeds such as for horses, dogs, goats and pheasants. Another example of forward thinking was the provision of a private pension fund many years before it became common practice.

Another first was the installation of a punchcard system for the selection of raw materials for manufacture. This gave great accuracy and control, and was the precursor of computer-controlled processing. This, again, was way ahead of the field at the time.

Several other businesses were purchased and added to the company during the 1960s and 1970s, including the Torbay Mill Co. of Newton Abbot, T. Daw & Sons of Kingsteignton, Ward & Co. of Crediton and W. Rowse & Sons of Bissoe, near Truro in Cornwall. Other companies were formed within the livestock industry during the 1970s and 1980s to provide tied outlets for feed, including egg production and packing, and bacon production. These enterprises were invariably in association with a company already experienced in their particular field such as the Fatstock Marketing Corporation, for bacon, and Stonegate Farmers, for egg marketing.

The company's fleet of immaculate lorries were a familiar sight throughout the West Country in their distinctive leaf green livery and gold lettering. It was unusual to make any journey without meeting at least one en route.

In 1965 the company purchased the old Bovey Pottery buildings after that company had gone into liquidation. Various ancillary enterprises grew on this extensive site, including warehousing, the storage of grain and raw materials, cereal seed processing, calf milk replacement production, egg packing, grain drying and cereal micronising, producing flaked maize and peas. This was the only plant in this field west of Bristol.

However, during the late 1980s the pressure of governmental control and bureaucracy, together with huge changes in the methods of feeding livestock on the farm, caused it to become clear that the days of profitable feed manufacture by a family business in the West Country, with its small farms and long, tedious lines of communication, was drawing to a close. The unpalatable decision was reluctantly made to withdraw and sell the business. That this was, in fact, a wise one was born out by the contraction of the industry during the following few years.

The buyers were Hillsdown Holdings PLC, a national conglomerate with extensive interests in animal feed and food processing. But, within six months, they, too, had seen the writing on the wall and sold the business to the national feed firm, J. Bibby PLC, who have, of course, closed the mill entirely. The site is now a housing estate and the Bovey Pottery has become the House of Marbles.

Wyatt and Bruce Reunion

In February 2003 Francis Chudley and Arthur Weeks organised a reunion of Wyatt and Bruce employees and 118 people from various parts of the country turned up. Photographs were hung around the walls of the Dolphin and memories were exchanged. Wonderful parties at Christmas time were remembered. Stories were told about farms visited; the time when Francis Chudley's lorry went down a well-shaft in a farmyard and the farmer only said, 'I knew there was a well somewhere but didn't know where'. Adverse weather was remembered. One afternoon the floods were so torrential the feed all had to be lifted off the ground. Coke from Jeffrey's next door washed into the mill and covered the floor. In the early 1960s the snow was so bad several lorries got stuck in drifts and couldn't be moved for days. Eccentric farmers were talked about; the way so many of them developed bad backs as soon as a load of feed needed to be lifted from the lorry!

Francis Chudley and Gilbert Hookway were both lorry drivers of the year in the early 1960s, and Francis Chudley, Mike Hicks and Stan Hinckley won the team prize, having lovingly prepared their Wyatt and Bruce lorries for the event.

Some of the 118 people who came to the Wyatt and Bruce reunion in 2003 (Francis Chudley)

Heath Brothers

The firm of Heath Brothers, as Wyatt and Bruce did, employed many people in Bovey and had a good reputation, but has now disappeared except from people's memories. The two brothers, William and Henry, had their business, a timber and building firm, on the site next to the Dartmoor Hotel, which was later taken over by Bowdens and is now a new development of houses. William Heath was noted for his ability to look at a tree and tell exactly how much wood was in it. Les Harris's father, William, was in charge of one of the horses using for pulling the wood, which meant that he had to work seven days a week caring for the horse.

Noel Lavis, who started as an apprentice there, remembers Henry and, in particular, his powerful voice. As a perk, he allowed the men to take home one log at the midday break and one at the end of the day. To make sure no-one sneaked out an extra log, Henry stood at the exit bellowing 'one man, one log'.

Heath Brothers were responsible for much interesting work around Bovey. They built most of the Cornish Unit houses locally. In 1948 Len Webber and Bill Beer repaired the waterwheel at the Riverside. Len Webber remembers going into the chapel roof at Devon House and finding an enormous honeycomb there; it fed the men with honey for some time. Noel Lavis had to remove the pitch pine roof lining from the chapel there and replace it in the library at Buckfast Abbey. It was

Heath Brothers' outing in 1925 (George Gribble)

a difficult job as the wood had to be shortened by three inches at each end. Noel was at Buckfast Abbey for six months and enjoyed every morning when the monks produced a large bowl of very strong, black coffee.

Phil Waldron worked as a saw-doctor for Heath Brothers, and one of the people he trained was Michael Caunter. They both remember what a dangerous job it was, especially when items had become embedded in trees as they had grown and would be revealed only when the saw hit them. These included extraordinary things such as bullets, bits of shrapnel, old musket balls and, on one occasion, even a horseshoe.

When Henry died the business was put under management and began to decline. Later, Keith

Cheril being built by Heath Brothers in the 1940s. Percy Webber, Len's father, is centre right (B.T. Heritage Trust)

Heath Brothers' dinner at the Dolphin in the late 1940s (Lil Moore)

Honor took over the business with his father. Noel Lavis, who had left to work for Zealley's, returned to Heath Brothers. The plan to save the firm was to develop and design wooden-framed, prefabricated houses. One of these was installed in only eight hours on Avenue Road, where it remains standing today, the owner reporting that the timbers are still sound. But the grand plan failed because of government limits on timber importation in these immediate post-Second World War years, and this was what hastened the end of the company.

Heath Brothers' yard in 1963 (Bert & Betty Bowden)

✳ ✳ ✳ ✳ ✳

Transport

In a period when we take it for granted that we can fly to the other side of the world, it is almost unthinkable for us to imagine a time when walking, for many, was the only method of getting around. Armitage Hargreaves tells several stories of people walking long distances, including the man who walked from Brimley to Hennock every day until he was over 70 and the man who worked on the granite tramway, walking to work from his home in Exeter in the mornings and returning again at night. The coming of the railway, which opened Bovey up to the rest of Britain and the world, completely changed this way of life.

The Railway
by Mike Lang

The railway line that used to pass through Bovey Tracey was part of a very picturesque branch line that ran between Newton Abbot and Moretonhampstead, a distance, by rail, of just over $12^1/4$ miles. It was first opened to passengers on 4th July 1866 by a company known as the Moretonhampstead and South Devon Railway, whose directors all had local connections. They were the Earl of Devon, Thomas Wills, William R. Hole, John Divett, who owned Bovey Pottery, Elias Cuming and Thomas Woollcombe.

A view of Bovey Station at around the end of the 19th century showing the arrival of a train from Newton Abbot hauled by a 1076 class 0-6-0ST (Lens of Sutton)

Always known simply as Bovey, as opposed to the town's full name of Bovey Tracey, the station was originally one of only three along the entire branch - the other two were at Lustleigh and Moretonhampstead - and also the only place where two trains travelling in opposite directions could cross. However, soon afterwards, on 16th December 1867, a new station was opened at Teigngrace, and this was followed, on 1st July 1874, by another at Heathfield, which was originally called Chudleigh Road Station. Much later, and in a bid to stem increasing road competition, the Great Western Railway, which had formally absorbed the South Devon Railway Company in 1878, also provided unstaffed 'stations' - halts - at two more locations along the branch. The first, which

Above left: Ted Godfrey and his three children at Brimley Halt in the 1950s (Eric Godfrey)

Above right: Large prairie tank engine No. 4150 makes an abrupt and noisy exit from Bovey Station with the two-coach 10.15 a.m. train from Moretonhampstead on 19th February 1959 – too abrupt as it happened, for an important letter had been overlooked and the stationmaster (the late Arthur Yendall) is attempting to hand it to the guard of the morning train. Alas, it was too late! (Peter W. Gray)

opened on 21st May 1928, was at nearby Brimley, and the second was on the outskirts of Lustleigh. This was opened on 1st June 1931 as Hawkmoor Halt but renamed Pullabrook Halt on 13th June 1955, because visitors to Hawkmoor Hospital, imagining that the halt was close to the hospital, were finding that they had a lengthy walk.

Originally, the line was built with the rails placed 7 feet $0^{1}/4$ inches apart (Brunel's broad gauge). But, during the weekend of 20th to 22nd May 1892, this distance was reduced to 4 feet $8^{1}/2$ inches after a decision made by the Great Western Railway to convert all of its lines in the West Country to the English standard gauge.

In its early days traffic was slow to develop on the line, but soon after the turn of the last century the future of the line began to look brighter, especially when the Great Western Railway started running omnibuses to Chagford in connection with trains at Moretonhampstead. This was in 1906, and within another four years there was a marked improvement in passenger services, which continued until the economies brought about by the First World War resulted in a reduction in the number of trains. After the war things picked up again, and during the 1920s and 1930s the station at Bovey took on added importance as being the starting point for day trips across Dartmoor, using road vehicles that would be parked in the station yard awaiting the arrival of the trains.

The Second World War, inevitably, had another adverse effect on the branch, from which recovery proved to be slow in the extreme. Problems with recruiting staff generally and the coal shortage meant cutbacks, and when the railways were nationalised at midnight on 31st December 1947 it made no appreciable difference. Furthermore, little serious effort was made to build up business, and road competition came increasingly to menace the future of the branch.

One of the problems in these latter years was a fairly inflexible timetable, with four trains running in the morning and four in the afternoon on most days. It was not always possible to make connections with main line trains at Newton Abbot and the council minutes mention these issues, particularly with regard to commuting schoolchildren. In spite of these difficulties the eventual withdrawal of passenger services in 1959 came as a blow to many of the townspeople, the last public train leaving Moretonhampstead at 9. 17 p. m. on Saturday, 28th February of that year.

Goods services began some three months after the opening of the line to passengers simply because the goods sheds at Bovey and Moretonhampstead were not ready. Many years later, in the early 1960s, the daily goods train was cut back to three times a week only, although Bovey did have an additional service from Heathfield on Tuesdays and Thursdays. At that time Bovey's last stationmaster, Arthur Yendall, was still in charge, but he had been designated a 'depot clerk': his duties were to clear up and dispose of all the fixtures, fittings and stationery at the station, and also attend to the administration of the goods traffic. Even before he eventually retired in 1965, however, the section of the branch north of Bovey was closed to all traffic, on 6th April 1964, and the track lifted, and on 1st May 1970 the dwindling goods traffic at Bovey also came to an end.

As the lights were switched off and the station buildings locked for the last time, no-one knew that the Bovey bypass would, one day, cover the route of the railway through the station, or that the station building would become the town's heritage centre.

0-4-2T No. 1466 arrives at the 'down' platform with the 7.50 a.m. train from Newton Abbot on 28th February 1959 – the last day of passenger services (Peter W. Gray)

Bibliography

Mitchell, V. and Smith, K. *Branch Line to Moretonhampstead*. Middleton Press, 1998

Jenkins, S.C. and Pomroy, L.J. *The Moretonhampstead and South Devon Railway*. Oakwood Press, 1989

Owen, John. *The Moretonhampstead Branch*. Waterfront, 2000

Kingdom, Anthony R. and Lang, Mike. *The Newton Abbot to Moretonhampstead Railway*. ARK Publications (Railways)*

*Due to be published in autumn 2004.

Bovey Station as seen in the 1950s

Bovey Station staff c.1958. Left to right: Signalman Derek Aggett, Stationmaster Arthur Yendall, Porter Cecil Fowden and Motor Driver Jack Heale (the late Arthur Yendall)

The railway station at Bovey is very picturesque and well maintained, with floral displays, some in hanging baskets below the canopy, and a rose garden - just inside the level crossing and wicket gates on the eastern side of the line - adding to its overall charm. There are two platforms, both 300 feet long, although the 'down' platform is normally used only if a goods or passenger train from the Moretonhampstead direction is being crossed. It is connected to the 'up' platform by a timber foot crossing located at the southern end of the platform ramps, and has a finished surface of tarmac chippings edged with concrete slabs with rounded shoulders on the lineside. Throughout most of its length the facing is of granite, but when the platform had been extended in the 1890s the additional 110 feet was faced with bricks supplied by Candy & Co. At about the midway point stands one of the two station nameboards, together with a tall concrete post from which an oil lamp can be hung, while just beyond it is an open-fronted waiting shelter, again built of bricks supplied by Candy & Co., and equipped with seating and a hearth. This has a pitched roof of grey slate, with plain ridge tiles, that extends towards the lineside in order to provide extra protection from the elements, and a single chimney of matching Candy brick. A flat-roofed extension at the northern end of the building once served as the gents' toilet, but this had been sealed off in the 1930s. Finally, beyond this point the rear of the platform has a white-painted, wooden fence of four-feet high slats, their tops cut to an apex, which is in complete contrast to the southern side of the waiting room, where the platform is backed by a natural hedge.

The main station building is situated at the southern end of the 'up' platform, immediately beyond a round-topped, corrugated iron store that had originated as a waiting shelter for bus passengers taking day trips across Dartmoor during the 1920s and 1930s. It is constructed in a most attractive manner of partly dressed granite blocks and, apart from the wings at either end, which are both flat-roofed, has a conventional pitched roof of grey slate, with plain ridge tiles and two squat chimneys; unusually, these are octagonal in shape and immediately differ from one another inasmuch as the chimney at the southern end has only one flue compared to the two of its more northern counterpart. On the platform side, the building's many interesting features include arched window recesses, a doorway (also arched) in the Gothic style and a wide, timber canopy supported

The station garden and level crossing gates viewed from the southern end of the 'up' platform (Dave Lewis)

A general view of Bovey Station looking towards Newton Abbot, as seen during the summer of 1957 (Geoff Howells)

The rear of the main station building (Courtesy of Anthony R. Kingdom)

by six ornamental wrought iron wall brackets, while, at the rear, part of the roof extends outwards in a similar manner to that of the waiting shelter on the 'down' platform. This, in turn, provides a small porchway, or canopy, shielding two of the five arched windows on this side of the building and also the entrance doorway (again in the Gothic style) which leads into the booking hall and general waiting room, the station office, parcels room and ladies' toilet. The gents' toilet, on the other hand, is situated in the northern wing and can only be reached from the platform by entering a prefabricated concrete lean-to with a sloping corrugated roof.

The goods shed, situated a little to the north of the main station building, is a substantial structure built in a similar manner. Its walls, however, consist of a smaller proportion of granite and more grey and brown shillet, the roof is of corrugated iron and it has only one chimney; this protrudes from near the south-eastern corner of the roof. There are three large openings provided with heavy wooden sliding doors, one at either end and another on the eastern side, and three windows. Two of these, both with arched recesses, are on the platform side to give added light inside the shed when the doors are closed, and the third is to be found at the southern end to allow light into the office of the goods clerk, where there is also a hearth. Inside the shed, apart from this office, is a wide, full-length loading platform served by a goods siding (this terminates by a multi-purpose loading dock situated immediately beyond the southern end of the shed), a two-ton crane and, lastly, a goods loading bay for road traffic, which is accessed from the adjoining station yard.

The yard itself is quite a spacious affair and is served by a second goods siding. Known as 'Back Siding', this is connected to the other by facing points near the permanent way department and sleeper-built coal store at the northern end of the station site. From there, it continues past the station's platform-mounted four-ton crane, which is used for transferring timber and other heavy items between road vehicles and railway wagons, runs alongside the premises of R. E. Glanville & Son (a firm of agricultural merchants and engineers) and terminates just short of Station Road by the premises of another firm using the railway, Wyatt & Bruce (grain millers and seedsmen).

Returning now to the 'up' platform (constructed to the same specification as that of the original part of the 'down', except for the finished surface being of paving stones around the front of the main station building), the northernmost structure is the 17-lever frame signal box. This is situated next to the goods shed and is built mainly of timber under a pitched roof covered with slate and finished with ridge tiles. The rear wall, however, is of brick, as are parts of the end elevations and also its tall chimney stack, which protrudes from near the south-eastern corner of the roof. All-round vision, apart from the rear, of course, is accomplished by multi-panelled sliding windows that run the whole length of the western (platform) side and by further windows at either end; the latter are completed to the apex with lateral wooden planking. At the northern end there is a partly glaze-panelled wooden door and a step, and at the front, below the sliding windows, is a standard GWR cast-iron nameplate.

Beyond the signal box, the rest of the platform is backed by a white-painted, wooden fence in like manner to that on part of the 'down' platform. This same type of fencing has also been used to bridge the gap between the main station building and the goods shed, where a gated recess leads down to the loading dock in the goods yard. Here also stands the other station nameboard and another tall concrete post from which an oil lamp can be hung.

Overleaf: A map showing the route of the former railway line from the south-eastern outskirts of Bovey to the northern side of where the station was sited, superimposed by the route of the bypass opened in 1987 (Reproduced courtesy of Roy Wills)

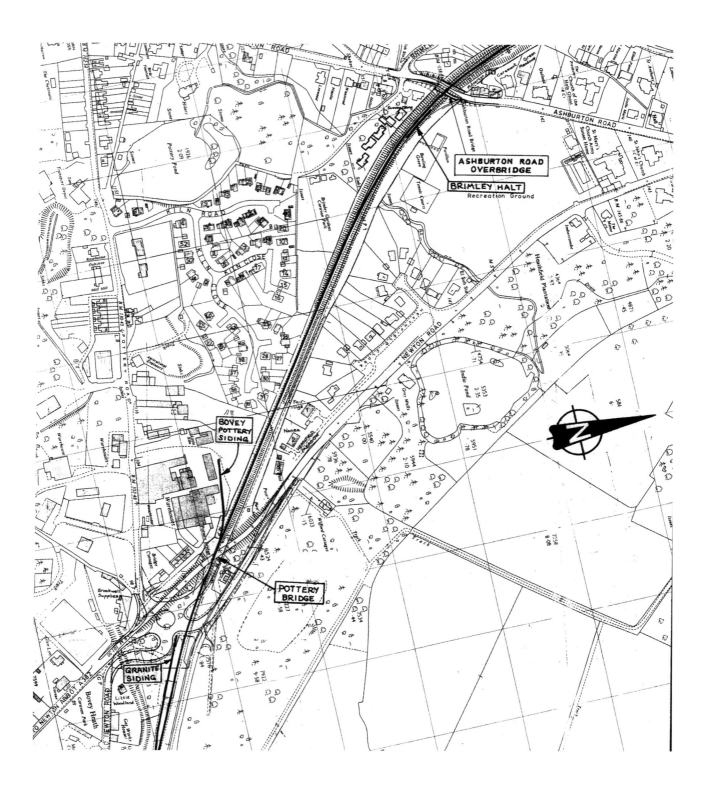

As indicated by the map, the whole of the trackbed of the former railway line from a point immediately adjacent to the western end of Granite Siding to just beyond the site of Bovey Station was used for the bypass. The trackbed then veers off north-westwards towards Moretonhampstead and, in parts, is now well used by walkers.

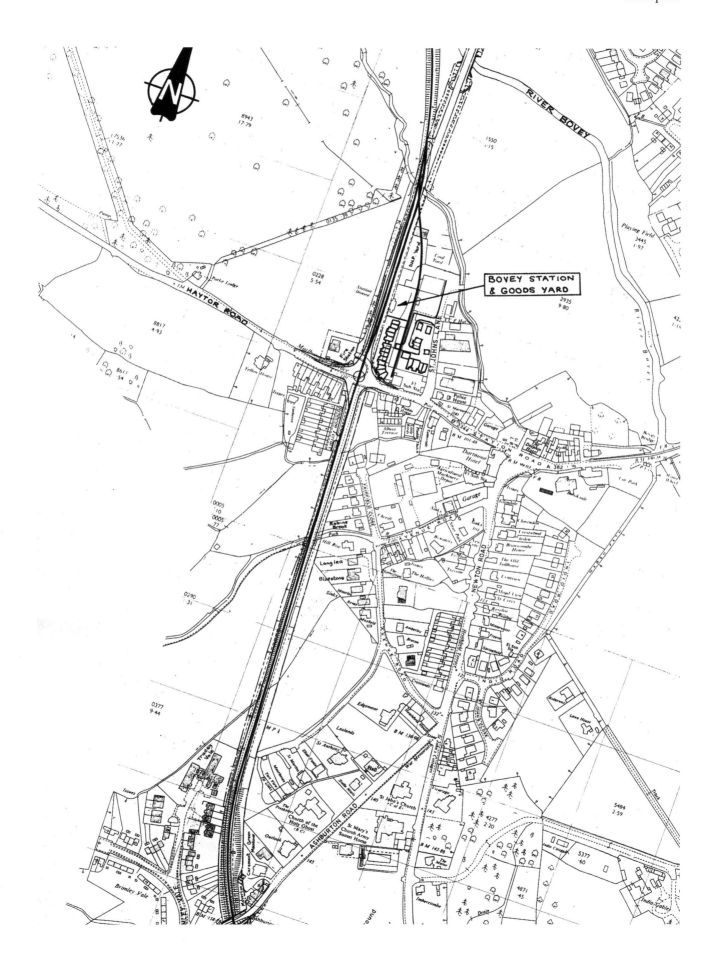

Highways
by Roy Wills

Apart from the period between 1866 and 1959, when rail travel was an option, the only means of travel to and from the parish was by road. Today's road network has evolved from the footpaths and cart tracks of old, with one of the most dramatic changes coming about in the middle of the 12th century when the Saxon open-field system was abandoned and fields were enclosed by the building of hedge banks and stone walls. This often resulted in the line of well-established routes being diverted, giving us the often seen sharp deviations in the roads we drive today.

By the 16th century royal roads had been established countrywide - the King's highways - although none of these went through the parish of Bovey Tracey. All other roads were termed common highways, for which no contribution for maintenance was made by the state. It was at this time that the principle was established which gave travellers the right of way, or free passage, on the King's or the common highways, the upkeep of the latter being the responsibility of the landowner adjoining such roads. Many 'sunken lanes' were created at this time, a common feature in Devon and evident at many locations in this parish, where the adjoining landowner complied with his obligations by merely scraping off the road surface when it became a muddy morass and piling it at the roadside.

Rivers were still mainly crossed at this time using fords or crude 'clapper' bridges, formed by the spanning of large stones, usually as found locally, but made of hewn and dressed stone in later years. Dartmoor provided a particularly good source for these stones known as 'clappers'.

It is recorded that in 1326 Bishop Stafford left 100 shillings for the repair of Bovey Bridge. Then Henry VIII introduced a 'Statute of Bridges 1531' to ensure that 'decayed bridges should not lie long without amendment to the great annoyance of the King's subjects' merely because of lack of knowledge as to who should maintain them. This enacted, amongst other things, that unless it could be proved that 'a hundred riding, wapentake, city, borough, town or parish, nor what person certain or body politick' should by right maintain a bridge, then the shire had to maintain it. This Act stood until 1888, when the county councils were formed. To raise money for bridge repairs, the Act authorised that a rate could be levied on all the inhabitants of a county or borough; this being the first occasion on which such a levy was made across an entire administrative area and the origin on which today's system of rating is based.

Local bridges subsequently improved under this Statute were Bovey Bridge, which is dated 1642 on an incised stone on the upstream parapet wall, and Drakeford Bridge on the parish boundary with Lustleigh, which has a stone set in the downstream parapet which reads 'THIS 168(4) BRIDG WAS REPARD BY THE COVNTY', although the bridge to be seen today dates from 1810.

The roads for 300 feet either side of bridges maintained under the 1531 Statute also had to be maintained by the shire, and in 1831 Devon magistrates required that the extent maintainable by the county be marked by 'bound stones', generally formed of locally gained stone about a foot square and three feet high and incised with a 'C'.

A Statute of Highways of 1555 had made parishes responsible for roads passing through their parish, with the exception of bridge approaches as previously described. The churchwardens were required to appoint an unpaid overseer of highways from its parishioners, and labour was to be provided by parishioners, also unpaid, who were required to work for four days annually to upkeep the highways. This was increased in 1562 to six days due to the increasing workload. This arrangement continued until 1654, when the payment of rates was introduced to maintain highways in the same manner which had been introduced in 1531 to maintain bridges.

A late 17th century Act required parish surveyors to install at crossroads stone or timber posts with the names thereon inscribed of the next destination. Bovey Tracey has a unique style of such stones at many crossroads, some bearing colloquial spellings of the destinations, such as 'Widdicombe' on the stone at Five Wyches Cross. This stone, and the one at Reddaford Water on the Manaton road, both have inscribed on them 'S. Bovey' from the days of the three Boveys – North, South and Little Bovey – when there were no other means of distinguishing them. Similar stones can be seen at Coombe Cross, the junction of Newton Road and Ashburton Road, the junction of Bradley Lane with the B3344, Slade Farm just off the A382 and, just outside the parish, at Woodhouse Cross, Ilsington.

Today most junctions are provided with fingerpost signs of somewhat mundane design when compared with those of the earlier part of the 20th century, which were often of cast iron with ornate features included in the casting, or crafted timber posts and finger arms. The names of many junctions are of interest; probably the most curious is Little Helston Bench Cross on the Bovey/Hennock Parish boundary, possibly named by a homesick Cornish miner who emigrated east to Devon to work at one of the many mines in the Hennock area.

The only visible difference with the style of fingerposts used now is the use of timber posts on such signs within the boundaries of the Dartmoor National Park, those elsewhere having metal posts finished in white.

Two scenes from the days when the main road linking Newton Abbot with Moretonhampstead passed through the town. Above: Union Square in the 1930s. Below: Dolphin Square around the mid-1980s (Roy Wills)

The main road through the town, linking Newton Abbot with Moretonhampstead, became a Turnpike road in the 18th century, allowing tolls to be levied on road users to improve and maintain such roads. The Old Toll House still stands on Newton Road.

The Turnpike Act required that milestones be erected showing the distance to the towns in either direction, and all those in the parish are still in existence – on the Bovey Straights, in Newton Road adjacent to the cricket field, set in the wall opposite Cross Cottage in Mary Street, Kings Cross and north of Slade Cross.

The Highways Act of 1835 abolished forced labour for highway maintenance and clarified many of the requirements of previous Acts, and in 1887 and 1888 other Acts were introduced which made county councils responsible for main roads, which would have included the Newton Abbot to Moretonhampstead road.

Two photographs taken of Pottery Bridge during the construction of the bypass. Above: The two arches of the bridge being used as part of a temporary diversion of traffic into and out of Bovey. Below: The bridge partly demolished (Roy Wills)

Other Statutes of note were the 1753 'Broad Wheels Act', invoked in an attempt to reduce wear and tear of the highway and requiring a minimum wheel width of 9 inches, and the 1865 'Locomotives on Turnpike and Other Roads Act', which introduced the first speed limit of 4 mph. This Act was also known as the Red Flag Act as it required mechanical vehicles to be preceeded by a man carrying a red flag. An 1896 'Locomotives on Highways Act' repealed the Act of 1865 and increased the speed limit to 14 mph; this was subsequently reduced to 12 mph.

The maintenance of roads was mainly undertaken by parish lengthsmen, who would primarily ensure that the length of road for which they were responsible was draining freely, generally via holes through hedges - 'buddle holes' – and ditch systems, water then, as now, being the cause of most damage to the fabric of the road. When more extensive works were required the county council had travelling gangs, complete with caravans for accommodation, who would traverse

Two photographs taken of Ashburton Road Bridge during the construction of the bypass. Above: The bridge still intact while earthworks are in progress. Below: Work commences on the demolition of the bridge (Roy Wills)

large areas of the county to carry out resurfacing and improvement schemes.

Devon County Council to this day is the Highway Authority and is responsible for all 'roads maintained at public expense' within Devon, excluding those in the Torbay and Plymouth Unitary Authority areas, and trunk roads which are directly funded from central government. The A38 dual carriageway between Drumbridges and Clay Lane, Chudleigh Knighton, comes into this category and is partly within the Bovey Tracey Parish. Today all highway maintenance is carried out by contractors under the supervision of engineers in the county council's Environment Department: this includes parish lengthsmen working to the same principles as their forebears, only instead of a number of lengthsmen per parish, the lengthsman now covers perhaps a dozen parishes on quarterly visits.

The greatest change to Bovey's highways in recent years came on 16th October 1987 with the opening of the bypass. This removed from Newton Road/Fore Street/Mary Street the increasing volume of through traffic which, at times, had resulted in gridlock in the town centre and at Town Hall Place. On some occasions HGVs grounded on the sharp bend into Mary Street, or others became wedged against the town hall when attempting to turn into Fore Street at its junction with East Street and Mary Street. The bypass followed the route of the former railway track bed from Pottery Road to a point just north of the former site of Bovey Station, but sadly necessitated the demolition of the beautifully constructed Pottery Bridge and Ashburton Road Bridge, the former built of limestone and granite and the latter of granite only. Beyond the station site the bypass crosses the River Bovey over Hole Bridge, named in recognition of the late Major Hole of nearby Parke House, who was a very generous benefactor to the town. It then heads due north through what was previously pasture to rejoin the Moretonhampstead road at Beara. The 'A' class status of this road from thereon belies its physical nature, becoming single track at many places on its route to Moretonhampstead and beyond, and frequently surprises first-time users who expect a much better standard for a road of this classification.

The opening of Le Molay-Littry Way in the mid-1990s, linking Fore Street from the Methodist Church to Bradley Road, south of the existing built-up area, was funded by developers and opened up the area south of Fore Street for building, also relieving the town centre of through traffic in the Chudleigh direction and particularly benefiting those living in East Street and Bradley Road.

At the time of writing it seems unlikely that there can be much expansion of the road network in the town, the total length of which has doubled since the beginning of the 20th century, mainly resulting from the building of the many housing and industrial estates which have hugely increased the urbanised area of what was originally a small town. Indeed, the only likely area of significant development in the foreseeable future is that north of Southbrook Lane, but as our ancestors, in their day, could not have envisaged Bovey being as it is now, only the passage of time will tell.

Work on constructing the bypass in progress at the site of the former railway station (Roy Wills)

Churches

The Parish Church of St Peter, St Paul and St Thomas of Canterbury
by Sheila Winckles

As the town's oldest and largest building, the parish church stands at the highest point overlooking the town, and is thought to have been built on the same site as the original small, wooden Saxon church which was burnt down by Danish pirates in 1000AD. The typical Saxon dedication to Saints Peter and Paul was passed on to a larger and more permanent church in Norman times. It is the addition of St Thomas of Canterbury which makes the church one of great interest and speculation, and gives it an air of mystery. There are few English churches which can boast of a possible connection with one of English history's most significant incidents which rocked both throne and Christian beliefs. The murder of Thomas à Becket in Canterbury Cathedral on 29th December 1170 has a dramatic link with our small town and its parish church through one of the perpetrators of that dreadful crime, Sir William de Tracy, one of the four knights who murdered the Archbishop of Canterbury. It is suggested that the church built during the 13th - 14th century was commissioned by Sir Henry de Tracy, the first lord of the manor of Bovey Tracey, and descendant of William's elder brother, Henry, as a means to expiate the sin of their kinsman and the curse put upon the family by the church hierarchy:

Wherever by sea or land they go forever the wind in their face shall blow.

The first Sir William de Tracy was the illegitimate son of Henry I, who gave his son lands in and around Devon. Certainly he was given the barony of Bradninch near Exeter together with the manor of Morton(hampstead). He married a rich heiress and adopted her name of Traci - the name of a town in Normandy and a title held by her forebears who had come over to England with William the Conqueror.

In 1258 Henry de Tracy gave the church and advowson of Bovey (the right of presentation to a vacant benefice) to the Bishop of Exeter, who, in turn, passed it on to the Master and Brethren of St John's Hospital, Bridgwater. They held the advowson until the dissolution of the monasteries during King Henry VIII's reign, when it passed to the Crown, and it remains a Crown living to the present day.

During the 14th century the church, together with many parish churches up and down the country, fell into a sad state of neglect and poverty. This was probably due to the French wars and constant outbreaks of the terrible Black Death which swept across England, destroying half the population.

Yet again, a fire destroyed the Norman church, and all that remains, apart from the tower, is a small piece of the arch over the Norman south chancel door - now walled up inside but retaining an early English doorway with an old studded door on the outside.

In the 15th century the church was transformed from the usual cruciform shape to the present 'hall plan' which incorporated the transepts into the north and south aisles, excluding, of course, the outer north aisle (added in the 19th century). The church also has its share of Green Men, which 15th century builders felt were necessary in places of worship. During this period the prosperity of the wool trade is shown in the richness of the building and the furnishings of the church. The 'Exeter Lands' owned by Lady Margaret Beaufort, Countess of Richmond and Derby and mother of King Henry VII (1485 -1509), meant she was associated with this parish through the Brethren of St John's, Bridgwater. It is thought she was the benefactor who gave the beautiful screen and pulpit in the middle of the 15th century, the detail of which is thought to be above average in character. Lady Margaret Beaufort is also thought to have been responsible for founding the College of Clerks,

Bovey Tracey Parish Church bell-ringers in 1953. Back row, left to right: Reg Ballenger (as an ex-boxer he had been Freddie Mills' sparring partner), Jack Heale, Frank Lavercombe and Walt Holman. Middle row, left to right: Stan Blackmore and Alf Yeo. Front row, left to right: Bert Blackmore (vice captain), William (Bill) Brooks (captain, who went on ringing until he was in his 90s) and Noel Lavis (who rang for 45 years) (Noel Lavis)

Sacristans and Singers, who resided close to the church until the closure of the chantries during the reign of King Edward VI. It was during Edward's reign that the rood and loft were removed from the top of the screen.

In 1628 King Charles 1 appointed a Scotsman and ex-army chaplain, James Forbes, to be vicar. He was ejected during the Commonwealth, and his stipend cut to a fifth. He had the reputation of being something of a firebrand who made his feelings known to the parliamentarians and the 'intruder parsons' who preached in his church. The Reverend Mr Forbes is reputed to have saved the 15th century brass eagle from the parliamentarians by sinking it in a pond.

After the Restoration, Reverend James Forbes was returned as vicar and he and Sir John Stawell, the lord of the manor, together with Sir John's son, William, did much to restore the church. William Stawell became a successful Member of Parliament for Ashburton, retaining his seat for nine sessions. The Stawell Gift was his way of thanking the people for electing him. He gave £10 each year to be spent on linen cloth for 50 poor people in the parish, who were to be chosen by the trustees; the cloth to be distributed on Christmas Day after morning service. This continued until the early part of the 20th century. The 'shirtings' were placed in the church porch and guarded by the town crier until they were distributed.

The 19th century is notable for the long incumbency of the Reverend Honourable Charles Leslie Courtenay (1849-95). He was instrumental in restoring and renewing much of the church fabric as it is today. This included replacing the old pews, removal of the galleries, the addition of the outer north aisle, the restoration of the screen and the rebuilding of the church school. In 1885 Canon Courtenay called a special vestry meeting to consider certain proposals regarding renovation and alteration at the parish church. The meeting was hostile to him and one of his parishioners said that his teachings savoured more of the papacy than of the Church of England. The canon was so upset that he decided to resign, but pressure was brought both locally and in 'high places' and he stayed in place.

During the renovation in 1858, when the whitewash was removed from above the arcades on the north aisle, a series of 15th century paintings were discovered, but they soon faded away. Copies of these paintings were made by Miss Hole and these are now framed on the west wall with an explanation beside them. Contemporary themes are represented as shown in the Moralities - Three Living and Three Dead Kings and the Dance of Death. Also shown is the Blessed Virgin Mary as the Protectress of the Souls in Purgatory.

In the 20th century the church suffered its share of war damage. The east window was damaged when a land mine fell in a field near Devon House on 18th November 1940. This had been donated by Canon Courtenay in memory of his father. Until the end of the war the main lights were filled with plain quarries.

The other stained-glass window worthy of mention is the war memorial window on the south

The choir in 1951. Back row, left to right: Roy Burgess, Noel Lavis, Bill Fouracre, Louie Lavis, Grace Lavis, Barbara Weeks, Len Fouracre, Michael Steer and John Ellis. Middle row, left to right: 'Titch', Les Steer, William Brown, Reverend Owen Duxbury, Horace Mountford, Frank Lavis and Sydney Weeks. Front row, left to right: Anthony Powlesland, Andre Schneider and Peter Wedden (Dave Wedden)

Bell-ringers from Bovey Tracey Parish Church in the ringing chamber of the Church of St Mary the Virgin, Laira, Plymouth in 2003. Back row, left to right: Austin Evans, Phil Hodder, Graham Downing, Diana Horne and Guy Holding. Front row, left to right: Bob Brown, John Horrell, Ron Garland and Barry Trevethan (Sheila Winckles)

wall. This was presented by the parishioners as a lasting memorial to those lost in the First World War from Bovey Tracey. Among the diamond quarries are 55 specially marked, showing the initials, service badge and date of death of each serviceman who died. The full names are recorded on the memorial on the north aisle wall. Bovey Tracey parishioners also donated funds for the organ to be rebuilt in memory of their war heroes.

To celebrate the birth of Christ 2,000 years ago the town council commissioned a stained-glass window, together with a machine-embroidered banner, depicting the Bovey Tracey coat of arms, whose motto reads: 'Look back with Pride, Forward with Confidence'.

Sources of information
Tregoning, Lance. *Bovey Tracey an Ancient Town*. Cottage Publishing, 1993
Teignbridge National Association of Decorative and Fine Arts Societies. Church Recorders

The Catholic Church of the Holy Spirit
by Monica Waldron

The interior of the original Catholic church, the Church of the Holy Ghost, Bovey Tracey (Monica Waldron)

Before there was a Catholic church in Bovey Tracey the Catholics who lived here had to walk to Ugbrooke in Chudleigh to celebrate Mass in the chapel there. In the late 19th century Mrs Chamberlain bought Rosario in Challabrook Lane, and took a great interest in the Catholics who lived in Bovey. A priest from Ingsdon Convent cycled over on Sundays to conduct Mass in her house.

In 1904 some ground was rented from Squire Bentinck of Indio. A little church, consisting of corrugated iron sheets for the outside walls but lined with wood, was built. At this time the church was known as the Church of the Holy Ghost. The priest still continued to come over from Ingsdon to conduct Mass. The church could be used for baptisms and funerals but it was not licensed for marriages, so Catholics from Bovey were married at St Joseph's in Newton Abbot.

In 1929 Father McLachlen was sent to Bovey Tracey for the sake of his health. He decided that the church was inadequate so, in spite of being unwell, started negotiations for building a new one. After various difficulties, particularly financial, which were overcome largely by the generosity of Mr and Mrs Dahl and other parishioners, the foundation stone was laid by Bishop Barrett in 1935. Less than a year after the church's consecration in 1936, Father McLachlan died at the age of 42.

After the new church was built the old church was used as a parish hall, and whist drives, social events and Christmas parties were held there. During the Second World War, when Father James Weeks was the parish priest, the hall was used as a temporary school for evacuee children. By the time Canon Power replaced him the hall was in need of repair and decoration, so a few men of the parish got together and did all the work to restore it. It was then named St Peter's Hall and used for many social occasions before ultimately being demolished.

During Canon Power's time there was a grotto to Our Lady in the garden of the church where the processions ended with benediction. At that time the girls and nuns of Ingsdon Convent and the Polish people from Stover Camp, in national costume, also joined in the processions.

Monsignor Tobin took over as parish priest and was here until he died in 1977. He was also Vicar General of the diocese for over 20 years, including during the period of the Vatican Council.

Father Charles Foley, parish priest from 1977 until 1990, served as an army chaplain in the Second World War and was a witness to some of its horrors when he entered the Nazi concentration camp of Belsen. In the mid-1980s Father Foley organised the building of the church hall. Within 12 months it was badly damaged by a falling tree, so he had to set to and organise a rebuilding. He later retired from Bovey Tracey and spent the remaining years of his life at St Margaret Clitherow House,

The silver jubilee of the Church of the Holy Spirit, Bovey Tracey, with Colin and David Waldron altar servers with visiting clergy (Monica Waldron)

Torquay, where he celebrated Mass daily in Latin. He was an expert on the Shroud of Turin and frequently lectured on it.

Father Michael Considine was parish priest for 12 months, but bad health took him back to his native Ireland. He was followed by Father Paul Kimber, who was also here for only a year. From then, until 1994, Bovey was without a resident parish priest, but Father James from Buckfast Abbey and Father Mark Skelton from Newton Abbot came to conduct Mass on Sundays and Holy Days.

From 1994 until 1999 Father Michael Murphy was parish priest. In 1996 the church's diamond jubilee was celebrated. The year began with a special Mass on New Year's Day and then, in May, the Right Reverend Christopher Budd, Bishop of Plymouth, celebrated the sacrament of confirmation, with a party in the hall afterwards. Mrs Angela Devonport arranged a very successful jubilee flower festival over the Whit weekend.

In December 1999 Monsignor Adrian Toffolo became parish priest. He had been rector of the English College in Rome for several years and, while he was priest in Bovey, was involved with the Catholic Diocesan Education Programme based in Exeter as Episcopal Vicar for Formation. Before he left Bovey there was a celebratory Mass to which ministers of all the churches in the town were

May procession in honour of Our Blessed Lady, with Polish women in the 1960s (Monica Waldron)

invited, and after which there was a farewell party in the hall. Father Adrian left in February 2003 to move to a larger parish in Barnstaple.

Monsignor George Hay is now the parish priest. He came from St Marychurch, Torquay, and is well known in the diocese.

The church is due for reordering, and a committee is in place to consider the way forward. The windows are gradually being replaced with stained glass, the work of artist Andrew Johnson, some donated by parishioners in memory of deceased relatives.

As the present Catholic parish in Bovey Tracey started in 1904, the parish is celebrating its centenary in 2004, remembering with gratitude all the priests and people who have built it up over the 100 years.

The Baptist Church
by Doris Collins

For more than two centuries the Baptist Church at Bovey Tracey has been involved over a wide area beyond the boundaries of the town. Among some of the earliest Baptist churches in the country, it is known that Baptists were meeting in Pludda - somewhere between the railway station and Dolphin Square - as early as 1658, or even before, with baptisms by immersion in the river. According to notes given by Miss Bent, the minister lived, at one time, in a cottage on the riverbank close to the bridge.

The church has, from earliest times, it seems, had connections, which waxed and waned over the years, with non-conformists in Moretonhampstead. In 1681 a certain Reverend Mr Jackson, a baker and serge maker living in Moreton, was the minister. He was imprisoned in Exeter Gaol for six months for preaching the Gospel; his wife continuing the serge making to support the family in his absence. When released from prison he walked home and, while crossing the graveyard on his way, was met by a stranger, who, having established Reverend Mr Jackson's identity, gave him £50 and an order for serge for a friend, to be collected at a given date. This was done, and a further order given, paid for and collected, but the identity of the customer was never discovered. The business flourished from then on. A letter written in 1831 by a descendant of Reverend Mr Jackson vouched for this story.

It seems that this early church was disbanded for a while until being reconstituted in 1773, then meeting in Hen (Hind) Street and using a building which may have been part of an old monastic building. Though part of the surrounding wall has been located, Cromwell Arch and the graveyard gate (once the church porch) are the only visible remains.

Between 1797 and 1806, as membership increased, the meeting house was first enlarged and then extended by the purchase of an adjoining cottage. Initially, the cost of the extension was anticipated to be in the region of £130, but the final figure proved to be £190, of which £54 was raised by local subscriptions and the rest by other Baptist churches. During this period, in 1800, some ground was also purchased to enlarge the burial area and a wall built around it at a cost of upwards of £28, which, again, was funded by subscription.

The Reverend Mr Sprague started his ministry at the church in 1795, was ordained in 1796 and remained for 43 years. During this time a much-loved and respected deacon, Moses Savory, also served the church well until his death in 1817, and a plaque in the church commemorates his life and service.

The Baptist church in Bovey drew people from a wide area. Places as far afield as Exmouth, Teignmouth, St Marychurch and Kingsteignton are mentioned from which folk came for baptism and church membership. Members were sent out in 1798 to assist a newly-formed church in Ashburton (the building, with its baptistery, is still there), and again in 1819 to plant a 'daughter' church in Newton Abbot. There are references in the records to 'the villages'. Among others, a cause was started in Ilsington and a work begun in Heathfield, which continued until the early 1960s, when children were ferried in to the Bovey Sunday School for a short time. During the 1830s the Bovey Sunday School grew from 70 to 117, and by 1872 the congregation numbered 291.

In 1822, having outgrown the enlarged buildings in Hind Street, the present building to seat 400 people was planned, and the foundation stone laid. In 1823 the new meeting house was roofed and, although not quite finished, was opened for public worship on 16th September 1824. This was a mammoth undertaking for a small group of relatively poor people, many suffering considerable hardship. A letter written in 1812 speaks of low attendance because many, living at some distance, were 'too weak to walk and too poor to ride'. The Reverend J.R. Way (1905-16), nearly a century later, also recorded difficulties he experienced. His salary, paid quarterly and being not much more than £85 per annum, was insufficient for basic needs in furnishing and decent clothing. He mentions inadequate footwear for the family, and his own 'best' trousers were a black pair his wife had turned. The menus for meagre meals were comprised mostly of bread and vegetables, with occasional stewed bones or rashers of bacon. They had difficulty in affording penny stamps to correspond with friends.

Despite the hardship, it was decided to build a church house for the minister. The ground, further up the hill from the church, was bought for £10 and the cornerstone laid on 8th September 1874. The building costs were in the region of £275, but besides having to raise the necessary funds there were other difficulties. When the walls reached nearly roof height, the end wall was blown down in a fierce windstorm. Nevertheless, Chapel House, as it was known until 1906, was completed, bills paid and

The Baptist church, built in 1824 (Baptist Church archives)

debts cleared within four years. It later became known as The Manse and remained so until the early 1990s, when it was sold and became Hind Street House. A new manse was then purchased in Churchfield Drive.

In 1915 the centenary of the Sunday School was celebrated in June with three services on the 27th, followed, on the next day, by a thanksgiving service, a public luncheon in the schoolroom, and games and tea for the children in a field adjoining the manse. The scholars numbered more than 80, and each one, as well as the teacher and visiting preacher, was presented with a Bible at the final service in the evening.

Until the mid-20th century the church was, like others, typical of a small Devon town, supported almost entirely by local Devonshire people. However, the second half of the century saw the arrival of the first of the 'incomers', who were graciously welcomed and encouraged by the older members to make their contribution. Among these older members were the Tucker family, whose connection with the church extended through 150 years. Miss Elsie taught in the local school, and 'Uncle' George Tucker was a much-

'Uncle' George Tucker (Stuart Hands)

loved Sunday School superintendent until well into his nineties, despite resigning earlier. He lived to be 103. Mr Ernest Wyatt, with his wife, Renee, followed his father as secretary of Lustleigh and Bovey chapels, and their involvement and loyal service lasted from the end of the First World War until retirement from business took them from the area in 1969.

Miss Winifred Snow also followed in her father's footsteps and held, at one time or another, most offices in the church, including that of treasurer. She also played the organ for over 50 years until she reached the age of 80. She was a great woman of prayer, who researched the records and correlated the church history, and to whom we are indebted for much of this information.

Mr Cyril Wreford was a well-known figure cycling through the town. He taught in the Sunday School for as long as possible and diligently put up the hymn numbers before each service. He also took many photographs.

Between 1960 and the end of the century many further changes, structural and otherwise, occurred. These included moving back the early gravestones, the construction of a ramp at the side (once main) entrance, and improved access for the disabled. Perhaps the most significant recent alteration is the new more welcoming porch at the Hind Street entrance.

During this time not only has the Sunday School continued, but other youth organisations, including the Boys and Girls Brigades, youth clubs and Crusaders have flourished. A toddler group, known as the Sunbeam Club, was started in 1981, and a pre-school group in 1991. These continue to meet daily throughout the week, and have never known a time

Win Snow at the organ. This instrument was installed in 1942, replacing the original organ. It was in use until the 1990s, when it was sold and the interior of the chapel modernised (Baptist Church archives)

without a waiting list. Other activities have included a luncheon club for older folk.

The drought in 1976 meant that water could be used only sparingly, so a baptismal service was held in the home of members, using a swimming pool which had been filled just before restrictions were enforced. In September 1984 there were more drought conditions and, this time, baptisms took place at Teignmouth, when the sea was so rough that troughs between breakers had to be waited for. Barbara Guthrie, one of the four candidates, remembers how cold it

Mrs Win Stevens cutting the 200th anniversary cake in 1973. Mrs Nellie Jones is on the right (C. Wreford, from the Baptist Church archives)

was and how, on noticing a ship lying offshore, she hoped it would pick her up if she got washed out to sea! All was well despite the strength of the tide, but it took courage to make a public witness under such stormy conditions.

In 1976 the East Dartmoor Baptist Church was formed to become one church comprising five congregations. At first Bovey, Lustleigh and Moretonhampstead were united, and then they were joined by Chudleigh and Christow - thus continuing old traditions and the much earlier vision for the needs of the villages.

The Gospel Hall
from notes by Gordon Symons,
secretary to the trustees and
preacher for 50 years

A small, yet important part of Bovey Tracey's Christian community is the Brethren congregation which meets in the Gospel Hall in Mary Street. The Gospel Hall stood on the site of a former cottage which, in 1865, was sold for the erection of the British School. The school's trustees included the minister of the Congregational Church and Edward Divett, who played a major part in this project. After the British School closed in 1910 the building and adjoining land was sold to a Mr Heath, who built a house on the land and sold the school to the Brethren in 1912. The secretary was Mr James Loveys Black of Pottery Road. The trustees, in 1941, vested the property in the Western Counties and South Wales Evangelisation Trust under an order from the Charity Commissioner to rectify the glaring omission of an inappropriate trust deed on the original purchase by Mr Black and other trustees in 1912.

Although the premises have changed little, there has been some modernisation during recent years, including the installation of a new kitchen and toilets.

The congregation in the inter-war years numbered around 35 and included a number of young farming families. During the Second World War some of the young people were scattered from the area, and several of those who did national service did not return. During these years additions to the congregation were small, and by the 1960s numbers had dwindled to fewer than a dozen. Over the next two decades the congregation increased again as new families moved into the town, and staff from Heathercombe Brake, a Christian school near Manaton, joined the church. The congregation now numbers around 20, with Mrs Mary Manley being the current secretary.

The Manning family has played a significant part in the history of the congregation, with Albert, a local farmer, as an original trustee. Albert's son, Theo, who formed a farming haulage business at

GOSPEL HALL, MARY STREET,
BOVEY TRACEY.

Scripture Union

Special Meetings for Young People

WILL BE HELD (D.V.) IN THE ABOVE HALL

every THURSDAY at 7.30 p.m.
(Winter Months only)

starting Thursday, September 29th.

A warm welcome is extended to all Young People.

"Thy Word is Truth." – John xvii, 7

Topical Papers - Discussions - Bright Singing, etc.

An advertisement for the Gospel Hall (Dave Lewis)

Dawlish, was a loyal member of the church. This level of commitment carries on to the present generation. Other members of the congregation included the Luscome family and Ken Hooper, who joined the fellowship about 40 years ago while living and working in Brimley. Having retired and moved to Newton Abbot, he continues to attend meetings at the Gospel Hall. Other long-standing members of the congregation include Audrey Partridge of Brimley, whose husband, Eric, died some years ago but who was prominent in the church for nearly 40 years.

The Methodist Church

taken from anonymous notes prepared for 'celebration 90'

In 1806 a request was made to the Lord Bishop of Exeter to have a house in Mary Street registered as a place of worship for Methodists, and on 20th November of that year a licence was granted. However, the first known formal services were not held until 20th November 1811. In 1880 the chapel was sold for £34 0s. 5d., and a new chapel, also in Mary Street, was built for £785. During the interim period, services were held in the Temperance Hall in Fore Street, which had been built in 1877 for £600. By 1887 all debts incurred by the construction of the new chapel were cleared and Bovey Tracey moved from the Buckfastleigh circuit to the Moretonhampstead circuit.

An organ was purchased in March 1891 from Guests of Exeter at a cost of £40. At the turn of the century the trustees acquired land next to the chapel and had a schoolroom built at a cost of £290. In 1923 Charles Steer of Paignton left the trustees £200 for the Sunday School.

By 1950 the membership had been reduced to six and the chapel was becoming untenable, needing many repairs and being less than ideal in opening directly on to the street. In 1967 the Congregational Church in Fore Street came up for sale, and so was bought for the Methodists at a cost of £6,500. The move was completed in 1969, and a short time later an extra schoolroom and new kitchen were added.

On 30th November 1975 a reed organ was bought for the church, but this had to be replaced five years later after damage by flooding. Further problems were uncovered when rot was found in the building, and in 1983 a fund-raising campaign was successfully launched for the interior of the church to be changed to its present configuration. In 1992 plans for the addition of a hall for use by the church and the community were drawn up, and fund-raising began. The final work was completed in December 1995.

A whole range of church activities now takes

The Congregational (now Methodist) Church being built in the early 1930s (Dave Lewis)

place in the hall, which is also used for hosting various interest societies. The membership of the church is about 80 and the average attendance 80 plus.

The Parish Church of St John the Evangelist
based on notes by Ernest Upham, a churchwarden at St John's, with extra information
from Barbara Mugford and David Carpenter, current churchwardens

Bovey Tracey is unusual for a town of its size in having two Anglican parishes, and the story of how this happened is another intriguing aspect of Bovey's history. The 19th century was a period of great religious revival but, at the beginning of the century, most people accepted and practised a form of Christianity, the basis of which was Biblical, with self-improvement as perhaps the most highly valued virtue. Sacraments and ritual were not emphasised, but preaching was. During the 1830s John Henry Newman, John Keble and Edward Pusey created by their writings and sermons what came to be known as the Oxford Movement. They emphasised the importance of the Catholic roots of the Church of England. Its opponents denounced it as Romanism in disguise and, in 1845, as if to confirm this belief, Newman joined the Roman church.

At the height of these controversies, in 1849, the Reverend Honourable Charles Leslie Courtenay, subsequently appointed as Canon Courtenay, and referred to as such throughout this section, was appointed vicar of Bovey Tracey. Shortly after his arrival he decided to build a new church. This church, to be dedicated to St John the Evangelist, was to serve as a Chapel of Ease to the parish church and, he claimed, was necessary to provide for parts of the parish distant from the existing church. He argued that Bovey Tracey's population had increased and there was insufficient accommodation in the parish church, adding that the potteries were likely to afford employment to a large number of people and result in an increase of population in the neighbourhood. While all these arguments were valid, many people believed that Canon Courtenay only wanted a new church so that he could hold ritualist services there without offending the congregation at the parish church. It is certainly true that St John's very quickly became an advanced ritualist church, and it is claimed by Nigel Yates that, along with Frome in Somerset, it was the most important ritualist centre in the south west of England.

The land for the new church came from the Courtenay Trust. When the building was first proposed much local feeling was aroused by the rumour that the new church was going to be built on the winnowing field where the townsfolk used to thresh their gleanings. However, it was built on the apex of the road to Teddy Hill (now Newton Road) and the road to Ashburton, both open tracks over Bovey Heath at that time.

The architect was Mr S. Carpenter, who was responsible for many Tractarian churches, and the builder was Richard Locke of Bovey Tracey. In September 1851 work began. Three generations of the Daymond family worked on the building as masons, and afterwards three of them sang in the choir. The church was consecrated and dedicated by the Right Reverend Henry Phillpotts, Bishop of Exeter, on 16th June 1853, and attended by a large number of senior church figures as well as the Earl of Devon, the Duke of Bedford, the Duke and Duchess of Somerset, Lord Russell, the Earl of Portsmouth and Lord Somers. Many local landowners were also in attendance.

Parish records show that the first baptism in St John's took place at the time of the consecration. Edwin Tapper wore a christening robe made by Lady Caroline Courtenay, with the smocking around the yoke done by Queen Victoria.

The first organist, Mr Drake, who came from Chelsea, formed a choir and for many years it was looked upon as one of the best in the county. In 1870 the choir went to Windsor and sang in St George's Chapel in the presence of Queen Victoria and other members of the royal family. In 1906 Dr Wood, former organist of Exeter Cathedral, wrote to the *Western Times* saying St John's choir had been a revelation to him in its singing of Stainer's *Crucifixion*. Sir Walter Tapper, the surveyor of Westminster Abbey and York Minster, sang in the choir as a boy.

St John's has been described as a rare gem of ecclesiastical art, with its reredos at the High Altar designed by Sir Gilbert Scott (this, it is believed, replaced the original), its mosaics by Salviati, and its rood designed by Fellowes Prynne and carved in Oberammergau. There are other interesting details as well. These include the Icon – believed to have been in a Moscow church, having been presented by Miss Rodd, whose brother was the last British Ambassador to the court of the Czars – and the Crucifix, which had been bought in Naples during the Garabaldian revolt by Mrs Bentinck's father.

St John's was not to everyone's taste and it remained the centre of controversy for many years. There were frequent attacks on it in the local press. In 1857 its services were attacked as being a mere aping of Roman Catholic ritual. The *Daily Western Times* described it as the lead centre of the priestly conspiracy of the county against Protestantism. It commented that visitors to the church noted that the 'reredos is a mass of imagery which renders it illegal'. The newspaper noted that there were 16 lighted candles on or around the altar, a picture of the Crucifixion over the pulpit and Stations of the Cross on the walls; the services were intoned and there were processions with banners. The Bishop of Exeter, Henry Phillpotts, was basically sympathetic to ritualism 'if it were done with discretion and due consideration of the ability of your people to receive it', but he was very concerned not to break the law.

Another extraordinary event in the history of St John's occurred in 1885. After a dispute with the parishioners at the parish church, the canon persuaded the church authorities (the bishop, the ecclesiastical commissioners and the patrons) to surrender the right to appoint priests at St John's to himself, as a private individual, and to allow that right to be transferred to Keble College, Oxford on his death. A formal legal agreement to this effect was duly signed before the end of the year, and thus the canon became the patron of St John's. This paved the way for St John's to become a separate parish – which happened in 1895, just months after the canon's death. Father Wickham was appointed the first parish priest.

Canon Courtenay's death did not end the controversy about St John's. In 1906 Henry Wickham and Miss Frances Fox, the churchwarden, had to appear before the Bishop of Exeter. The proceedings were private, but the statement issued to the press after the meeting said that various items, including two statues, three lamps, and the Holy Water stoop, were to be retained. It was ordered that the word 'Mass' be omitted from all church notices, the Lady Chapel, as such, was to be closed and the Sacred Heart be obliterated. The bishop recognised the great love the congregation had for its church and the splendid way everything was kept, but said he would not

The interior of St John's in the 1940s (Chapman & Son, courtesy of Dave Lewis)

be able to visit it while incense was used and other 'offensive practices' carried out. In practice, not all the measures demanded were carried out.

By the time Cecil Torr wrote *Small Talk at Wreyland* in 1918 he was able to be more tolerant. He wrote of an earlier visit to the church that

> *at the old church the service was very plain indeed, and [Canon Courtenay] preached in a black gown; but at the new church it was ornate, and he preached in other things. And people said he preached rank Popery there, though he preached sound doctrine at the old church. I have some reason to believe that the sermons he preached at the new church were the same that he had preached at the old church in the previous year. The black gown covered the Popery, if there was any there.*

In 1919 the patronage of St John's was transferred from Keble College by Lord Halifax, who was Canon Courtenay's executor and also his nephew-in-law, to the Guild of All Souls, still patrons today.

The erection of the large crucifix, St John's Calvary, outside the church caused controversy in the 1920s. A public lecture was held in the town hall, and the Reverend Mr Bloomfield from the Baptist Church took the opportunity to make a public protest. He said:

The choir at St John's in 1943. From left to right: Mr Payne, John Ireson, Ted Godfrey, Alfie Cadman (an evacuee), Geoff Wills, Donald Riddell, Father Hughes and Eric Godfrey (Eric Godfrey)

> *If people would have certain forms of images as objects of worship let them have them…but they should support them out of their own pocket and keep them within the walls of their own places of worship. If the Vicar of St John's, or Viscount Halifax,…thrust their peculiar forms and chosen images on the public, then they were overstepping the bounds of religious liberty, and making themselves trespassers on the rights of others.*

In the town there were many who supported this view at that time. Mercifully, today there is much more tolerance of differing religious views, and the present Christians Together in Bovey is a strong and united organisation.

Father Wickham continued as parish priest at St John's until his death in 1935, by which time he had served the parish for over 40 years. He was succeeded by Father Hughes, who came down from London. Father Hughes presided over the controversial transfer of the organ to its present position at the west end of the church where, sadly, it obscures the west window. He also guided the parish through the dark days of the Second World War. In all, he served the parish for over 30 years before his death in 1969. Father Hughes was then succeeded by Father Ker, who retired in 1980. He lives in retirement in Folkestone, and still maintains regular contact with some parishioners.

Father Pease succeeded Father Ker and was vicar at St John's when another great controversy arose in the Church of England over the ordination of women to the priesthood. The General Synod gave its approval to the ordination of women in November 1992. Following this, many Anglo-Catholic priests and lay people left the Church of England, and Father Pease retired in 1993.

The present vicar, Father David Stanton, arrived in 1994. By the mid-1990s the Church had created special measures by which the faith of those, like St John's, who were opposed to the ordination of women was protected. Since then St John's has continued to play a prominent part in what has become known as the Traditionalist group in the Church.

In conclusion, it is fair to say that the Catholic revival that so inspired Canon Courtenay in the 1850s has flourished at St John's over all of the last 150 years, despite various ups and downs. In June 2003 its 150th anniversary was celebrated with special church services, and, in September 2003, a flower festival was held at which all the treasures of the church were displayed.

David Carpenter and Barbara Mugford are planning to produce a new history of St John's in the near future.

St John's as it is today (2003) (Vernon Morgan)

Bibliography
Torr, Cecil. *Small Talk at Wreyland*. CUP, 1918
Yates, Nigel. *Anglican Ritualism in Victorian Britain 1830 - 1910*. OUP, 1999

✳ ✳ ✳ ✳ ✳

Schools
by Barry Jarvis

Bovey Tracey has been blessed with a variety of different types of schools over the years, each with different objectives and aims and built to cater for the various aspirations of the parents and children of the town. Most of the schools have been well supported by the people of Bovey. Some particularly noteworthy benefactors, who will be mentioned as the chapter unfolds, were instrumental in establishing Bovey's early schools. A theme common to all of the schools was a lack of finance; nothing changes in educational circles. Fortunately, on most occasions, local worthies and local institutions came to the rescue to provide education for all in our town.

The first educational records show that a school for seven poor children was established in 1713 as a result of a contract of February 1st and 2nd of that year between John Smith, John Bawden and Thomas Coniam and the vicar and 12 others. This same contract also made provision for the annual rent from various properties in Bovey to be donated for the education of the children. The trustees

> *should, for ever, employ the rents and profits of the said premises, for and towards the keeping constantly and continually to school seven poor children of the said parish successively for ever.*

The contract further decreed that the schoolmaster should be paid from this trust and that books and equipment should also be provided. This first public licensed school was given a further boost in 1715, when a certain Thomas Tothill gave to the schoolmaster, Thomas Durston, Wise's meadow, for the education of another six children. The children

> *were to be regularly kept to school and there carefully taught, and especially in the said church catechism.*

The schoolmaster was also told to teach reading, writing and arithmetic, and if he failed in these duties then the trustees would use the rents for 'pious and charitable uses'. Even in those days the schoolmaster was under pressure and accountable to his employers!

Things were really looking up for the school when yet another benefactor, William Stawell, in 1725, gave the profits from Manning's meadow to the vicar, Reverend Samuel Maynard, and eight trustees for the payment of the schoolmaster at the English School, as it was called. There are no more useful education records until those of 1822, which record that the schoolmaster received the princely sum of £35 12s. from the existing trusts. The records mention a dwelling house that the schoolmaster occupied and 'a room adjoining built about ten years ago for the purpose of a school', at the expense of a Mr Hole, on the condition that the schoolmaster instruct an extra two children appointed by Mr Hole. It was also mentioned that the schoolmaster also taught ten children under the Madras system. The school, according to Lance Tregoning, was sited in Fore Street where The Pink House now stands.

As always in educational circles, controversy raged and around 1822 the poor expressed dissatisfaction because the schoolmaster was charging the parents for stationery. He had the effrontery to charge 2s. 6d. per quarter for pens, ink and paper or they had the option of providing these materials themselves. After protest, this was reduced to 2s. per quarter at Michaelmas 1822. The matter was finally resolved when the parents bought the books themselves, but as the schoolmaster was not receiving all the rents due to him things became peaceful again. Little other information is available about Bovey's first venture into education, but in 1839 money from Hele's charity was paid to the school and in 1874 a scheme was drawn up whereby this first ancient free school, which was also claimed to be a grammar school, became Bovey Tracey Grammar School and public lands were given for its upkeep.

Bovey Tracey Grammar School

Mr Hole again featured in the life of the grammar school when he provided the site for the new school. The original building has now been developed as the Edgemoor Hotel. The Charity Commissioners, who administered the charities previously mentioned, financed the school, constructed in 1879 at a cost of £2,831 3s. The school had a constant battle throughout its history to obtain the rents due from its various lands and it kept the local solicitors well employed. The school comprised two large dormitories to accommodate 25 boys, a master's house, a schoolroom, a chemistry laboratory, a classroom and a dining room.

The age limits for the school were 7 and 16 years, and numbers fluctuated widely during the course of its history. The quality of its head teachers varied judging by comments recorded in the governors' minutes. One head teacher was given notice for having the audacity to rent out the head teacher's house without permission during the summer vacation, a practice which became common-place in later years when finances were constantly stretched. The unfortunate Mr Birchall was told by the governors that they were

dissatisfied with the general management of the school especially with reference to irregularities in time and to the boys' daily lessons not being heard as soon as practicable.

They also complained that he did not look after the grounds properly. Numbers, of course, went down accordingly and Mr Birchall resigned soon afterwards. Reverend R. Wellington Menneer from Cheshire, who inherited a run-down building with only 16 scholars and poor attendance, replaced him in 1898.

Towards the end of Mr Menneer's time in office the school had grown considerably in every way, the number on roll being 57, comprising 39 boarders and 18 day boys, of which 3 were awarded scholarships by examination. The scholarships were awarded to children of poor parents who earned less than 30 shillings a week.

During this time Mr Menneer had the school enlarged and was allowed to advertise far and wide for new pupils. He also introduced the teaching of natural science as a prerequisite to receiving a county council grant to enlarge the dormitories and teaching space. The governors in 1901 wrote:

The governors have great pleasure in passing a vote of confidence in the Head teacher, who has in a few years raised this school to a highly efficient state and so increased the numbers as to make enlarging necessary.

When Mr Menneer resigned to become Head of Newton Abbot College things declined to such an extent that an inspection report in May 1908 stated that the teaching staff was inadequate and the work extremely poor, even though the head teacher described the examination results as good. The staff comprised the Head, an assistant, a visiting art master, a drill sergeant and a teacher who had formerly been master on HMS *Worcester*. The boys themselves were a sickly collection: some were delicate or extremely delicate and their attendance was sporadic; some were backward and found the work beyond their reach.

At this time the new Bovey council school was about to be built and the numbers had fallen to 14 boarders and 10 day boys. The county council also withdrew its annual grant because of the poor inspection described above. The school was consequently closed in August 1908 and the premises, known then as Edgehill, were rented out. The Charity Commissioners used the money in hand to establish *The Bovey Tracey Exhibition Foundation*. The exhibition was keenly contested by examinations in reading, writing, arithmetic, history and geography by pupils resident in the parish of Bovey, who, in the opinion of the governors, were in need of assistance to pay tuition fees and travelling expenses to Newton Abbot Secondary School. Three boys and two girls were initially selected, but later the best five in the examination results, regardless of sex, were awarded the scholarships. Bovey Tracey has always moved with the times: the Great Western Railway was asked to run a convenient train for pupils attending Newton Abbot Secondary School.

According to Lance Tregoning, many of the local farmers' and tradesmen's sons were scholars here, some of them riding to school on horseback. The grammar school was a far cry from the first school, which was opened for poor children.

The Church Schools

The churches have always been prominent in helping to provide education for everyone and in 1834 Mr Francis Berry, a wealthy woollen mill owner, donated a garden adjoining the churchyard on which a school could be built where children would be educated according to the principles of the Church of England: he also generously gave £250 towards the building costs. According to a newspaper report of the opening ceremony,

The children were regaled with a plentiful supply of that good old English fare, roast beef and plum pudding, given to them by the octogenarian Vicar.

The school developed rapidly and attendance was always praised, diocesan inspectors decreeing it to have the best attendance record in the district. Attendance statistics were very important as they, together with tested academic performance, were used to calculate the grant that the school could obtain each year. A stick and carrot approach was used to encourage attendance; one girl, Susie Moore, was given a dress for full attendance for one year, and there are many records of prosecutions for poor attendance.

The good start made by the school led to expansion across the road into a new building in 1868, initially for the boys only. The girls remained behind in what we now know as the church rooms, and the privileged boys were ensconced in what is now the house called Panorama. The girls did move across in 1884. The school was, until 1914, administered as two separate entities, each having different head teachers and staff. The girls and infants of mixed sex were taught together, and the junior and senior boys were taught in a different room. The two schools did come together for Empire Day, when the flag was raised and saluted by all the children as they marched past it and patriotic songs were sung.

Not surprisingly the teachers were more concerned about the quality of teaching in religious education than anything else, although the children were examined in composition, spelling and dictation, recitation, geography and arithmetic. Diocesan inspections were frequent and the children were examined in catechism, Old Testament, New Testament, prayers and collects, seasons and scripts and hymns. There were frequent inspections by HMI and these were almost always complimentary. The various vicars spent a lot of time in the school, teaching, moralising and checking registers as well as witnessing punishments.

It appeared that children from St John's Infant School had to take an examination in order to attend this school, and one poor child was returned to St John's for a second time because he was not up to scratch. The Head complained bitterly about how backward the St John's infants were on arrival. He also had trouble with the half timers, the so-called 'Pottery children', who worked half time in the pottery. Their reading skills were always a source of concern. Some children were admitted from the British School and some gained exhibitions for Newton Abbot Secondary School. The children left school if they achieved enough attendances for a certificate of attendance, although some were exempted from this.

The school routinely closed for carnival, then held in October, and for Bovey Fair in July. Days off were given for such things as the Co-operative Society fete, Mayor's Day, Union Jack boys' outing, school treat, following an HMI inspection, and for ploughing and thatching contests. The boys who belonged to either the parish church choir or St John's choir frequently had time out for weddings, funerals, saints' days and so on. Half days were taken for Ascension Day. Children were often sent home with suspected diphtheria, and some deaths were recorded from this scourge. The school was closed for a month for scarlatina and the building cleansed and whitewashed in 1913. A strange absence for goitre among nine children occurred in May 1925. Absences were common for bad weather, especially floods, at harvest-time and in the fruit season, when the children were ill from eating too many apples; one child scoffed eight apples in one morning and suffered the consequences!

Numbers at the school began to decline when the council school became established: children also attended the council school for such things as domestic science lessons. Finally, when the number on roll fell to 14 in 1939, the school was closed and the furniture transferred to the council school. The original schoolroom is now used for church and parish functions, but it was used again as a school when the evacuees arrived during the Second World War.

The British School

This school evolved due to the crusading of the formidable Annie Croker, who campaigned relentlessly against the teachings of the established Church of England. She was opposed to Tractarianism, High Church philosophy and influence. Miss Croker stated that Bovey was

a very dark country village where Tractarianism in its worst form prevails...

She was continually constrained by a lack of money and pleaded constantly for financial help, not easily available in Bovey, 'the principal families here being all Tractarian'. She wrote to newspapers and journals, especially the non-conformist press, and opened a penny subscription. From small beginnings in hired premises in 1861, with seven children on roll, she accumulated enough money to open a new building in Mary Street (now the Gospel Hall). Miss Croker was not able to be a manager of the school because she was a female, but was an extremely dominant secretary and organiser of the school. The school was run on non-sectarian lines using the educational philosophy decreed for British Schools by Lancaster and Bell, two renowned Quaker educationalists.

It was considered that the school could accommodate 250 children, but fortunately it never held more than 160 because the dimensions of the school were a schoolroom 40ft by 24 ft, a classroom 20ft by 12 ft and a cloakroom 10ft by 5ft. Nearly half of the children were under 6 when the school was opened. Even though the school was now established, Annie was always alert for High Church intrusions and she was wary of the Devon House Sisters of Mercy who, she said, canvassed for children for the Church School. She became very suspicious when a new curate arrived in Bovey and visited the school without saying who he was and asked questions and showed great interest. Annie wrote that

a perfect looking Jesuit lately came to work among the children...the last new dodge of the ritualistic Vicar...a wolf in sheep's clothing.

Staffing was always a problem for Annie and the school because of lack of money. The school could not afford to pay a competitive salary and therefore could not attract or retain staff of very high quality. Although quite a high grant was earned because of attendance and measured academic performance, the full grant could not be taken, as the school could not match this amount from its own money-raising. Consequently the school had 26 teachers in charge in 28 years before Miss Kingcombe stayed for 11 years, 'an energetic and painstaking teacher'. Eight teachers stayed less than a year.

Miss Croker always preferred female head teachers and had many battles with the managers who had different views. One male teacher, a certain John Fiddes, did the male sex no favours when he stayed for three days only. He was described as a charlatan who used false testimonials and left leaving unpaid bills. He was said to be

an apparition in a tall box hat, shabby black clothes, a pile of books in leather, straps in hand and a black cane.

He spent his time in school doing private writing and left after a deplorable fracas in the street in which his landlady's son seized his bag to stop him going off without paying his rent, with Miss

Croker trying to intervene unsuccessfully. Miss Croker also had a battle with a Mr Parsons when the managers insisted on appointing a man. He ingratiated himself with a letter of Uriah Heap-like proportions to the managers. Annie disliked his

stiff cold formality, his religious exercises, his slack discipline and his sardonic and supercilious manner and his scoffing at her simple faith.

Mercifully for Annie he resigned when she refused to pay him monthly and not quarterly and at a higher salary, as he demanded. Annie said that, 'this was providentially permitted to facilitate his exodus'. A more useful and famous member of staff was Mr A.J. Coles, better known to us as Jan Stewer, the author of Devon dialect stories.

Miss Croker tried to recruit her staff from non-conformist training colleges and by advertising, but she frequently had to have supply teachers to fill vacancies between appointments. A Miss Barnecutt from Yorkshire was recommended to her but this lady wanted £65 per annum, far too much for Bovey funds. The matter was resolved when the noble Miss Barnecutt agreed to come, having turned down £100 a year from a Bradford school. She came on a salary of £50 and hoped to supplement this with a night school enterprise which failed dismally. At a later date Miss Barnecutt received an extra £5 a year from the managers, and a parlour and two bedrooms were rented for her. Miss Barnecutt formed a close bond with Miss Croker, who called her 'good Miss Barnecutt and the best teacher that the school had in 30 years'. Miss Barnecutt left to take care of her dependent family when she took over her father's school in Llanelli for £70 per annum. She had just broken up with a long-standing fiancé, calling him worldly and uncongenial. There were tears all around at her departure.

Despite the constant search for staff and the financial difficulties, the school seems to have achieved good standards judging by the HMI reports. Many concerts, or entertainments, were given to the public in The Temperance Hall, comprising recitations, songs and drills. These were highly praised in the local press.

The school was eventually closed as a British School on 2nd June 1911, when the school marched down to the new purpose-built council school in Abbey Road, which, of course, is the present primary school.

Bovey Tracey Primary School
The first head teacher was Mr George Lamacraft who had previously been in charge of the British School. He was obviously delighted with his new building, describing it as 'one of the most advanced and envied schools in Devon'. The school began with 176 pupils from the Gospel Hall site and some from the overflow building in Spion Kop. The pupils were thrilled by the new wood-block floor marked out with a map of the British Isles and were impressed with the motto above the separate boys' entrance of 'work well done is its own reward'.

Children aged from 3 years attended the school if they lived close by, but had to wait until they were 6 if they had to travel any distance; the usual leaving age was 14. The school bell, which is now displayed in the Heritage Centre, rang out to warn children that the starting time was imminent. The curriculum for the oldest children was very practical, the girls having cooking lessons and needlework and the boys having woodwork and gardening.

The school flourished under the benevolent Mr Lamacraft, and the tranquil atmosphere that prevailed in the school was often praised by visiting inspectors, as was the leadership of the school. The number on roll reached 200 in 1914, when there was a great deal of movement of children from the Church School and from outlying schools such as Lustleigh. Several scholars passed away from a variety of illnesses, including the son of the head teacher. Children were excluded for mumps, and scarlatina was still prevalent.

During the period of the First World War the children knitted gloves, socks, scarves and so on and sent boxes containing these items, together with chocolate and stationery, to the front line troops and to the crew of HMS *Falmouth*. Letters of thanks were received. Produce from the now

The infant class of 1912. Miss Martin, later Mrs Pring (infant teacher), is on the left and George Lamacraft (headmaster) is on the right. Back row, left to right: Leslie Heath, Bill Mountford, Jack Webber, Stanley Petallick, Kate Tolley, Millie Hawkes and Gwen Tucker. Middle row, left to right: ?, Walter Wallen, Eddie Johns, Murray Steer, Doris Pascoe, Bill Payne, Ruby Carpenter, 'Norry' Noakes, Dorothy Richards and Reggie Gale. Front row, left to right: Bertie Redstone, Irene Underhill, Herbert Godfrey, a visitor and Roy Stancombe (B.T. Heritage Trust)

well-established school garden was also sent, and egg collections were despatched to wounded soldiers. The children were taken to the square to see wounded soldiers passing through the town. A war savings scheme was established when Baron and Baroness Bouck visited the school and gave each child a shilling to start the scheme off. During the war years one member of staff was called to the colours, and the headmaster received call-up papers on two occasions, later revoked, before eventually joining the army in July 1918. A temporary Head then took charge until Mr Lamacraft's return to school in January 1919.

Things progressed smoothly after the war and Mr Lamacraft left to become head teacher at Dawlish in July 1920 to be succeeded by Mr Charles Bint from Birmingham, who was also given a recently purchased house at Orchard Terrace to live in. Numbers on roll remained fairly constant at around 210, and the woodwork room was used for lessons for children from Blackpool, Chudleigh Knighton, Heathfield and the Church School. Cookery and needlework were also offered to these other schools. The school garden continued to flourish despite the occasional disaster caused by marauding sheep. The children could sell some of their own produce from their individual strips of land.

Milk was delivered daily by Mr Dart in his pony and trap and was warmed in the cookery room for 11 o'clock break. School hours were altered according to the seasons, with children allowed to start and leave at variable times during inclement weather. A school orchestra was formed, comprising mostly violins, and a Welfare Association met in the school on a regular basis for the benefit of mothers and their babies. The Red Cross Society came into being and examinations were successfully taken in first aid. Prefects were appointed and one ex-prefect recalls having the privilege of collecting the Head's newspaper and whisky from the local shops on a daily basis.

War again reared its ugly head and school routine was interrupted from 1939. In September of that year 80 children from Acton arrived as evacuees, as well as many unofficial evacuees from other areas. Forty of these children were sent for lessons in the old Church School. The number on

The highly productive school garden, with Mr Bint supervising, circa 1920 (B.T. Heritage Trust)

roll now reached 279, comprising 216 from Bovey, 25 unofficial evacuees and 38 official ones from Acton, together with 37 based at the Church School. The school was kept open during the summer vacation, with the teachers taking it in turns to supervise 'war work' – collecting paper, metal, cones and wood as well as knitting and sewing. Money was constantly raised for the Spitfire Fund: a Spitfire named the City of Exeter was purchased. Gas masks were frequently checked and refitted. The children also regularly undertook air raid practice, which involved diving under the table clad in gas masks when given the word of command, and sold newspapers to American soldiers based at Bovey for inflated prices, as the Americans had barely grasped the true value of British currency. The Americans reciprocated with sweets and film shows at Devon House.

In 1944 Mr Northway replaced Mr Bint, who had served for 23 years. Mr Northway remained in post until July 1951, when he became head teacher at Watcombe. The war effort continued with copious amounts of jam being made from hips; 87 pounds were made in one day. The children were paid one penny per pound for collecting the rose hips. After the war, with the return home of the evacuees and their teachers, the number on roll was 210 and there were classes of 40 plus; one class was held in the hall. The PTA was formed in 1947 and has grown from strength to strength. During this time school radio broadcasts began and school visits went further afield, including one to London.

Mr E.R. Vinnicombe arrived as Head in 1951 and remained in post until 1976 to continue the tradition of long-serving and devoted head teachers. He had to oversee the change in status from an all-age school to a primary 5-11 establishment. At the time some of the people in Bovey were unhappy to see their school have its status altered, and the change did not come about without a fight.

The building was altered to accommodate the new age range, and the infants were housed in the room previously used for domestic science; the old woodwork room became a craft room and a new staffroom was formed. A visiting HMI was most impressed with the new organisation. The children, on reaching the appropriate age, now attended either Newton Abbot Grammar School or Ashburton Secondary School according to the results of the dreaded 11-plus examinations.

As a result of the change of status, the school roll was 147, but as the new school became established the average number on roll increased to about 170. Then, in 1964, when the children from Lustleigh were first admitted following the closure of their school, the number on roll became 210.

The present school field was first used in 1963, which saved the long trip to the recreation ground. During the next few years the teaching methods were considerably changed, T. V and radio broadcasts were commonplace and the old regimentation was succeeded by much more individual attention. School clubs and societies were expanded, including a pottery club.

School summer fete in the mid-1960s with, from left to right, Mr Vinnicombe (headmaster),
Mrs Way, Mrs Vinnicombe, Mrs Kitson and Dr Thompson (H.R. Rivers)

Mr Ted Atkinson succeeded Mr Vinnicombe in 1976 and he said that Mr Vinnicombe was a difficult act to follow. The staff was very stable during his tenure and he expanded the curriculum by using the expertise of various part-time staff instead of employing a permanent teacher. During this time several children were taken on cruises on the educational cruiser, HMS *Uganda,* and the school was involved in the first twinning ceremony. Mr Atkinson had many battles to try to improve the school building and to develop a community hall on site. He retired in 1983 to be succeeded by Mr Max Quick.

In 1986 the school was extensively refurbished when a large hall was constructed together with a new administrative wing and changing rooms for the children. The classrooms were modernised and a new play area constructed on part of the school field. During Mr Quick's time at the school the number of classes has grown from six to ten as the number of houses in Bovey has radically increased, and the school roll is in excess of 300. The school has coped with the ever-changing educational philosophies of the government of the time and has had two very successful OFSTED inspections; in June 2001 the inspectors said, 'Bovey Tracey School is a very effective school and provides its pupils with a good education'. It was also praised for its good leadership and fine community links as typified by the recent production of 'Tracey and the Timekeeper', a truly community drama production involving parents, governors, staff and pupils. The school has also been awarded the coveted Investor in People accolade and the blue flag flies proudly from its flagpole. This reflects the school's concern with the needs of its most valuable resource, its staff. Other awards include Education Extra for its range of extra curriculum activities, Healthy Schools for Citizenship and a School Achievement award for SATS results.

The buildings have received another refurbishment but, with an army of children under five now living in the new developments and waiting to be educated, how much longer can the school continue to absorb such high numbers in a building originally designed for a maximum of 200 children?

Other Schools
There have been some other schools worthy of note in Bovey's educational history but, to date, not much detail has been discovered about them.

Brimley School
This school was sited in Upper Brimley, in a lane just above The Prestbury. It is now the bungalow called The School House, situated in Stentiford Lane, and is thought to be part of the original Colehayes estate. The school was built to educate the workers' children who lived in nearby cottages. A photograph still exists of this Dame School, but the main records were destroyed in a fire. The photograph given to the Heritage Trust by Mrs Tregoning shows the whole school of about 20 children with their headmistress, Miss Treleaven: there are some plans of the building in the heritage centre. The late Mr Dick Wills, a local historian, once told us that the first head teacher in 1850 was a Miss Levitt, a relative of the family living at Colehayes. Two sisters assisted her, the Misses Cambell, one of whom translated the words of that popular hymn, 'All Things Bright and Beautiful', from German.

St John's Infant School

Typical school apparel of 1900 captured at St John's Infant School, with the schoolmistress, Mrs Hellier, and her assistant, Winnie Staddon (later Mrs Bond) (B.T. Heritage Trust)

This small school was built in 1860 opposite St John's Church and catered for infant aged children who took a test before they could be admitted to The Church or National School. It did not come under LEA control after the 1902 Act but continued as a private school until about 1919. The average attendance was 22 and Mrs Hellier was in charge as shown in the photograph.

The Retreat

This was a preparatory school staffed by Misses A. and A. Warner. It only catered for junior aged children, several of whom transferred to Ingsdon Convent School when they became aged 11.

Miss Bodkin's Kindergarten

The school was in the Indio grounds and was a mixed school for pupils aged 5 to 7. Some of the former pupils recall that there were two classes, each containing 12 children, and that the curriculum was very narrow. One pupil says that she was always miserable there and was referred to as either Lucy Drip or Carol Tapwater as she constantly wept. The school was in existence during the 1940s.

So ends the story of education in Bovey over the last 200 years, a story still changing in order to come to terms with the many developments in educational philosophy. With the arrival of a new generation of devoted educationalists and a constantly increasing population, the future will be interesting.

References

School documents from County Record Offices, *The Report of The Commissioners concerning Charities, Volume 2.*

Minute Book and Headmasters' reports from Bovey Grammar School

School Log Books from the Church Schools, the British School and the County Primary School.

Sellman, Roger R. *Bovey Tracey British School in the nineteenth century.*

Tregoning, Lance. *Bovey Tracey: An Ancient Town.* Cottage Publishing, 1993

Tregoning, Lance. *Bovey Tracey In Bygone Days.* Devon Books, 1989

✳ ✳ ✳ ✳ ✳

Buildings

An Architect Walks Through Bovey

To walk through the streets of Bovey Tracey with architect Peter Hall is to become aware of its multi-layered history. Very little is what it appears to be. Many of the houses have Georgian or Victorian facades, but they hide much earlier structures. Cottages with slate roofs still have remnants of thatch in their roof space. When out and about doing the shopping it is easy to walk past buildings and have no idea of their history, but Peter's discerning eye draws attention to the palimpsest that is Bovey. For instance, the Spice Bazaar and the barber's shop have Georgian fronts and modern windows, but when they were repaired about ten years ago elegant medieval oak-frames with rendered lathe and plaster walls were revealed.

As we walk up Fore Street we pass houses which have been hacked about and altered, but signs, such as chimneys earlier than the main building, indicate an interesting past. Peter Hall finds the listing of the town hall something of a mystery as he sees it as a poor example of a municipal building of that era. However, he is ready to acknowledge that it does have its defenders.

Opposite the town hall is a simple group of four little shops, which he sees as a lovely piece of streetscape, and, although their integrity is perhaps compromised by their 'sensible' aluminium windows, he thinks they should be better appreciated by the people who casually pass them.

Walking further up into East Street, passing Little Front House, Front House and Summerfields, there is much to delight the eye and feed the imagination. Various signs indicate that these houses are hiding much older houses. For instance, the roof of the Manor House has ancient oak timbers blackened with soot from before the time of fireplaces.

Next we come to Ashwell, which is a Georgian gem. It is clear, in every detail, that the whole place was carefully planned before construction began. The Georgian modules of the house are echoed in the rhythm of the pillars of the verandah. Peter Hall says it is rare to see a verandah so carefully related to the proportions of the house. All the rooms are classically proportioned, too.

Bell House is fascinating, with its Georgian roof and brick chimneys, and Victorian bay window overlooking the garden. But all this Georgian and Victorian endeavour overlays the small medieval cottage buried within: oak-cruck frames hidden within the thickness of the new walls support a complete set of ancient roof timbers and old cob walls that sit above the much newer ceilings. A magnificent medieval fireplace was hidden for years behind a mean 'modern' fireplace and is now once more opened up to give the ancient heart of the house a new life. The main entrance has an old oak door frame which leads into a stone-flagged cross passage with the remnants of an oak screen. At the base of the entrance, the bedrock protruding above the tarmac footpath hints towards this house being a place where people huddled in a much simpler hut built to exploit the natural landscape and where, over the generations, it grew slowly into today's house.

Church Steps is a house that has seen many changes in very recent years and, although it has lost its rendered walls and its inside has been reorganised, its roof has been rethatched using local thatching techniques with a simple laced ridge instead of the rather chocolate-box method of thatching imported from other counties.

Peter Hall recognises that changes have to take place; people have to live in their houses, and needs change from generation to generation, but he finds some changes distressing, such as plastic windows and drainpipes, or false details on thatched roofs. The Victorians started the craze of removing the waterproofing render from walls to show the more romantic stones and, ever since, people have been trying to waterproof walls that were only built to be rendered. Similarly, the present-day tendency to strip paint off woodwork usually exposes relatively poor quality timber and workmanship that were always meant to be painted. The stripping also destroys historic paintwork that could have divulged fascinating and important information about the changing lifestyles and living patterns of the many previous inhabitants. He sees these as being unsympathetic to the story of the house as well as being inappropriate building. Using traditional materials, such as lime, timber, cob and wooden windows, can contribute significantly to the longevity of our historic buildings and shows proper respect for our heritage, which he sees as being particularly rich in Bovey.

Below is a selection of some interesting houses in Bovey Tracey.

Church Hill, Colehayes, Cross Cottage, Indio, Parke, Whitstone, Wolleigh and Yarner
by Sherryl and Susie Healey

Church Hill

Church Hill is one of the finest examples of Georgian architecture in Bovey Tracey. The present house dates from about 1851, but there is evidence of an earlier building on this site. The Land Tax Assessment of 1799 indicates that the property, then called Bull Hill, was owned by John Harris and occupied by the Timewell family for nearly 30 years. A search of the parish burial records reveals that George Timewell was buried on 1st November 1789, Jno. Timewell on 4th January 1807 and Sarah Timewell on 11th July 1820: she was aged 63.

The 1839 tithe map shows a building which legend says was burned down in the early 1840s. An article in the *Exeter Flying Post* on 1st March 1841 confirms a fire in East Street, stating that this occurred in a thatched cottage adjoining the home of Mr Brown, the courier, and destroyed three other properties. The cause of the fire was hot ashes being thrown out in the back of the premises. It is believed that a Mr Roberts, a miner, lived in Bull Hill in 1841.

The new house, grander than the cottage preceding it, is built of granite and slate stone rubble, with a red brick chimney stack in the end gable. The centre door has a cement surround and the windows all have moulded stucco architraves and eight-pane sashes. Inside there is an elegant wooden staircase, and some rooms have plain moulded-plaster cornices. Upstairs there is a prime example of early indoor plumbing, which was installed in about 1891.

John Harris sold Bull Hill to the Loveys family, the whole site fetching £31. The Loveys owned the property from the 1850s to 1903. Thomas Loveys, a Bovey Tracey man, was the land steward to Mr Adair at Colehayes. His wife, Susan, who was born in Lustleigh, ran a girls' boarding school at Church Hill with her two daughters, Anne and Caroline. In 1881 they had pupils from the Teign Valley, Torquay and India, all aged between 12 and 17.

During the Second World War, after Dunkirk, the house was requisitioned as a sergeants' billet. One story from that time tells of a soldier cleaning his rifle inside the house. The rifle was accidentally discharged and the bullet went up through the ceiling, narrowly missing a man in the room above.

Colehayes

The estate agent's details in 1913 described the Colehayes estate as 'one of the most attractive estates in South Devon, extending to about 470 acres'. The house is in a beautiful, secluded position half a mile down a drive, well away from the main road and surrounded by woodlands.

From 1540 to about 1780 Colehayes, or Colehouse as it was then known, was a small house with some surrounding land. The name is variously written as Colhouse, Colehouse, Coal House, Cole House, Colehays and Colehayes. In old English 'Col' meant charcoal, so this was probably a house where charcoal was produced. 'Hay' derives from 'Gehaeg' in old English, and by 1870 the name changes to Colehays, meaning an enclosure or fenced in wood.

By the middle of the 19th century there was small estate and a modest Georgian country house, which was then turned into a Victorian gentleman's large country seat. The house remained a private residence until 1952, the lands having been sold off successively in the period after 1913. Both the shrinkage of the estate and changes in the use of the house were due to economic and social factors, locally and nationally.

As usual the Bovey Tracey Church and Poor Rate and the Land Tax Assessments proved an excellent source for ascertaining the names of previous owners. These included, in 1540, Thomas Pinson and, in the 17th and 18th centuries, the Puddicombe family. Then, in 1788, Charles Fanshawe, a Recorder of Exeter, purchased Colehays from the Puddicombes and left it to his son, Reverend Charles Fanshawe.

The next owners were the Adair family. Alexander

Church Hill (B.T. Heritage Trust)

Adair, the third son of William, was born in 1791. He married Harriet Eliza Atkinson of Westmorland on 17th June 1828, and it was his father who bought Colehays for the young couple. Alexander and Harriet had six children between 1829 and 1843 – Alexander William, Harriet Camilla, Robert Desmond, Hugh Jemson, Allen Shafto and Henrietta Mary, probably all born at Colehayes. When William Adair died in 1844 Alexander and Harriet moved back to their father's house at Heatherton Park, near Taunton. Alexander William and his grandson, Gerald, born 1865, followed them there and Colehayes was sold.

From 1880, when Theophilus Levett lived there, Colehayes changed hands approximately seven times until being purchased in 1952 by Mr R.F. Lucas. Mr Lucas ran the place as a hotel for several years. In 1966, under different ownership, there was a country club and a hotel at Colehayes. However, the two did not always co-exist happily and, in February 1966, Mr Showell, proprietor of the hotel, opposed renewal of the licence of the club. He said the club was 'fully active as late as 7 o'clock in the morning, and there was an occasion when members were going home at 9.15 a.m.' Three members of the club, Wing Commander H. Watkins, Mr L.J. Copp and Mr P.D. Freeman said the club, 'with a membership of professional and business men, was efficiently run and gave no cause for complaint'. As the hotel had three flats, ten bedrooms and the normal ground-floor rooms in addition to the club lounge bar, it is easy to see how problems arose when the licence for a club was granted originally. The club lost its licence.

The property became the Dartmoor Field Studies Centre under the ownership of Bill and Rosemarie Longfield. At the time

Colehayes (B.T. Heritage Trust)

there was planning permission to convert the house to 10 flats. Mr and Mrs Longfield saved the estate from the possibility of unsympathetic development and built up an extremely successful business. The students' accommodation consisted of 20 centrally-heated bedrooms, some large enough for eight beds, a 40ft panelled hall and log fire plus a bar with an original fireplace and a dining room for 70 covers.

The house itself is early 19th century with later additions, built of granite ashlar under slate roofs. There is a central front door within a Greek Doric porch.

Cross Cottage

The property takes its name from the cross in the wall outside. This cross originally stood at the junction of the old Moretonhampstead road and the lane to Higher Atway (*Transactions of The Devonshire Association* vol. 70, p. 369). Dr John Croker had the cross removed and built into his wall when the road was widened.

The house itself was built in the mid-1700s of stone and some cob, with rendered walls and slated roof in parallel ranges. It appears to have been a cottage with a new extension on the front, and a previous owner, Mr J. Lloyd, said he believed the house was either an extended cottage or two cottages converted into one house.

Dr J.G. Croker was married to Mary Ann Hole of Stickwick in 1816. The Hole family later lived at Parke. Their first child, Mary Grace, was born at Cross Cottage in 1817 and this family still lived in the house in 1906. Over the following 23 years, four daughters and three sons followed. Dr Croker experimented in smallpox and whooping cough vaccinations, using his children as guinea pigs. He kept detailed notes on the condition of each child after vaccination and these were found in the house. Despite Dr Croker's modern approach to vaccinations, he still attributed the death of one of his young sons to 'a short illness in a violent bowel complaint, caused by the strong smell of sea air at Dawlish'.

As well as being the local doctor, John Croker was a keen geologist and historian. In 1867 he found two spindle-shaped, blue Serpentine Celtic moulds during a dig on Bovey Heath. He also co-wrote a book called *Letters Historical and Botanical* with Dr Frazer Halle. Less than enamoured of his fellow humans en masse, Dr Croker complained about the steps cut into the rock at Haytor because they enabled 'the enervated and pinguitudinous scions of humanity of this wonderful nineteenth century to gain its summit'.

His only surviving son, Samuel, married and lived in Bovey Tracey. His name was given to the Crokers Almshouses, and his wife donated the bells to the parish church in his memory, raising the money for this with a two-day fete at Parke.

Another daughter, Annie, founded the Bovey Tracey British School. She remained actively involved with the school until her death in 1906. Her sketchbook survives today, leaving simple pictures of 19th century Bovey Tracey for us to enjoy.

Indio

Indio or Indeo, also known as Yenyeo, means 'a house of God' in Latin. The property is said to be called this because the first building on the site was a priory. There does appear to be some doubt about this, but it is known that there was a nunnery on the site during the reign of Henry II. At this time a lane, bordered by high hedges, ran from Indio to the parish church to enable the nuns to attend church without having to go through the village and risk being distracted by the inhabitants. At this time the land belonged to the Priory of St John, Bridgwater. During the early 19th century Joseph Steer of Indio began legal proceedings to have the right of way (Drakes Lane end) re-established, but was unsuccessful due to lack of money.

At the dissolution of the monasteries in 1535 John Southcote of Bovey Tracey owned the whole property by purchase from the Crown. He later built a new house on the site. John Southcote had made his fortune as a steward, or tithe holder, for several monasteries in Devon. He was agent for the St John Priory, on which he held the lease until the dissolution.

Indio remained in the ownership of the Southcotes for several years, passing first to John's son,

Thomas, and then to his eldest grandson, Robert. Mrs Eveleigh of Parke was the daughter of John Southcote of Indio. In 1625 Sir John Stawell, lord of the manor of Bovey Tracey, owned the house.

Cross Cottage (B.T. Heritage Trust)

As may be expected the house has had a varied history. It has often been used as business premises as much as a family home and has been remodelled on several occasions. In 1766 George Tufnell founded a pottery at Indio using the clay extracted from the nearby heath field. Well-known local historian, William Ellis, often claimed his grandfather started the pottery, but no deeds or records are known to exist to confirm this. In 1775 the Indio Pottery endured a visit from Josiah Wedgwood himself. It seems that the wares he saw did not overly impress him.

The Indio potters celebrated Martinmass with a feast of goose cooked in the kiln, large amounts of beer and bladders of, reportedly, smuggled French brandy. One man, Isaac Youlden, had a good excuse for being drunk at the feast. He said it was to 'stop the quacking o' the gander'.

In 1850 Indio underwent another change of ownership. The property passed into the ownership of the Bentinck family. Charles Aldenburgh Bentinck was a magistrate who hired the architect David MacKintosh of Exeter to design a new house. The outer stone arch bears the Bentinck heraldic emblem, the initials CAB and the date 1850. The house remained the home of the influential Bentinck family until its sale in 1939. Mr Bentinck was lord of the manor and, like most of the owners of the big houses, a large employer, with a cook, housemaid, lady's maid, butler and kitchen maid to see to the family's needs, plus outdoor staff.

The sale details at that time describe Indio as a 'charming residential estate with 1.5 miles of trout and salmon peel fishing in the River Bovey and 400 acres'. The estate included Lambels Cottage (off Station Road), Townsend Cottage, the Old Toll House, the land on which the public conveniences stand in Station Road car park, the recreation ground, including the cricket club, two lodges, Grey Walls and Wifford Farm.

The gardens at Indio were said to be a showpiece in the Bentincks' time. They were under the capable control of a Bovey Tracey man, Fred Edgecombe,

Indio (B.T. Heritage Trust)

from 1923 until 1938. During this period the gardens included orchards, vegetable gardens, a walled garden with fruit trained against the walls, heated greenhouses, including orchid houses, a 72ft peach house and a carnation house. Mr Edgecombe reported that the owner expected a fresh carnation for his buttonhole each morning. The estate employed twenty staff, five of them in the gardens.

Indio House, as it stands today, is a grade II listed, early Victorian, Gothic-style manor house. It is built mainly of local granite, with a slate roof and stone chimneys. The windows have Bath stone mullions and surrounds with oak casements. The interior has extensive oak panelling, oak staircases and doors. The fireplaces are either granite or marble. Local rumour has it that Indio is haunted by the ghost of a Roundhead soldier, who has been seen leaning on the mantelpiece. This is quite some feat as the mantelpiece in question is well over shoulder height.

Another mystery surrounds the granite pillars which stand in the garden. The origins of these six pillars are not known, but it has been said that they may have come from the butterwalk structure which once stood in the town. It was noted that they are similar to the pillar which stood outside the Manor House in East Street for many years. This was also said to have come from the Butterwalk.

During the Second World War Indio House was used as a guesthouse for refugees and an assembly point for American forces before the invasion of Europe.

Today, Indio is still yielding its secrets - recently the new owners found a treasure trove of beautiful dresses in the attic!

Parke

Parke is a house with a long and interesting history. One of the earliest mentions of a house at Parke was in the 11th century, when King Harold owned the manor. Harold's sons, Goodwin and Edmund, lived at Parke, South Bovey and at the manor house lower down the river on the opposite bank. Later, Parke was given to George, Bishop of Coutance, and then, early in the reign of Henry II, the manor came into the possession of Sir William de Tracey. Thomas à Becket is said to have spent two or three summers at the house with Lady Tracey, and this is the connection which gave rise to the story that William de Tracey built (or rebuilt) the parish church as penance for the murder of Becket. Certainly this link led to the name South Bovey being changed to Bovey Tracey.

In the 15th century Henry Holland, Duke of Exeter, owned Parke. Holland died without heirs and the property was granted to Margaret, Countess of Richmond, for her lifetime. In 1571 it was leased to Thomas Southcote. Peter Southcote was in residence and the estate, listed as The Parke, is

Parke in 1912 (Chapman & Son)

mentioned in the survey of 1596.

The two big houses of the time were Parke and Indio. A close connection began when Nicholas Eveleigh lived at Parke in 1618. Nicholas was a steward of the Devonshire stannaries and his mother was the daughter of John Southcote of Indeo.

In the 17th century people living at Parke included Elizaeus Hele, who married Nicholas Eveleigh's widow, Alice, after Eveleigh's death when the Court House at Chagford collapsed. The Heles owned Bovey Tracey mills. The couple had no children, so the house passed to John Maynard of Exeter in 1637. In 1658 Sir John Stawell of Indeo moved to Parke. His son, William, succeeded to Indeo, strengthening the tie between the two houses.

A contemporary account described it as a 'fair large mansion house and gatehouse with all suitable convenient outhouses in good repair, a pound house and coach house'. In March 1703 an advertisement appeared in *The Post Man* for

The Barton Mansion House and Capital Messuage of Parke, the Mannor and Royalty of Bovey Tracy with the Fairs and Markets and Custom Mills, the Mannors of Knighton and Hennocke, and the Barton of Indio (all lying adjoining) in the County of Devon.

The precincts of the manor at this time were more than 23 miles – with plenty of game, except red grouse. The estate was seldom without red deer, duck, mallard, widgeon and teal. Snipes bred in the heathfield, and the timber and trees of the woods were surveyed in 1701 and valued at £1,400.

The next family to settle at Parke was John Langdon with his wife, a sister of the Powderham Courtenays. Their only daughter died young. Distraught, John Langdon allowed his stepfather, George Hunt, a lawyer, to take over his business affairs. On John's death, Hunt ejected his widow. The dispute over this raged for nine months but without resolution. Hunt and Langdon's mother had had two daughters and they became the co-heiresses of Parke. To settle this problem, each daughter was given a candle and the one whose candle burnt out first would inherit. The winning daughter was the wife of George Clapp. Later Clapp's son's widow sold Parke to John Gould. Gould does not seem to have lived there as he leased the property to William Hole of Stickwick for one year.

At the end of that year Hole bought the estate and a long association with the Hole family began. William's sister described the old house as being built in the 14th century, saying it was a large irregular place of two and a half storeys with a gabled main block. A dozen stone steps in the outer court led up to one large entrance door. An inner court was divided off from the outer by high walls with a tall narrow gatehouse in one corner. The gatehouse had an arched and mullioned window above a very wide oak, nail-studded door pierced by a wicket; stone seats ran along the internal side walls, and the date 1620 was cut in its pavement. Buttresses, mostly of the Elizabethan age, supported the walls of the house. 'In some of the inhabited rooms were handsome ceilings adorned with plaster showing the arms of Eveleigh, Southcott, Courtenay, Bray and Vaux.' The front of the old house was near the present drive, and in dry weather one can see marks on the lawn where the house stood.

William Hole had the dilapidated house demolished. A story is told that whilst this was being done someone approached Mr Hole. He wanted to know where the old chamber had been. Apparently, his relation had been a mason who had worked on the old building years before when a hidden chamber had been found. In this was a group of figures sitting around a table with musical instruments in front of them. Once the air reached them they fell to dust. Mr Hole did not know of the chamber but was much amused by the tale, wondering if the musicians had been so out of key that they merited walling-up!

The new building was square-looking, with mock-Egyptian pillars on the portico going straight down to the ground without a plinth, which was a popular design at the time (1826). The house had a lead roof that needed protecting from leaks. Men wearing soft boots had to clear the snow from the gutters to prevent problems. On one side of the house stood a large conservatory, now demolished.

James Raisey, gamekeeper at Parke in the 1930s (Alan Raisey)

William Robert Hole had one son, William Gerald, who owned the house until his death in 1974. During his ownership the house was occasionally leased out. After the First World War Baron John Augustus Bouck installed electricity and heating, and replumbed the house.

In the 1920s Parke was run as an hotel, and during the Second World War it was a convalescent home, the Hole family not returning until 1951. Between the wars the estate was quite productive. Grapes, oranges, peaches and nectarines were grown in the greenhouses, and in the conservatory were a vine and a passion fruit. Vegetables, mushrooms and corn were produced in the walled garden, and cider was made on the premises as well as at Southbrook Farm. It was at Southbrook that cream and butter were made for the house. There were, at times, fifty to sixty ewes, twenty to twenty-four head of cattle, a couple of pigs and six dray horses.

Pheasant and duck shoots were held; also, an otter hunt met, but it is recorded that the otter hunt hardly ever caught anything. After a shoot there would be about 40 people for dinner. The cook had two maids to help with the preparation on these occasions. Point to point races were held, too, in the marshy field by the river. Locally it is remembered that 'there was always a beer tent'.

Major Hole left the estate to the National Trust in 1974. The house was too big for a private residence but too small to open to the public. The county council agreed to renovate the building at a cost of £100,000, of which the government paid 75 per cent, and the Dartmoor National Park Headquarters was established there in 1979. The DNPA only leases the house and driveway, and the rest of the land is let for grazing. At one time a rare breeds farm was a tourist attraction on the site, and the property has been used in the filming of the Two Ronnies Christmas Special in 1975 as well as a short feature called Futtocks End. Now the grounds are open to the public, with comfortable walking alongside the river.

Whitstone

Whitstone today is a cluster of buildings looking across to the splendid slopes of Dartmoor. Whitstone Farm was once an active farm with several outbuildings surrounded by an enclosed yard. Access came only from Furzeleigh Lane, which climbs from Bovey to Hennock. The present access road that climbs up from the Moretonhampstead road was put in around 1840.

The size of the farm fluctuated over the years. At times Whitstone incorporated Beara Farm to the west, Furzeleigh Plantation to the north and stretched as far as Crownley in the east. The name Whitstone is thought to be derived from 'whetstone', a stone against which knives were sharpened. The Bovey Tracey Church and Poor Rate 1596-1729 mentions Whitstone. The assessment shows that Johane Cove (who is not referred to as a widow, but must have been listed as occupier of the farm) was assessed at a rate of 'one shilling ten pence and one shilling three pence for Whitstone and half of Beare or Beara'.

In 1641 Whitstone comes into clear public view, appearing on the so-called Guliemus map. This map shows all of that part of Bovey Tracey that belonged to the manor but excluding the land that falls within the borough of Bovey Tracey. On the map Whitstone Farmhouse appears to have been facing due west, and thus was in a different position from the present south-facing house. This would indicate that the present farmhouse was rebuilt after this period.

George Barclay getting ready to spray the Whitstone vineyard vines in the mid-1980s (Laura Barclay)

The present house is constructed of granite and shillet, perhaps taken from the Whitstone quarry, which is close to the house. It has an outer wall, which is three feet thick. The roof, which must once have been thatched, was slated at a later date and more recently tiled. Built in a similar style to a longhouse, it is one room deep with three ground-floor lateral rooms, much the same size, and has a cross passage running from the front to the back of the house between one of the rooms and the other two. This means it was probably built before, or at, the turn of the 18th century. The three rooms would have been termed the parlour, the hall and the kitchen, or lower room. Signs of charred walls and floors found in 1954 suggest the present house may have been rebuilt on the same site as an earlier one. At a later date a dairy was added on the north side and an outshot (or small room) to the east, with a floor drain for washing the milk churns.

The farm belonged to the Stawell family in the 17th century. (The Stawells also owned Indio and Parke.) Then a period of ownership continued with the owners of Parke. Later, Whitstone (also known as Whitestone at this time) was bought by Charles Heath in 1718. In 1743 it was conveyed to Gilbert Yarde, whose daughter, Mary, married the Reverend Christopher Beeke in 1743. His other daughter, Rebecca, married Mr Nicholas Tripe, a surgeon, in 1750. By 1749 the Reverend Mr Beale owned Whitstone and Mr Tripe owned Beara: in both cases the occupier was John Ellis.

In 1805 the Reverend C. Beeke was both the proprietor and occupier of Whitstone and Beara, and since he married in 1743 must have been quite elderly. It may well be that he died within the next

Harold and Kevin Heale at Whitstone vineyard in 1991 (Laura Barclay)

few years. In any event, in 1814 Robert Hole of Stickwick bought both properties. After his death his son, William, became the listed owner. First Mr William Honeywell and then, in 1830, Mr Howard are given as occupiers of Whitstone and Beara.

Later, in 1834, James Langmead and his family took on the farm at Whitstone. The 1851 census shows they then had 140 acres of land. By the 1881 census, 30 years later and just before grandson William Langmead decided to leave Whitstone, they were farming 480 acres. The decision to leave was in order to search for richer farmland, as Whitstone soil was not particularly good and the land is very hilly and difficult to work.

After the Langmeads left, Whitstone was farmed by William Pinsent and then, around 1903, the Manning family went to live there. Albert Ashley Manning, the elder son, and his wife lived at Whitstone from 1924 until 1943. The family was strongly evangelical and supported the Gospel Hall in Mary Street. The Mannings used no motorised vehicles: ploughs were drawn by horses. Some of the land was arable, and wheat, barley and oats were grown as well as turnips and potatoes. Cider apples grew at Whitstone and the circular walk for the horses around the press can still be seen. The cider press, although in existence, was not used as the apples were sold to cider merchants.

Ashley left school at the age of 15 and his job was to hand-milk the cows and ride and drive the horses. He remembers being thrown off one pony, galloping up the lane. Flung onto a stone wall, he broke his pelvis and had to be carted away in a wheelbarrow. Being young, he made a good recovery and was up and about in six weeks. In 1928 he disposed of part of a field for the construction of Bovey Tracey Hospital. Then, in 1938, more land was sold on the Moreton-hampstead road for bungalows.

In 1954 Colonel Ratcliffe-Jones bought Whitstone Farm and, in 1969, he split it into two houses, Old Whitstone and Little Whitstone. The name Whitstone Farm lives on in one of the nearby houses. Nowadays most of the land has been sold off to neighbouring farmers and the various barns converted into houses, creating a hamlet with stunning views.

Much of the above information relating to Whitstone was kindly researched by Rosemary Wurtzburg.

Wolleigh

Wolleigh in 1998 (B.T. Heritage Trust)

Wolleigh House – Wolleigh meaning wolves' wood or clearing – is hard to distinguish from Little Wolleigh and Wolleigh Cottage in an historical context. The first mention of a property on this site must refer to the property now known as Little Wolleigh, or, perhaps, Wolleigh Cottage.

Wolleigh House itself was built during the early 1890s for Mr Henry Tanner Ferguson. Henry Ferguson was a railway engineer of the Royal Institute of Engineers. Henry and his wife, Beatrice, lived at Plumley before moving across the valley to Wolleigh after its completion in 1893. They had eight children, the youngest ones being born at Wolleigh. Henry was very involved in Bovey Tracey life; for example, he was treasurer of the Devon House of Mercy for some years.

The house remained in the ownership of the Ferguson family until the 1970s. It is not recorded how much it cost Henry to build Wolleigh, but the house and 46 acres of land were sold in 1979 for £80,000.

When it was built Wolleigh had eight bedrooms, four bathrooms and four reception rooms. It also had a flower room and several smaller sculleries and pantries, and was set in 75 acres of pasture and woodland. Wolleigh itself is a large property with immense cellars. The kitchen and principal rooms are on the ground floor, with the main bedrooms and bathrooms on the first floor and further smaller rooms in the attics.

Wolleigh has been under the ownership of a diverse range of people during its 110-year history to date. During their 80-year ownership, the Fergusons sometimes let the house, with one family living there on and off from 1935 until 1957. During this time it is known there was a hard tennis court in the grounds, surely the venue for many Sunday afternoon tennis parties.

Following its sale in 1979, the house came under the ownership of a family from the Sudan, who lived in it for several years. It has been said by local tradesmen who worked at the house, when the family moved in, they had the bathrooms completely refitted with gold taps and gold showers. It has also been said that the bathrooms were highly decorated: the ceilings and the walls were covered in swathes of patterned silk. Locals who worked at the house say that many of the principal rooms in the house had similar ceilings, and walls covered in silk hangings – perhaps not quite the style Henry Ferguson would have envisaged for his much-loved house!

Local rumour has it that, during this time, the house stood empty for large parts of the year. When in residence, it has been said the family camped out in it rather than actually using it as a functioning house. They apparently painted much of the ground floor in black paint and, when the fires were lit, they opened the windows to let the smoke out rather than having the chimneys swept. We do not, of course, actually have any first-hand proof of these stories; maybe somebody knows differently!

The current owners bought the house in the mid-1990s. Before then Wolleigh had not been lived in for several years. A lot of hard work and effort must have gone into restoring both the house and garden to their former glory- something of which Henry Tanner Ferguson would surely have approved.

Yarner

Yarner is situated at the end of a long driveway on the edge of the Dartmoor National Park, about 800ft above sea level, and has wonderful views. Somewhat remote, it has, nevertheless, always been part of the life of Bovey Tracey. For instance, the granite tramway – built in 1820 by George Templer, whose family lived here for some years – passes through the estate, and the shale that was used between the granite rails came from the Yarner quarry. A little later, sometime prior to 1850, the pottery leat was constructed and then, in 1898, the first Bovey reservoir was built at Trendlebere, ensuring an excellent supply of clean water for the town.

The first part of Yarner House was built in Tudor times as a hunting lodge and is mentioned in an inventory of the King's forests in 1547. The name means variously 'eagle bank or slope' or 'where eagles soar'. It passed through several owners until the late 1700s, when longer periods of ownership began with the Templers.

In 1856 operations began on a copper mine on the estate, George Templer having leased the mining rights, in 1829, to one Joseph Reynolds for 1,000 years. Yarrow Mine, as it was called,

Yarner in the 19th century, showing the now demolished wing (B.T. Heritage Trust)

employed 50 people by 1862 and, by 1865, had produced 2,300 tons of copper ore. It was equipped with a 60-inch Cornish pumping engine, two waterwheels with a diameter of 40ft (12m) and 25ft (8m) respectively, a winding machine and an ore crusher, but, unfortunately, the mine went out of production in about 1867.

Yarner estate was sold in 1878 to Henry Chadwick, who renamed it Chadwycke. It is recorded that under his ownership the wood was keepered and pheasants reared at Yarner Wells. There was abundant wildlife with rabbits, red squirrels and buzzards. One of Henry's sons was the Reverend Percival S. Chadwick of Torquay while another was Alan Chadwick, an actor, musician and garden designer. Gardens to his credit can be found at Admiralty Gardens, South Africa and Carmel, California, home in later years to Clint Eastwood.

The name was changed back to Yarner when Sir Harry Trelawney Eve bought the property in 1902. Sir Harry Eve was a judge and Member of Parliament for the old Mid Devon division. He employed a woodman, Mr Knowles of Merryleigh, and a rabbit catcher. There was no keeper at this time. During the First World War much timber was cut for the war effort.

Richard Henry Lee bought the estate after the end of the war, in 1919. Like most large houses Yarner has been altered over the years, and Mr Lee had the sizeable terrace constructed in front of the house. He also added a wing to provide a ground-floor dining room with a drawing room above and the servants' hall behind the kitchen.

At this time it had five main living rooms downstairs plus a bathroom, kitchen, scullery, servants' hall, larder, dairy and storeroom. On the first floor were the drawing room and five big bedrooms, two dressing rooms and a bathroom. The second floor housed the billiard room and six extra bedrooms.

The outdoor staff included a cowman, woodman, coachman, chauffeur, gamekeeper and gardeners. The chauffeur, Jack Shepherd, married a local girl and lived at Pottery Road. He is particularly remembered for keeping the cars immaculate and for taking the boys of the family fishing. Bert Treeby was the coachman, who also married locally. He was a talented man who, apparently, could turn his hand to anything, even standing in for the butler on occasions. The gamekeeper, Fred Toby, and his wife lived in Lower Lodge on the estate. Mrs Toby would sometimes replace the cook up at the house. Another character from the outside staff was Mr

Heathman, the head gardener. Described as a quiet man who wore glasses, he had a glass eye that constantly dropped out, necessitating a search amongst the plants. Consequently his colleagues called him Winkie. He had the last laugh; while the others toiled up the hill to work on bicycles, Mr Heathman rode from Ilsington on his motorbike.

The indoor staff was numerous and included a nanny, parlour maid, housekeeper, under housemaid, a scullery/kitchen maid and cook. The cook was, apparently, brilliant at milk puddings and stewed fruit, chocolate cakes and jellies.

Mr and Mrs Lee's daughter, Evelyn, married Captain John Catterall Leach RN. When Mr Lee died Mrs Leach and her mother stayed on, with Mrs Lee having responsibility for the house and Evelyn Leach for the garden, which was her pride and joy. The acid soil of the garden encouraged rhododendrons, azaleas, magnolia and primulas. There was also a rose garden and herbaceous borders. The rock and water gardens were of local granite, and the huge specimen trees were a feature, including a copper beech by the rock garden and a Scots pine in the centre of the lawn. In the kitchen garden was a mix of soft fruit and vegetables. Around the walls were apple trees.

Early on in the war, in 1941, Captain Leach was killed in action whilst commanding the battleship *Prince of Wales* off Malaya. His wife lived at Yarner bringing up their family, who remember it as a wonderful place to grow up even during the war. Yarner Wood was used for infantry exercises at this time and in 1942 the central part of the wood was burned when an incendiary bomb started a fire. This time was really the end of the rather feudal life at Yarner. The men were away. The lawns became chicken runs; the fields planted with swede, corn and potatoes - digging for victory!

A few years after the end of the Second World War, on 14th December 1950, the house and estate were put up for sale. Nature Conservancy bought the wood and a new era began. The house survived but, nevertheless, large-scale alterations were carried out: a wing was demolished to leave a house of more manageable proportions and a large sitting room with gallery was built of recycled materials. This room is now licensed for weddings, and the estate provides a beautiful backdrop to the celebrations.

Grey Gables
by Joan Robertson

Grey Gables in the 1920s (Dave Lewis)

Grey Gables in Bradley Road is a grade II listed building and was built in the early 1850s for the Reverend Honourable Charles Leslie Courtenay. He had come to the living in Bovey Tracey in 1849 but found the vicarage so dilapidated that he decided to rebuild it. The architect for this project was Charles Fowler of Middlesex and in his report he wrote that

> *the roof is greatly sunk and distorted, the floor and ceilings are out of level, the walls bulged and the whole so completely decayed and insecure as to be past repair...I feel it my duty to recommend that the whole be taken down and rebuilt.*

The architect's specifications give some idea of the work undertaken and included

> *the walls to be built of the rough stone of the country, hammer dressed and pointed on the face, having granite quoins... the best stairs and landings to be of Portland stone...the best rooms on the ground floor to have marble fireplaces and those in the best bedrooms to be of Portland stone, the others to be of slate...the stairs to offices to be of oak...two water closets to be fitted...the privy in the court to be fitted with an oak seat...painting four coats to all the wood and iron work.*

All this was estimated to cost £1,549.

The new vicarage comprised cellars, a ground floor with scullery, kitchen, servants' hall, butler's pantry, Lady Caroline's wife's room, study, drawing room, dining room and housekeeper's room. Stairs led to the bedrooms on the first floor. There was also a chapel, which has since been deconsecrated. External buildings consisted of a coach-house with a room above, cottages, stable and hayloft. The bell tower and bell on the west side of the house and the terrace with steps to the lawn on the south side are still in existence today.

In the 1940s the vicarage was sold to become a private residence. Much of the 7 acres of glebe (land) belonging to the vicarage was also sold, and properties, including the present vicarage of the parish church, built on it.

St Mary's
by Veronica Kennedy

St Mary's is first mentioned in the census of 1881 when Adela Divett, described as living off income from land and dividends, is listed as the owner. She had six servants, including a kitchen maid of 13 and a page of 13, living in. Adela was the daughter of Edward Divett, MP for Exeter, and the niece of John Divett, the owner of the potteries. We know that she was closely involved with St John's Church as the brilliants around the Cross were worn by her at her presentation at Court. In 1871 she had the choir vestry built, which fulfilled its duties as a vestry until 1897, when it was used as a lady chapel. In 1873 she had a window representing the Annunciation installed in memory of her parents, Mr and Mrs Edward Divett of Bystock.

Before he died in 1894, Canon Courtenay must have owned St Mary's because he left it to his niece, Agnes, who was married to Charles Wood, second Viscount Halifax. Agnes was the daughter of the 11th Earl of Devon and had met Charles Wood in 1860. He immediately fitted in with his new in-laws, sharing with Canon Courtenay a keen interest in the Oxford Movement, and both were to be bearers at Dr Pusey's funeral in 1882. Agnes and Charles lived mostly in Yorkshire but often came to Powderham to stay with Agnes' family. Whilst there they made many happy visits to Canon Courtenay to 'enjoy the simple pleasures' of Bovey Tracey. A few months before his death the canon wrote to Agnes and Charles and said: 'You neither of you can tell how, to us, you have filled up the gap in our lives of having no children.'

The Halifaxes loved St Mary's, although Lord Halifax's biographer, Lord Birkenhead, described it as

> *... a solid unattractive house in local stone, standing at the end of a straggling village on the edge of the moor with a fine view behind it from its Gothic windows towards Hay Tor. Inside was that curious wood*

smell of Victorian houses in which pitch pine predominated.

St Mary's in 1913 (Dave Lewis)

In April 1919 Lord and Lady Halifax celebrated their golden wedding in Yorkshire, although Lady Halifax was seriously ill. Then, in May, the Halifaxes went down to Bovey Tracey as usual, where they spent nearly a month hoping that they could live again in the atmosphere of the past. 'We spent the most delightful month,' Lord Halifax wrote to a friend, 'almost the happiest month of our lives. Edward [his heir], Dorothy and their children Charles and Anne came down to us; each day was finer than the last.' In their last two days in Devonshire, when he and Agnes were alone, Halifax was conscious of deep contentment. Then, in July, Lady Halifax died, leaving Lord Halifax heartbroken.

At first it was painful for him to return to Bovey Tracey, but then he began to come back each May and soon the memory of his life with Agnes at St Mary's brought him solace rather than affliction. 'I do so like being here,' he told Edward; 'I am so fond of this little house and all that is in it. …The past lives again almost more than it does anywhere else.' Many Bovey residents, including Jack Wills and May Moir, remember him at this stage of his life when he used to go to church wearing a cloak with his little dog, who sat on a cushion in the pew with him and never moved.

In 1933, when Lord Halifax was 94, he let the Church Army have St Mary's for a peppercorn rent. He died in 1934. In 1936 an article appeared in the *Western Morning News* entitled 'Church Army's Scheme: an Experiment in Devon', which was about the problem of meeting the needs of elderly men and women in general, particularly those in reduced circumstances. It then went on to say that

the Church Army have begun in the last five months an experiment in Devonshire…where in pleasant and friendly surroundings, elderly men and women with small incomes may find a happy refuge from the cares of housekeeping. St Mary's Sunset Home has been designed to accommodate women of 60-65 and upwards who pay a graded subscription towards their board, varying from 15s. to 25s. a week.

The writer of the article described the changes that had taken place in the home.

Central heating gives a welcome warmth as one steps inside the door, and electric lighting is another necessary modern adjunct. The sunny drawing room was already divisible into two, and the cosiest end is now in occupation by the four residents.

The article finished by suggesting how its readers could show a welcome to the newcomers in their midst by providing the occasional 'small entertainment to break the quiet evenness of life in a backwater'.

In 1945 the third Lord Halifax, who had been viceroy of India in the 1920s, foreign secretary in the Chamberlain government and ambassador to the United States, and who had spent many happy holidays at St Mary's, decided to sell the house to the Church Army. One of the Church Army sisters remembered that, whenever he came to visit friends in the West Country, he always attended St John's Church and came to visit St Mary's. On one occasion he said St Mary's didn't feel like home without his mother's portrait there, so he sent paintings of his mother and father, and also two pastels of Canon and Lady Courtenay, to be hung there.

Many people in Bovey have had friends or relatives living at St Mary's or attending the day centre which was built out of the old stable blocks, partly by local subscription, or they have worked there. Summer fetes were held in the garden with stars such as Eric Sykes opening them.

In 1999, with increasing government regulation, the Church Army could no longer maintain St Mary's and sold the house to a developer. After failed planning consents it was sold on to another developer and the main house was divided into four homes. The new block and the lodge were turned into two more homes. And so a new cycle of life begins for St Mary's.

Bibliography

The Earl of Birkenhead. *Halifax.* Hamish Hamilton, 1965
Lockhart, J.G. *Viscount Halifax.* Geoffrey Bles, 1935

❋ ❋ ❋ ❋ ❋

Devon House of Mercy in 1911 (Chapman & Son)

The Devon House of Mercy
by Janice Wallace

The Devon House of Mercy is a prime example of a Victorian institution. This fine building stands as a testament to mid-19th century religion and what was perceived as a strong need or defect in society. The occupants of the Devon House of Mercy were all female. The 1891 census lists eight Sisters of Mercy and eleven supplementary staff along with eighty 'inmates', typically around 20 years old. Although the nearby cities of Plymouth and Exeter feature as the places of origin for some of these inmates, the majority came from the rest of Britain. Different contemporary accounts refer to these inmates as penitents or fallen women, and the purpose of the institution was to provide a house of 'moral correction' in Victorian terminology.

Situated a short distance from the parish church, yet out of view of the main road, the former Devon House of Mercy is known today as Devon House. In October 1868, a year after its official opening, the Earl of Devon, at a thanksgiving lunch, described the work undertaken there as having a threefold purpose:

Primarily, its object is of a reformatory character, secondly as a means of reformation, its object is to promote the education of the inmates; and thirdly it has the character of an institution for industrial training, in such a way as to make those inmates useful, and to enable them when they return to the world to earn their living in an honest manner.

Why such a large building, devoted to reforming women through 'industrial training' by taking in washing on a commercial scale, came to be placed in Bovey Tracey was explained in the St John the Baptist Magazine in 1883:

It was calculated that in the county of Devon alone, those needing the shelter of such a House numbered many hundreds, and the existing Penitentiaries in Exeter and Plymouth could receive but a small proportion of the number.

Concern over levels of inner city prostitution linked up with the desire to help or offer a sort of safety net to vulnerable females, and the challenge had been taken up by the Church Penitentiary Movement. Responding to a situation prevalent throughout the major cities of England, a religious dimension of saving the souls of prostitutes added to this essentially social problem. It was also believed that removal of women at risk into a rural area placed them out of temptation whilst simultaneously training them for domestic service. On a far smaller scale a similar enterprise had been set up at Chapple Farm, Bovey Tracey, in May 1863. Less than a year later, 40 requests for admissions were made but, unfortunately, the house could only offer accommodation for 20 women. Apart from having to turn applicants away, other insurmountable problems had appeared, including the impossibility of carrying out the laundry work which had been intended to help finance this project: there was only one stove to heat up the irons and, in wet weather, there was no space to dry the laundry. In addition, the water supply originating on the moor could sometimes have a high copper content, which meant that the washing subsequently suffered from staining.

Chapple Farm was run by the successful Anglican Order known as the Convent of St John the Baptist, founded in 1852 and based just outside London, at Clewer in Windsor. Bovey Tracey became the first major outpost of the Clewer organisation. Charles Leslie Courtenay, the vicar of Bovey Tracey, also held the position of Canon of Saint George's Chapel at Windsor Castle. He had first-hand knowledge of the sisters' enterprise and invited them to come and work in Bovey Tracey. Courtenay was extremely influential. His father and, then later, his older brothers were earls of Devon, so he had excellent social contacts whilst, on a more pragmatic level, he donated land to the sisters. The sisters also opened a mission house in Fore Street in 1879 for the people of Bovey Tracey;

here they offered religious instruction along with giving more practical assistance to the sick and needy. Whilst many must have been thankful for such beneficence, others were not. Annie Croker seemed deeply suspicious of the sisters' intentions and wrote about their teachings in her diary.

The Girls' Church School is in a sad state - teachers sent off home and two Sisters of Mercy in charge, teaching confession to the Priest and bowing to pictures and priestly absolution.

In retaliation, in 1867 Annie Croker set up the British School in Mary Street, near the centre of Bovey.

The Devon House of Mercy, which superseded Chapple Farm, remained the sisters' most ambitious undertaking in Bovey Tracey. Unfortunately the house's history is far from clear with much of what we do know relating to its perennial problem of finances. Apparently the call for donations echoed in churches throughout Devon until enough money had been collected to complete the initial phase of the house and admit the first occupants. The continued need for monetary assistance meant that the house featured prominently in the local press. *The Torquay Directory* of 30th October 1867 gives an early description:

The house is in plan a parallelogram running east and west, with two principal wings projecting to the south, the chapel being an extension of the main building to the east. Being built on a sharp declivity, there is a basement under the western end of the house containing the kitchen and other domestic offices etc. A large laundry and washhouse extending to the north or back of the main building contain all the modern conveniences for carrying out that branch of industry by which it is hoped that the inmates will be able to earn funds towards their support. In fact, every care has been taken to make the office and laundry arrangements good and simple for work, and a loft has been arranged with a turntable to communicate from the kitchen yard to several storeys of the west wing. There are two entirely separate staircases, and great attention has been paid to ventilation by flues which pass from several parts of the building to a main ventilating shaft, which contains a stove to create draught, and is also used for heating the baths. The western wing contains a large dining room, probationers' room and dormitories with the sisters' rooms annexed for supervision. On the ground floor of the centre block of the building are classrooms for the instruction of the inmates, and a porter's room, with dormitories and sisters' rooms over. The ground at the back will be used for drying.

The house seems to have been purpose-built to include the laundry, and features what must have been an innovative ventilation system. The sense of pride, which infuses the above description, suggests that the facilities provided were the best available by the standards of the day.

The architect was Henry Woodyer, who also planned the Clewer Sisters' founder house in Windsor, with Mr Locke of Bovey Tracey appointed as the main builder. The overall construction was of rough dressed granite with quoins of Bath stone and tall chimneys made from red brick. The building expanded as the money collected grew. After the early flurry of interest, problems occurred and at one point it seemed that the east wing might have to be abandoned.

With renewed calls for aid the work was completed, yet the demand for placements increased and in 1873 the half-yearly meeting reported in the *Exeter Flying Post* said that:

The House was full at the beginning of the year, and has remained so ever since. Although the House holds as large a number as 70, several applicants for admission have been necessarily refused owing to want of room.

After being filled to capacity for over two years it was decided to build an infirmary and, because of concern over the possibility of contagious disease spreading in the main house, a separate smaller building at the outskirts of the grounds was suggested. Infectious illness never seemed to pose any problem in reality and the one immediate outcome in the completion of the infirmary cottage was the extra available accommodation. The half-yearly meeting in the summer of 1878 reports that:

The infirmary cottage was opened a few weeks ago. In consequence your committee were enabled to

The laundry at the Devon House of Mercy (Chapman & Son)

The dining hall (Chapman & Son)

sanction an increased number of admissions, hence whereas on January 1st there were 79 penitents within the walls, on June 30th the number had grown to 84.

During the following five years the numbers rose even further, and at one point reached what must have been a very overcrowded 114 occupants. The house, however, seemed to thrive and the further call for charitable donations resulted in the final building, that of a subwarden's cottage, just outside the gates of the grounds, being completed in 1882.

The running costs of the Devon House of Mercy were quite well documented in the 19th century, but it is far more difficult to try and piece together information regarding its occupants. A newspaper cutting from the Devon Record Office suggests the criteria for admission 20 years after it first opened.

The committee desired to call particular attention to a large number of orphans; nearly one half of those in the House had lost one parent and more than one third (a larger proportion than in any former year) had lost both parents.

The creation of the Devon House of Mercy had arisen out of the wish to save the souls of sinners and the fear of the high level of prostitution. R. Newton in *Victorian Exeter* (1968) described Exeter's high street as 'swarming with prostitutes'. However, the drama seems to have faded 20 years later when the type of family background (and probable poverty) seem more important characteristics in the typical person admitted. Upon arrival, the girls were organised into groups, or 'sets', and each set had its own dining and living rooms. The rule was 'no talking' at mealtimes, although they were allowed to read. The youngest were trained at the infirmary cottage. In the main house there were three types of work – laundry, kitchen or embroidery. Most left to be employed in domestic service. The St John the Baptist Magazine in autumn 1883 states:

Since the work began in May 1863 six hundred and more poor girls have been under the Sisters' care. Of these, upward of 80 are now in the house, nearly 300 have been placed in service, 150 have been restored to their friends, 36 have been sent to different homes, 19 have died and the remaining 41 have either left under medical advice or at their own request.

David Ball, a family historian, has shed light on Dorcas Ball, who was listed in the 1881 census. Whilst Dorcas lived at Devon House, her one-year-old son was listed in the Dorset census as living with her parents. The child appears to have been born out of wedlock. After her time at Devon House, Dorcas married a widower in 1885 and the next Dorset census shows that she was reunited and living with her son. The legacy of the Devon House of Mercy can be seen with the statement listing her occupation as that of a laundress.

Unfortunately there are no daily records for Devon House, but the Roll Books for Clewer still exist and these occasionally mention Bovey Tracey. Anna Bennet in August 1870, at the very young age of 13, was brought into Clewer by her mother. The following November, Anna moved to Devon House. Grace Goring was a 27-year-old laundress who left Clewer during November 1874 and subsequently came to Bovey Tracey; she chose to leave of her own accord. Elizabeth Fragel spent three years at Bovey Tracey, only to perform badly in service. In 1872 Bertha, the Sister Superior at Devon House, took Elizabeth, now aged 20, to Clewer for retraining, but this proved unsatisfactory and Elizabeth also refused to stay. These few comments offer conflicting evidence as to standards of life at Devon House; not everybody wanted to stay, but then they also seem to have had the choice of leaving.

During the 20th century the option of leaving might have proved more difficult because girls did run away from Devon House and the church bell would ring in order to alert everybody. Life appeared to be hard for these girls, who were not allowed to stop work or talk to visitors. Even residents from Bovey Tracey who have fond memories of Devon House describe the intimidating air which permeated the main building, with its grand entrance door and long, dark corridors. Also the dormitories upstairs had prison-like sliding grills on the doors. It was rumoured that, after the sisters left and the house was redecorated, one room, which had very high windows, had holes kicked in the wall so as to provide a means of looking out. The implication was that being sent to this room, situated right at the top of the house, was regarded as a form of punishment for bad behaviour.

Many years after the Devon House of Mercy closed local people still recalled how the girls had gone out walking in crocodile fashion on the outskirts of town. They wore blue and white-striped dresses, with high necks, and thick white aprons topped with a cap-like bonnet tied under the chin. The girls did not have overcoats but only heavy grey shawls, which could be pulled over the head in rainy weather. Thick black stockings and boots completed the uniform. The sisters and lay helpers, namely Miss Barnett and Miss Cummins, supervised the off-duty hours and would take groups for walks to pick primroses or blackberries. When the girls went on their walks they appeared to be happy, and several people of Bovey recalled the high level of their chatter which, from the distance, could sound like a lot of starlings. One of the girls, Dora (not her real name), also recalled these walks fondly and that Miss Barnett had given her a ten-shilling note and a purse soon after she arrived at Devon House. Dora originated from London and when she became an orphan at a very early age she was apparently sent to Devon House for her own safety. Some time later a family staying at the Manor House Hotel, near Moretonhampstead, saw the girls out walking on the heath and enquired at Devon House if anyone wished to come to south-east England and work in domestic service for them. Dora was chosen. She then remained with this family for the rest of her life and often revisited Bovey Tracey.

Although an undeniable divide existed between the house and the local community, some Bovey residents made closer contact. In the grounds of Devon House stood a grand horse-chestnut tree which tempted at least one child to enter and gather its conkers. One lady remembers how she hid as the girls clattered down the drive with wheelbarrows, which they would fill up with coal stored in a shed situated between the infirmary cottage and the entrance. These heavy coal-laden barrows would then have to be pushed back up the drive to the main house, where the coal would then be used to heat the water for the laundry. Another family befriended Bessie, a lay sister who lived at the infirmary cottage during the 1930s. Bessie was always kind to the children of this family; she offered sweets and gave out Christmas presents, and is remembered with affection. Ada Elizabeth, one of the Sisters of Mercy in the early 20th century, agreed to become godmother and would welcome a visit from her godchild living in Bovey Tracey.

Many more people recall the laundry. A van eventually replaced the horse and cart, which not only increased the laundry service offered to the nearby larger houses, such as Parke and Indio House, but also meant that it became possible to collect from similar properties in Chudleigh. Despite expanding the laundry, funding remained problematic and the house never became the totally self-sufficient unit that was originally intended. The need to attract extra income resulted in open days, including the Christmas play, to an invited audience, and the summer fete. This latter event took place on the lawn where, underneath the cedar trees, the girls would serve strawberries and cream. High quality embroidery and needlework was also sold in order to raise funds. Gooseberries grew in abundance in the grounds and the cook would take these to make excellent jam, which was also for sale. Therefore, although the house and town can both be seen as separate, active liaison did, nonetheless, occur between the two.

There are very few individual details about the Sisters of Mercy. We know they all trained at Clewer before coming to Bovey Tracey. As novices they would have received instruction in church history, the Bible, Christian doctrine, mental prayer, rules of the organisation and how they should apply it to their lives. In the 19th century they wore black habits, a white linen wimple and, around the neck, a silver cross engraved with the *Agnus Dei*. The sisters had to pay to stay in the sisterhood and, although they made stipulated payments to Clewer, rule eight of the statutes indicates that they were also encouraged to make donations to Devon House. The sisterhood attracted a number of affluent middle-class families who all contributed £50 annually to the Community Fund; by the late 1870s the Clewer Sisters also included several whose families were titled or landed gentry. These women could choose either to become a choir novitiate, spending the maximum amount of time in religious devotion, or else opt to

Devon House in 2003 (Karen Lang)

become a lay sister and then supervise the practical running of the house. Sisters named in the 1881 census were aged between 29 years and 40 years and came from all corners of Britain and beyond. One sister, who had previously served at Devon House of Mercy, was described in the records held at Clewer. Her name was Sister Frances Constance and she had come from a well-established Unitarian family in Boston. Upon completion of her training in 1867, some of her work was undertaken at the Devon House of Mercy before she left England in 1874 to become the Sister Superior at a recently founded House of Mercy in the poorer section of New York.

In 1907 Sister Bertha, one of the three sisters working at Chapple Farm and the first Sister Superior at the Devon House of Mercy, died. The following years coincided with a general decline in the rate of occupancy and staffing levels. Eventually, the Clewer Sisters left Devon House in 1940, and first British and then American troops were billeted there during the war. From late 1946 to 1947 the house then was used by the Bovey Tracey Lignite Company to accommodate miners from Wales whilst they mined for lignite at Bluewaters. The house was later converted into 28 flats in the 1950s, which still exist today.

Many of the original architectural features remain, such as the window handles shaped into devils' tails in the belief that this would help to keep out evil. These handles, as is the whole building, are manifestations of Victorian society and its concerns about sin. We are fortunate in Bovey Tracey because not only do we have an unusually pure example of a Victorian institution, but also one that revolved around women in an era when women were granted little power or autonomy. Although we can see from the statutes of the house that men had ultimate control in major decisions, the census shows only female occupants, and it was the Sisters of Mercy who effectively devoted their whole lives in the supervision of destitute and vulnerable young women.

Bibliography

Bonham, V. *A Place in Life. The Clewer House of Mercy 1849-1883*. Windsor, 1992
Bonham, V. *A Joyous Service. The Clewer Sisters and Their Work*. Windsor, 1989
Newton, R. *Victorian Exeter*. Leicester University Press, 1968
Tregoning, L. *Bovey Tracey: An Ancient Town*. Cottage Publishing, 1983

The following Bovonians have recalled their memories of Devon House: Mrs Beer, Mrs Blackmore, Mr A. Brealey, Mrs N. Davis, Lady Hampton, Mr D. Lewis, Mr W. Mountford, Mrs M. Parry, Mrs K. Perrem and Mrs Ralph (with special thanks to her friend who was at the Devon House of Mercy).

The Second World War

Bovey Tracey Home Guard 1940 - 1944
by John Parnell

The situation in 1940 could be seen as a case of history repeating itself. Towards the end of the 18th century the nation was under threat of invasion by Napoleon Bonaparte's France. The 'Defence Lists' or Posse Comitatus lists of 1798 were prepared under the Defence of the Realm Act when all able-bodied men, together with their occupations, were required to be recorded by parish constables. Men aged between 15 and 60, and who were not already employed in a military capacity, had to be listed. A company of infantry was raised that year at Bovey Tracey, under the command of a Captain Crane. The unit was disbanded in 1802 following the fragile 'Peace of Amiens' and the resulting lowered threat of invasion.

On 10th May 1940 German forces invaded the Low Countries. Listeners to the BBC Home Service's 9 o'clock news on 14th May 1940 heard the recently-appointed Secretary of State for War, Anthony Eden, make this statement:

Since the war began the Government has received countless inquiries from all over the kingdom from men of all ages who are for one reason or another not at present engaged in military service, and who wish to do something for the defence of their country. Well, now is your opportunity. We want large numbers of such men … to come forward now and offer their services. … The name of the new Force which is now to be raised will be 'The Local Defence Volunteers'.

The eligible men of Bovey Tracey were as quick as any to respond to the government's plea. Within 24 hours, volunteers throughout the country totalled 250,000. One of their first jobs was to remove all road signs and anything that contained information about the local towns, villages and railway stations.

In July 1940 the Local Defence Volunteers were renamed Home Guard by Winston Churchill. From 15th August 1940 all Home Guard ranks were authorised to wear the badge of their County Regiment. The men of Bovey Tracey proudly wore the badge of the Devonshire Regiment with its motto 'Semper Fidelis' (Ever Faithful). The Devon Home Guard consisted of 25 battalions, Bovey Tracey being the H.Q. of the 14th (Moorside) Battalion, part of Mid Devon Sector (with the 6th, 7th and 23rd Battalions). The 14th (Moorside) Battalion was made up of men drawn from nearly 300 square miles of Devonshire.

Pat Tregoning remembers at the age of 17 how he and his friend, Les Steer, joined the LDV. 'We learned how to make and throw Molotov cocktails (petrol in a bottle) and how to stop a German tank with a hand grenade! Eventually the lucky ones were issued with rifles, but not a lot of ammunition.'

With the threat of an enemy airborne attack, a hut at Furzeleigh Copse was used by the local contingent as a parachute observation post. Dave Lewis, a Bovey schoolboy at the time, recalls the hut key being 'hidden' beneath a stone near the door, and how he and his friends would use the hut during the day for card playing. He also remembers that wooden poles were erected in the larger fields to reduce the space available for enemy glider landings.

When rifles became available firing practice was held in Whitstone Quarry. The Home Guard also used the rifle range located a short distance above the town cemetery in Coombe Lane. The armoury was located in the Coombe Cross area, but residential development has now removed all traces of it. The ammunition

Bovey Tracey Volunteers button (Adina Parnell)

stores consisted of a black-painted Nissen hut.

As the war progressed the 14th (Moorside) Battalion held joint exercises with units of the British army in the Haytor area of Dartmoor. Later on, the US army provided the 'opposition'. Mrs Norah Davis, the daughter of Captain E.L. Steer (Second-in-Command H.Q. Company) recalls how the back bedroom of their cottage in Fore Street was used as the Signals H.Q. during these exercises.

The need for the Home Guard receded when the Allies began the enormous task of freeing the overrun countries from their Nazi occupiers. On 6th September 1944 Sir James Grigg, Secretary of State for War, said that, from Monday, 11th September, compulsory drills and training for the Home Guard should be discontinued, and that any operational duties still required should be on a voluntary basis. Perhaps as a way of celebrating this relaxation of duties, a Home Guard cricket match was arranged for Saturday, 9th September between H.Q. Company (Bovey Tracey) and D Company(Chudleigh). The event, in aid of the Bovey Tracey and District Hospital, was held at the recreation ground and resulted in a win for the Bovey side. A grand total of £2 18s. 6d. was presented to the hospital.

H.Q. Company batted first and reached the very modest total of 87 runs, V. Coombes being top scorer with 37 runs. Fortunately for the Bovey unit, D Company was even less successful, managing to score a mere 39 runs. The H.Q. team consisted of the following: E. Steer, F. Baker, C.H. Mountford, V. Coombes, W. Wallen, J. Stoneman, C. Caunter, J. Webber, T. Coniam, W. Stoneman and C. Bunclarke.

The Home Guard officially stood down at the end of 1944. On Sunday, 3rd December 1944 King George VI, the Home Guard's Colonel-in-Chief, held a farewell parade in Hyde Park. The Stand Down Parade of the 14th (Moorside) Battalion, Devon Home Guard, took place at the recreation ground, Bovey Tracey, on the same day. The battalion's five companies, consisting of over 1,100 local men, paraded before its Battalion Commander, Colonel P.I. Newton, DSO, accompanied by his

Bovey Tracey Home Guard NCOs photographed at the rear of The Bell Inn. Back row, left to right: Joe Gribble, Bill Heath, Archie Martin, Alf Cann, Sid Hawks and John Fogwill. Front row, left to right: Alf Yeo, Alder Harris, Louis Steer, Francis King and Organ Edworthy (Norah Davis)

In the years when our Country

was in mortal danger

Alder John Harris

who served *from* 19·6·40 *to* 31·12·44

gave generously of his time and

powers to make himself ready

for her defence by force of arms

and with his life if need be.

George R.I.

THE HOME GUARD

A copy of the certificate given to Alder Harris in 1944 (Christine Gale)

Lieutenant George Black and Sergeant Alder John Harris outside Bovey cricket pavilion (Christine Gale)

Second-in-Command, Brigadier J. de Lisle Conry, CIE. Also on parade were the Women's Auxiliaries, supported by the full band of the Devonshire Regiment, brought along by Major W. Sparkes.

This is an extract from the colonel's farewell address, given from in front of the cricket pavilion:

This was the first time 14th (Moorside) Devon Battalion Home Guard [has] ever paraded together as a battalion. It is probably the last and I am delighted to see such a fine turnout ... I want to pay a special tribute to the original L.D.V. who, dressed in plain clothes and armed only with farm implements, were prepared to defend their country; though they must have known well, what would have happened to them if the Germans had got hold of them ... You have served for no reward and have felt the satisfaction of doing so. Go on doing it and persuade others to do the same.

A stand-down social, held at the Bell Inn on Saturday, 16th December 1944 to commemorate the official ending of almost four years of comradeship amongst the men of the town, was fully reported in the *Mid-Devon and Newton Times*.

Captain Steer rose to thank everyone for their loyal cooperation and said the unity had been marvellous, with very little quibbling or falling out. Lance Corporal W.H. Conian (vice-chairman of Bovey Tracey Parish Council) expressed the town's appreciation of their service to King and country and, in particular, to their own town. The principal event of the evening was the presentation of a cheque to Captain E.L. Steer, who, from a private, had risen to become their second-in-command. He was described as possessing tact, with a 'complete understanding of man ...' and was 'diplomatic in all his undertakings'.

That evening Lieutenant George Black was also honoured. Corporal J. Tremlett presented him with a cheque on behalf of the Mobile Reserve and said that 'they would have to a man followed him wherever he sought to lead and carried out his orders to the last man'.

Perhaps a short extract from a speech by Winston Churchill in 1940 would be a fitting tribute to those men who, in the dark days of war, were prepared to give their lives in the defence, not only of their King and country, but also of their neighbour.

If the enemy had descended suddenly in large numbers from the sky in different parts of the country, they would have found only little clusters of men mostly armed with shotguns, gathered around our searchlight positions. But now, whenever he comes, if he comes, he will find wherever he should place his foot, that he will be immediately attacked by resolute, determined men who have a perfectly clear intention and resolve to namely put him to death!

The War at Home
by Anne Broom

Geoffrey Coombes RAF with wife Betty and son Clifford
(Victor Coombes)

War left its mark on Bovey Tracey with several incidents imprinting themselves indelibly upon the minds of townsfolk. During the night of 18th November 1940 a huge explosion shattered the town's peace. Enemy action had resulted in a parachute landmine being dropped in the grounds of Devon House. The subsequent explosion caused a massive crater, breaking windows in houses as far away as the cricket field. Irreparable damage was caused to the town's parish church with the shattering of the finely coloured east window since no records survived to enable it to be rebuilt. Numerous shop windows in the town were damaged, and townspeople left their beds to crowd into the streets. It was believed that the town narrowly escaped a major disaster that night. A soldier on sentry duty and stationed at Devon House had spotted something descending from the night sky. About to take aim, he realised that it might be a parachutist. Had he fired his gun it could have resulted in massive damage for the town. Still visible today, the crater provided an exciting source of shrapnel for local youngsters.

On a morning in 1944 a German Focke-Wolf fighter plane flew low over the town, strafing the railway station where Stanley Dart, the signalman, was on duty. It swooped low over the Brimley area. Startled by explosions, Jack Wills, home on leave from the Royal Medical Corps, observed the scene from his bedroom window. The plane was flying so low that its pilot was clearly visible as he fired indiscriminately at houses along the road. One bullet went through the window of 9 Moor View. Mrs Ayres, the occupant, sustained a scar on her back as the bullet ricocheted through the wireless, becoming embedded in the woodwork. One of her daughters, who had been trying on a coat, had a lucky escape. As she leant against the mantelshelf, a bullet sliced through the cloth of her jacket below her armpit. Out in the road, milkman Jimmy Horrell was delivering the daily supplies, dipping the ladle into a churn perched on his cart. As 12-year-old Christine Holmes and her mother went out to collect milk, the sudden crackling of gunfire caused the frightened horse to bolt down the road, spilling milk everywhere. Neighbours rallied round to help, the horse was safely tethered, and the episode proved a major talking point for some time.

As a 16-year-old choirboy, Pat Tregoning, who three years later, in 1942, was to be called up to the Devonshire Regiment, clearly recalled the morning of Sunday, 3rd September 1939. At 11 a.m., as he sat in the choir stalls of St Peter's Parish Church, the vicar, the Reverend James Howell, told the congregation that from that hour the country was once again at war with Germany. Preparations were already well in hand, with the issue of gas masks and the evacuation of children from major cities. Regulation gas masks in their square boxes, and with unpleasantly smelling thick black rubber, were to become a familiar sight, carried everywhere on shoulders. That night, for the first time, black-out regulations were in place in the town. Air raid wardens patrolled to enforce the law. Walking through dark streets and being unable to recognise fellow walkers was an eerie experience.

Evacuees

Initially around 90 young evacuees came to Bovey Tracey, arriving from Acton in London on Friday, 1st September 1939 – two days before war was declared. Each child had a gas mask in a small square cardboard box and as many possessions as could be carried, packed in suitcases and brown paper parcels. Bewildered and tired, they then spent their first night away from families at the Wickham Hall in Ashburton Road before being welcomed into homes throughout the town. Although convinced that they would only stay a few weeks, many were to live with their new families for several years. Two sisters, 5-year-old Audrey and 8-year-old Joy Beattie, went to stay in Blenheim Terrace with Mr and Mrs Will Wotton, while their 10-year-old brother, Bertie, was billeted two doors away with Mr and Mrs Harding. They looked on the Wotton's daughter, Irene, as a big sister, helping ease her sadness at separation from fiancé Stan Blackmore, called up that day for full-time service.

After the shortages of London good food, including eggs for breakfast, ensured that the youngsters grew healthy and strong. There were few shortages in Bovey. Most people had gardens with vegetables, fruit and a few hens, and the Brimley allotments were extensively cultivated. Parents travelled down from London to see their children whenever possible. Host families were allowed eight shillings per week to feed and look after each child, their parents helping out by providing major items of clothing. Feeding and billeting the evacuees on arrival was difficult, but people generously gave food supplies. Soft fruit was plentiful that year, but when Mary Wyatt of the Red Cross brought a huge dish of freshly-cooked blackcurrants it was refused by suspicious London youngsters, who had never seen the fruit before. All the children were eventually found a home. Several evacuees never returned to London and continued to live locally. For instance, George Marks, at the age of ten, came to stay with Mrs Muriel Jope in Orchard Terrace. He remained in the town and, in later years, moved to St John's Cottages when he married Sylvia Mitchelmore, whose father, Eric, was a builder and undertaker.

In June 1940 Bovey received a second group of evacuees, this time from Eltham School in London. Over several days nearly 5,000 children arrived at Newton Abbot to be taken to towns and villages in the area.

Mr Frank Hicks, the town's Relieving Officer and Registrar of births, deaths and marriages, received a list of all evacuees. It was his task to sort out each child's financial situation. He issued food tickets for those in special need, to be exchanged for items on a list, according to money granted by the Guardians Committee. His daughter, Evalyn, later Mrs Rice, joined him as his assistant. In 1941 she was appointed Deputy Registrar and Assistant Relieving Officer for Bovey Tracey District, registering the marriages of soldiers and their fiancées, and the births of children.

When, in May 1995, the town celebrated the 50th anniversary of VE Day, the memories of many former evacuees were recalled in a souvenir paper published by Bovey Tracey Town Council. These included Mrs Margaret Swetman (née Caunter) from Portsmouth, who had arrived in Bovey in 1939 before the mainstream of evacuees. Together with her mother and father, who was in the Royal Army Medical Corps and posted near Bovey, she recalled being treated more as a villager, attending the village school instead of one set up at the top of the hill near the church. The family had rooms at Mrs Gay's sweetshop in Fore Street, becoming great friends with Mr and Mrs Heal and their son, Leslie. Mrs Pat Hoyle, now from Paignton, and her sister, then aged 9 and 10 respectively, were among the first evacuees to be sent to Bovey Tracey, coming to the town with the children of Derwentwater School, Acton. They experienced much kindness in this their first experience of the countryside and country people. Former evacuee Jean Walker lived in White Heather Terrace with Mr and Mrs White and their daughters, Joyce and Pat, attending Newton Abbot Grammar School. Writing from Warwickshire, Margaret Crump (later Mrs Richards) recalled coming from Acton with her brother, John, and sister, Evie. They stayed at Broad View, Brimley, now renamed Broad Coombe, with Mr Kilby and Miss Reddaway. Stepping back in time, Christine Holmes remembered many evacuees: high-spirited John Preston from Acton, who stayed with Mrs Emma Davey and made it clear he didn't like rice pudding; May Preston, who stayed at Gay's sweetshop in Fore Street; and Gill Rowlands and John Groves, who lived with Mrs Martin at Station Road and later married and raised a family. Miss Wallace, in Hind Street, took in six girls, some being sisters she did not want to see parted.

Getting into scrapes was part of growing up, but frequently blame for any misdemeanour was laid on the town's evacuees. On one occasion two lads rolled a huge boulder down a bank onto the Hennock road near the cemetery. Someone had seen the escapade, and they were reported to the police. Following a strong reprimand, each was fined five shillings with the stipulation that it should be paid to Bovey Tracey Hospital. When some evacuee boys helped themselves to a wedding cake made in the Co-op Bakery (now the Riverside Mill), the miscreants were sent to court and subsequently birched for their misdeeds.

Frank Surey, from Ferndown, Dorset, remembered happy years spent with kind folk. As an evacuee, he lived with Mr and Mrs Joe Gribble at Brimley Vale. With his father abroad in the army, he loved both Joe, a placer at Bovey Pottery, and Ma Gribble, describing her as the kindest and gentlest of people. In later years Ma Gribble told him how she had 'selected' him from the remnants of a group, of his somewhat scruffy appearance – as the youngest of five boys from a poor family he had been wearing handed-down clothes that were

Some of the evacuees staying at Lower Bradley. The boy at the front is Dave Wedden and the smaller boy directly behind him is Peter Wedden (Dave Wedden)

well worn – and of how she had just had to take him in. Frank, meanwhile, fell in love with South Devon and its people, but had eventually returned to London. It had been a sad parting and a return to a life he had willingly and easily forgotten. At the time he had carried with him precious souvenirs – some American army collar eagles, a US belt buckle and a Tom Pearce mug from the pottery.

Refugees

The town also became home to several refugees. At the end of June 1940, prior to the German occupation of the Channel Isles, Mrs Dorothy McKenney and her 10-year-old daughter, Stephanie (later Wills), came over from St Helier, Jersey. They were allowed one suitcase each, but treasured possessions and beloved pets had to be left behind. Travelling in a cattle ship, the journey took over 12 hours as they dodged German U-boats. Stephanie found Bovey a friendly place and attended Newton Abbot Grammar School.

Casualties were high when the island of Malta came under heavy German fire. Among those who escaped were Angela, Mario and Hugo Peenie, the latter remembered as immensely handsome. They came to live with Stella and Alfred Gale. Also from Malta, vivacious Delarose Calchie, recalled as rather like the film star Carmen Miranda, stayed in Pottery Road.

The Troops

The first British troops soon arrived in the town by train. They took over Devon House and the

Conservative Club, and also requisitioned several of the town's bigger houses. These troops, the first of the conscripted men, together with a few regulars who were mainly non-commissioned officers, underwent training before being moved on, to be rapidly replaced by other units. Some searchlight units were based more permanently off Chudleigh Knighton Heath, on the Hennock road.

As other towns and villages did, Bovey Tracey welcomed the arrival of soldiers from the United States. Gordon Lawrence, himself an evacuee from Lambeth, in London, recalled the friendships that were formed. They brought a new and colourful way of life with the lively dance music of the American Forces Network, including the bands of Glenn Miller, Benny Goodman and Tommy Dorsey. Always generous to the children, they shared chocolate, tins of biscuits, tinned fruit and meat, peanut butter and chewing gum. With their smart uniforms, Hollywood looks and Lucky Strike, Chesterfield and Camel cigarettes, the Americans were a big hit with all the girls. They camped on the heathland at Chudleigh Knighton, building a naval station at Heathfield. They sited an American serviceman's hospital base beside the golf course at Stover, surrounded by other units. All roads around the town were lined with soldiers and military vehicles, and, in the skies, Dakota aircraft were a familiar sight.

Les Brealey's clearest boyhood wartime memory was of standing in a long line of black American soldiers on the stairs of Bovey Tracey Liberal Club, waiting his turn to shake the hand of the heavyweight boxing Champion of the World, Joe Louis. His invitation came about through chance. Setting up camp at Bluewaters, a group of black Americans had asked the youngster where they could get something to drink. He told them of Farmer Harvey's cider, and was immediately dispatched to Langaller Farm with money, two five-gallon jerry cans and a trolley. This was the first of many trips for Les and for anyone who would fetch them cider. He was convinced that some of those landing on the D-Day beaches remained under the influence of Langaller cider. Unfortunately, the soldiers left behind potential killers in the shape of phosphor bombs which burst into flames on contact with the air. Local boys played dangerous games; standing the bottles up and throwing stones at them. Les's cousin opened a bottle with his teeth and his face was engulfed in flames. Another memory Les had was of returning home from army cadet drill at the Church School with other boys from Brimley, and teasing the Home Guard sentry on duty at the telephone exchange in Mr Jeffery's coal shop in Station Road. The sentry was scared stiff at the thought of being overcome by hordes of Germans, and the boys were never forgiven for their escapade.

Prisoners of War
A few years into the war a number of Italian prisoners arrived in the town. Diamond-shaped patches worn on their clothes marked their status and they were privileged to walk around freely. With limited English, they were always friendly, communicating in sign language with local people. There were also German prisoners of war and one, called Willie, worked for Mann's Dairy, driving the tractor and herding the cows. Remembered as a friendly giant with a warm smile, he happily carved toys, wooden dolls and trains for local children.

Daily Life
Despite rationing, the town's traders continued to serve the public, although queuing for provisions became a regular practice. Gordon Lawrence recalled that milk costing 1¹/xd. a pint was delivered daily, frequently poured straight into a jug left by an open window. A loaf of bread cost 3¹/xd., a newspaper 1d., Cadbury's chocolate 2¹/xd. a bar, a pair of men's boots less than a pound, a settee bed

Facing page: Some of the people from Bovey who served in the forces during the war:–

Top row, left to right: Murray Coombes, Leonard Coombes and Roy Coombes. Second row, left to right: Rodney Coombes, who died in 1941, and Laurence 'Bob' Moore. Third row, left to right: Austin Coombes, Sidney Mountford and Barbara Waldron. Bottom row, left to right: Victor Coombes and Walter Mountford (Courtesy of Victor Coombes, Lil Moore, Walter Mountford and Andy Waldron, and arranged by John Adey)

four and a half guineas and Embassy cigarettes 9d. for ten. In summer, with an abundance of fruit for free, children picked blackberries from hedgerows and whortleberries on the moors, to be made into pies and jam by thrifty housewives.

For youngsters a day at the seaside was an exciting event. Families with picnic sandwiches, flasks of tea and swimsuits boarded a train at Bovey Station, or further down the line at Brimley Halt, to travel to Torquay. On reaching their destination, they headed for a small stretch of sandy beach that remained free from obstructions and wire entanglements designed as enemy deterrents. With clocks on double summer time during the war, there was plenty of daylight, and a day spent in the sun, sea and sand, oblivious of the concerns of war, was a day to treasure.

On summer weekends Bovey Tracey's cricket team, immaculate in their whites, turned out to entertain, with matches played in a beautiful rural setting that on weekdays was used for military practice parades. With petrol rationing, few private cars were on the road. Bovey's five garages - Moir Davie's, Aggett's, Collins', Tucker's and Jarman's - each ran a taxi service. Daily life continued on an even keel despite the presence of military personnel. Occasionally enemy planes could be seen being chased out to sea by RAF Spitfires, and one afternoon a Typhoon fighter aircraft crash-landed in fields at the end of Brimley Vale on Challabrook Farm, its pilot fortunately unhurt.

Peace in Europe

On 7th May 1945 the unconditional surrender of the German armed forces was signed at General Eisenhower's headquarters in Rheims. Greeting the news on 8th May with great joy and relief, millions of listeners to wirelesses in Great Britain and throughout the British Commonwealth listened as the prime minister, Winston Churchill, broadcast to the nation. He told them that at 2.41 a.m. the previous morning, at Allied Headquarters, the unconditional surrender of all German land, sea and air forces in Europe had taken place. But, although there was peace in Europe, in the Far East in Japan the war continued.

In Bovey Tracey, as in towns and villages everywhere, people were wild with excitement, weeping tears of joy, smiling, waving and dancing in the streets, happy to be alive to see the end of hostilities in Europe.

Celebrations

Victory in Europe was marked as a day of celebration with peals of church bells and a beacon lit on Haytor. The town's churches held services of thanksgiving, streetlights were once again switched on, and many restrictions abandoned. With the ending of the black-out, headlight covers on cars were removed. Nearly every street in Bovey organised a party for the children. Although some food rationing continued, people rallied round to make cakes, jellies and trifles. With paper hats on heads, long tables set out-of-doors and decorated with flowers, and the sun shining, it was a day to remember. In the evening, dancing in Union Square and outside the Dolphin and Dartmoor Hotels continued until the early hours. Smart in their uniforms, the few American servicemen remaining in the area joined in as music played and the town celebrated victory and freedom.

Children enjoying tug-of-war at Brimley during the VE Day celebrations (Glenda Mortimore)

Hawkmoor – and the Treatment of Tuberculosis

by Janice Wallace

Hawkmoor Sanatorium was established in 1913 on the outskirts of Bovey Tracey and played a significant role in the town until its final closure in 1975. This chapter recalls the social and medical conditions that resulted in its opening and how it was developed to meet the changing needs of medicine and the hospital's patients.

George Orwell, Keats, the Bronte sisters and Robert Louis Stevenson are amongst the many famous people in history who have died from tuberculosis. But this ailment did not simply affect those with great literary talent; it stood as a massive threat to the whole population. So much so that in 1920 Dr J.C. Chapman, from the Ministry of Health, maintained 'that in England 140 deaths occur daily - one in every 10 minutes - from tuberculosis, and the disease is increasing'. Tuberculosis, also known as TB, or consumption, was expected to be fatal. Occasionally, the patient did get better, but for the majority of cases the prognosis was grim.

The creation and then the phenomenal growth of Hawkmoor can best be explained by looking at the wider picture of health and disease in England. Early in the 20th century local governments were empowered to take control of the spread of tuberculosis. One of the measures undertaken was to set up special institutions where sufferers could be segregated. All over the country units were built with a double benefit. Firstly, patients were offered a high standard of living in healthy surroundings and, hopefully, in time would be cured. Secondly, any further spread of the infection to the wider population would be curtailed. The main impetus emerged from the National Insurance Act of 1911, which specifically mentioned that care for tuberculosis through rest and care inside a sanatorium was to be made available for all. A year later it was reported to Devon County Council that its subcommittee had 'carefully considered the whole question of providing a sanatorium for the county' and had decided to 'recommend that an estate called Hawkmoor, near Bovey Tracey, be purchased'.

The estate offered to the council consists of 500 acres, and we are of the opinion that the dwelling house and surrounding buildings will, with the proper additions and shelters, be found to meet all the requirements of the county.

Hawkmoor Hospital was approximately 2^1/$_2$ miles from Bovey Tracey on the road to Moretonhampstead (Aerofilms & Aero Pictorial Ltd, courtesy of Dave Lewis)

Located approximately 2½ miles outside Bovey Tracey on the road to Moretonhampstead, Hawkmoor became Devon's premier specialised isolation sanatorium or hospital for the treatment and cure of tuberculosis, and eventually thousands of sufferers underwent treatment there. The original price was £11,000. The payment for each patient's care was to be financed from three sources. Some would be covered by insurance if it had been paid by the patient, with the remainder of the costs to be jointly met by the county council and the government. The patient was not required to pay directly for any treatment. Furthermore, once diagnosed, going into Hawkmoor was more or less compulsory. Devon's Public Health Committee said on 16th March 1920 that

tuberculosis being now recognised as an infectious disease, it is essential for the benefit of the Public Health that it should be dealt with as other infectious diseases, and, that all persons suffering from advanced pulmonary tuberculosis, not having or being able to provide or obtain proper isolated accommodation and treatment, or who are living in one room occupied by other people shall on the certificate of the Tuberculosis Officer, be removed (by order of a Justice of the Peace) to such a hospital as may be deemed suitable, at the public expense.

Years of growth

Under the county council's jurisdiction Hawkmoor underwent substantial expansion, which can be seen best in the building programme to increase the available facilities.

In 1913 there were 24 patients and by 1916 this number has risen to 40 patients. They lived in primitive conditions and were housed in small wooden huts, which measured only 8 feet by 6 feet. R. Bessell's short history of the hospital relates that 'there was no heating other than a limited supply of hot-water bottles and a few paraffin oil stoves. For some time lighting consisted of one hurricane lamp per chalet'. However, more permanent accommodation was under construction in this same period and initially two separate long wooden wards were built. They were each divided into duel occupancy chalets; one ward consisted of 80 beds and the other 50 beds. These wards became the male and female blocks and each had a verandah along the whole length of the building; the beds were pulled out whenever possible. By 1925 Hawkmoor accommodated up to 108 patients.

1938, in particular, stands out as a year when no expense seems to have been spared. Improvements included new equipment for the kitchens and laundry, a new telephone exchange, and the installation of a 'talkie' cinema projector. An extensive building programme appeared to be in progress and there was even agreement on providing a tennis court. A year later the sanatorium boasted several major additions, including, at the cost of £53,000, a nurses' home and two new surgical wards, both built to face the sun and containing 46 beds. An operating suite and x-ray department were also opened. Walter Elliot, the Minister of Health, conducted the official opening of the new buildings on 10th March 1939. The *Western Morning News* and the *Express and Echo* printed several photographs and particularly featured the art deco style nurses' home which, although constructed principally of brick with reinforced concrete floors, was equated with a 'white-painted river steamer'.

The opening speech by the chairman of the Hawkmoor Sanatorium subcommittee reported on the innovative nature of care given in the hospital.

Devon was one of the first counties seriously to take up the treatment of tuberculosis. Today [we have] passed from passive to active treatment, and [we are] proud of having an institution that [is] now one of the most up-to-date in Great Britain.

Demand escalated further and 3 years later, despite the number of beds increasing to 173, the county medical officer related how 16 of these beds were in the recreation hall and there was still a considerable waiting list. During the next 10 years Devon County Council saw Hawkmoor grow to its maximum capacity. Before central government assumed control after the National Health Act in 1948, another two-storey block of 80 beds had been commissioned and, in 1949, this opened, thus allowing care for 228 patients: the highest rate of occupancy in the history of the sanatorium.

(Courtesy of Dave Lewis)

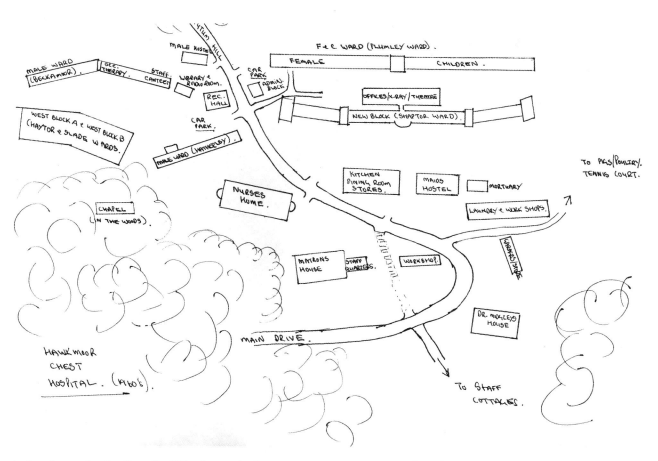

A plan drawn by Jim Bessell of Hawkmoor in the 1960s. New nurses were advised to invest in good macintoshes because of the scattered layout of the hospital.

Charitable Support

As well as public funding, private donations played an important part. The recreation hall was built in 1923 with the help of the Red Cross and St John charitable organisations. This hall was particularly popular for film shows.

More personalised acts of charity led to the chapel's creation. Behind the foundation stone, which was dated 27th February 1928, a letter was discovered in a lead-lined box, which described the very first donation of two years previously. It came in the form of a 'threepenny bit I got in my Xmas Pudding' and the benefactor was an 8-year-old girl patient. In total, the costs of the chapel amounted to £2,000, with the most sizeable percentage made by Dame Violet Wills' contribution of £1,300 along with the organ, the reredos, the altar table with Honiton lace cloth, and a stained-glass window depicting Christ healing the sick. The *Western Morning News* reported how this building was 'particularly interesting by reason of the fact that the church was designed by the Medical Superintendent Dr J. C. Smyth, and built entirely by the patients and staff'. Although provision had been made for payment of a Church of England chaplain to attend on Sundays during the late 1940s, the chapel seems to have been used mainly for Methodists, with the Church of England services taking place in the ward's restroom.

Dame Violet Wills' patronage also extended to offering a complete wireless installation in 1930 and, the following year, financing covered walkways between the sleeping pavilions and the dining room. Another longstanding benefactor was Mary Tickle, admitted as a patient with tuberculosis along with chronic arthritis and who remained at Hawkmoor for 28 years before her death in 1968. Despite being bedridden she became an active and successful campaigner for the patients' social club. The social club originally began at the suggestion of Dr Roy Midgeley, the newly-appointed medical superintendent in 1935, and 30 years later the *Mid-Devon Times*, on 30th July 1965, reported: 'the social centre had provided recreational amenities for about 6,500 patients since it was opened'. On an annual basis donations amounted to around £500 to £700, which covered all amenities not subsidised by public funds. Outside charitable bodies also became involved: some of the more notable were the Round Tables of South Devon, who, in 1956 alone, raised £1,500 for patient welfare, and also, from 1961, the League of Friends, who actively offered help. The British Red Cross librarians were also especially appreciated, along with Lustleigh's WRVS, who supplied and served afternoon teas on Saturdays.

Staffing at Hawkmoor

Much of the major growth at Hawkmoor happened shortly after the appointment of Dr Roy Midgeley as the medical superintendent. He was an extremely influential member of staff from 1935 until his retirement in 1970. Dr Midgeley lived in a house in the grounds with his wife and children. Other prominent doctors in Hawkmoor's history include Dr Jack Lloyd Griffiths, a consultant thoracic surgeon who lived in Teignmouth. His reputation was worldwide and often American doctors would come to Hawkmoor to learn new surgical techniques. Whilst numerous short-term surgical registrars worked on a temporary basis, some of the medical physicians, including Dr Norman Littler, appointed as deputy medical superintendent in 1946, stayed for years. Dr Littler, who lived at Manaton and came in daily, acquired the nickname of 'Flash', apparently because of the short amount of time he needed to perform certain medical procedures. However, in later years other explanations for his name include the high speed at which he tended to ride his motorbike and his habit of carrying a flashlight at night whilst searching for any patients who were unaccountably absent from their ward. The purpose of such a search was to deter 'courting couples', especially as males and females were strictly segregated by the hospital, although this rule was relaxed in later years.

Matron stood as the highest female figure of authority and discipline. She conducted a daily ward-round and lived in the grounds of the hospital in what was originally the estate house, an attractive building with an orangery at one end. Matrons bore responsibility for all the nursing staff, and amongst the individuals filling this position were Miss Long, Miss Greenhill, Miss Hammond and Miss Smith. It was usual for them to interview the ward sisters, in order of seniority, from 9.30

a.m. each day. Each sister presented a report and, when Nurse Kemble was promoted to sister, she recalls that, during the presentation, Matron 'would pass comment on what you were doing or what ought to be done, or didn't ought to be done'.

Apart from the medical superintendent and the matron, a third influential person at the top of the sanatorium's hierarchy was the hospital secretary. In the earlier years of the century the medical superintendent had been inundated by issues relating to the sanatorium's expenditure and so, in an attempt to reinstate the more medical aspects of his job, the position of hospital secretary was created to attend to the general running of Hawkmoor. Matron, similarly overburdened, handed over her role as overseer of non-nursing staff. Therefore, the hospital secretary assumed responsibility for the administrative and clerical department, catering, porters and ward orderlies, domestics, transport, farm and gardens, ancillary staff along with the pharmacy department as well as building, maintenance and engineering services. Bertram (although more usually known as Roy) Bessell became the hospital secretary from 1952 until his retirement in the mid-1970s. In his spare time, with his wife's help, he also formed and then organised the social club for staff outings and parties.

Not surprisingly, the pay of nurses was poor, and the matron often commented on its inadequacy. Perhaps because of this, along with the hospital's remoteness, recruiting and retaining adequate nursing staff remained a perennial problem. Reporting in February 1948, the matron listed vacancies for 30 fully-trained nurses. During periods of shortages, beds were closed down on the male block when nurses left, and then reopened when new nurses arrived. However, the West Block and the Surgical Block were less affected as these were given priority. The general lack of staff was especially acute on Sundays, and even in winter the lunchtime meal consisted of a salad with hot soup from an enamel bucket, and cheese for the last meal of the day. By offering specialised training, Hawkmoor did manage to attract nursing staff. During its earliest period of history, unqualified nurses were known as probationers and, in 1921, it was proposed that a 3 years' series of lectures by both the matron and the medical superintendent, followed by a successful examination, would result in a certificate and consequently a higher grade of pay. In later years the sanatorium enticed staff nurses by offering the training for the British Tuberculosis Association Certificate, which was a one-year post graduate course, and the 1945 Government Report stated that 'a schoolroom has been arranged' for the purpose. Soon afterwards student nurses could take the Thoracic Nursing Certificate as part of their general training and, in 1956, six nurses enrolled. Subsequent students came from all over the county to take a 12-week block of lectures, with practical experience in the nursing of thoracic patients in both medical and surgical wards: a month was spent on each of three wards. The choice of this 3-month secondment in training lay between chests, midwifery or mental health nursing. When Pat Kemble arrived as a student at Hawkmoor during the 1960s, she remembers that 'there were 12 of us from the Royal Devon and Exeter hospital, and there were 6 or 8 from Torbay and 4 from the North Devon Infirmary'.

Technical staff included the radiographer who, even in the 1950s, operated quite complicated x-ray equipment. Procedures were being used to visualise and evaluate the state of the patients' illness and treatment. There were, on average, 60 investigations per week. In a one-roomed x-ray department, simple chest x-rays of the thoracic cavity were supplemented by the more time-consuming tomograms, whereby several sections or levels of the lung were viewed, and by bronchograms, involving introducing a dye to establish the lung's validity and capacity. X-ray screening of patients who had had air introduced as a means of collapsing their lungs as part of their treatment plan, often occurred on a routine weekly basis.

Amongst the numerous non-medical staff 'chefs, cooks, seamstresses and farm labourers, the pig and poultry men, engineers, plumbers and electricians' were employed. Its size and remoteness meant that the hospital had to become as self-sufficient as possible. Yet the institution did not appear completely isolated and one of the more communal activities included the monthly dances for those working there. People came from outside, friends and acquaintances were welcomed and even the Royal Naval College at Dartmouth would occasionally be invited. All this ensured that these regular dances became a well-known event.

Staff Accommodation

Nurses in the lounge (Copyright Emap Healthcare. Reproduced by permission of Nursing Times)

Before the new nurses' home opened in 1939 the living arrangements offered were described as 'very inadequate, 2 and 3 nurses sleeping in a room'. The nurses' home changed this completely by offering individual rooms and excellent facilities for 50 people in attractive, light and airy surroundings. All the rooms were much the same, but the sisters tended to sleep on the top floor of the building whilst the night nurses slept on the middle level and the day nurses on the ground floor. Cleaners were employed to clean the rooms; nurse uniforms were washed, ironed and repaired if necessary in the hospital laundry and sewing rooms; and cooked meals were provided for the resident staff.

Other hospital accommodation included the six staff houses at the bottom of the hill near the main road, which had been built in 1925. These had been constructed for former patients who, now cured, had chosen to remain and work at Hawkmoor, particularly if they had families. In 1926 the medical superintendent reported 'that 19 of our present staff are old patients'. In reality, the houses appear to have been occupied by any members of staff with families willing to pay the rent; there were four houses priced at 6 shillings 6 pence a week, and the other two, which each had a parlour, cost 10 shillings a week. A further 10 homes were added in 1948, by which time the rent for the original houses was 9 shillings and 11 shillings, whilst the new cottages cost 15 shillings per week. As the hospital expanded, staff shortages were even more acute and offering adequate accommodation became essential. Mr Bernard Smalley, the radiographer appointed in 1956, cited one of these new cottages and its enviable position in the Devon countryside as the main attraction for taking up this post and moving across the country from Uxbridge. By the 1960s many of the homes had been extended and a new bathroom added. Most had three bedrooms, a lounge and dining room downstairs, along with a little kitchen. Members of staff living at the cottages included Mr Bessell, the hospital secretary, who, with his wife and children, arrived in 1952 from a similar tuberculosis sanatorium in Northumberland. He lived at No. 6, which was the largest one at the end of the row by the road. His son, Jim, worked in administration at the hospital and, when he later married, he moved into No. 4. Mr Aggett, the van driver, along with his wife and two children, occupied another of the cottages. Many ancillary workers commuted and one main use of the van was to transfer members of staff to and from their homes in Bovey Tracey.

The Patients

The treatment of children features heavily in the earliest discussions of creating a sanatorium at Hawkmoor and the provision of '50 beds for consumptive children' is mentioned in the plans of

1913 and onwards. However, adults always formed the majority of patients, and the Government Report of 1945 declared that the original children's ward had been taken over and 'used by adult female pulmonary cases'. In the late 1940s the typical patient would be in their twenties or thirties. The earliest patients suffering from tuberculosis stayed for months or even years, and part of their road back to recovery incorporated the theory that they should be allowed to work. One longstanding idea was that of an industrial colony, which was discussed as far back as 1919 in the minutes of the health sub-committee for Devon County Council, when it was thought that 'ex-service patients were suitable for training in farm work'.

On the terrace. The person stood to the right is Staff Nurse Miss M.G. Carlyle (Copyright Emap Healthcare. Reproduced by kind permission of Nursing Times)

The minutes relating to 1916/7 again discussed work done by long-term patients with regard to the construction of new paths – 'the work to be carried out by the patients as far as possible' – and the 'painting of exterior woodwork by the patients' on outbuildings. And, in 1920, following a review of similar sanatoriums, along with the idea of an industrial colony, it was recommended that at Hawkmoor 'such a colony is badly needed to bridge over the most critical period in the life of a consumptive i.e. the period between his leaving the sanatorium, and his becoming fit to take up full remunerative work without risk of relapse'. But, in later years, this philosophy only extended to a few patients and then only to those at the very end of long-term treatment.

Cases of tuberculosis came from all over Devon and they were admitted through a selection procedure. By the late 1940s it was most usual for the patient to be initially referred by their GP to a chest clinic. They would then see a consultant chest physician in places as far away as North Devon, Exeter, Plymouth and Torquay. These specialists had examined the patient and produced notes which the patient brought along with their x-rays to sit and discuss with Dr Midgeley. The merits and priorities of those needing admission to Hawkmoor were thus assessed. Philip Lyndon, diagnosed in 1946, had to stay at home in bed and wait seven months for a place to become available. The shortage of beds had been exacerbated by a rise in demand by returning servicemen as well as by many civilians who needed treatment in this post-war period.

By the 1950s the walls in the admissions office were covered in blackboards, each divided up into the various wards, and all the patients' names were written in different coloured chalks, depending on what was wrong with them. The tuberculosis patients were always written in white and others requiring thoracic surgery were written up in green chalk. The idea was that Dr Midgeley could come in with any of his colleagues and look around the walls of the office and know exactly how many beds were available. The boards were updated daily and proved efficient in illustrating just how many medical or surgical beds were available at any one time.

When a patient was called into hospital they were sent a standard letter telling them to attend on a specific date. They were also offered transport from the local hospital car service as long as they didn't live too far away. On Mondays, which was one of the main admitting days, there might be 15 patients waiting to be interviewed at the admissions office. They arrived at a set time, usually between 2 p.m. and 5 p.m. and were registered one at a time. Basic details were noted, typed out and placed in front of their case notes in a folder. The case-note folder was pink for tuberculosis and medical patients, and blue for other surgical patients.

Patients always had the visiting hours to look forward to, but in the 1920s the rules for visiting were extremely harsh. Adult patients were allowed to receive two visitors in each month, either two visitors on one day or one visitor on two separate days. Children were only allowed one visit a month and then no more than two visitors. All applications for visitors had to be made to the matron, who issued cards of admission without which no-one would be admitted. The visiting hours were between 2 and 4.45 p.m. Children under 7 were never admitted. These hours were extended in the early 1930s, and by the late 1940s were increased from 2 p.m. to 4.30 p.m. on every day except Christmas. Whilst in theory only two visitors were allowed, occasionally four or five turned up. Some nurses were lenient but, when the others adopted a stricter attitude, the visitors faced being farmed out to other patients.

The Patient's Day

Time at Hawkmoor was heavily planned and followed a set regime based on the grading given to each patient. The grades, awarded on arrival and then regularly reassessed by the medical superintendent, ranged from AR (Absolute Rest - in bed at all times, washed by the nurses) to BO (Bed Ordinary - mainly in bed but out as required: the normal grade for most patients) and to differing number of hours the patient was allowed up. The final grade was Work, but usually only long-stay patients were on this grade.

Although the idea of enforced inactivity might be perceived as intensely tedious, not everybody disliked this slowed-down pace of life. Philip Lyndon, who was first admitted in the late 1940s, reports that 'there wasn't time to get bored'. Fellow sufferers were also interesting in that they came from varied backgrounds and included farmers, policemen and servicemen from all three services. Added to this, the day's set itinerary helped to pass the time.

The daily routine on the four wards of West Block began with three early morning calls. One ward would be on a 5 a.m. call, when patients were woken up with a cup of tea. They were either washed or got up to wash themselves if they were so allowed. The next ward had a 6 a.m. call. The last two wards had a 7 a.m. call. Patients would be on 5 a.m. one week, then 6 a.m. the next, and the following fortnight they were awoken at 7 a.m. However, some of the fitter individuals might be permitted to sleep a little longer, providing that they made their bed before the day staff started.

Breakfast arrived at approximately 8.30 a.m. Mondays meant a weigh-in at about 9.30 a.m. Everyone was weighed to assess whether or not their weight had gone up or down, and, when weight went down, this was perceived to be a bad sign. In the morning some patients took the drinks trolley around the ward - one could have hot milk, cold milk, Ovaltine, Horlicks or Bovril. At 11 a.m., or 11.30, a handbell rang for the first rest hour of the day. In the rest hours, as soon the bell sounded, all patients had to get on their bed, regardless of the grade they were on. Whilst patients did not have to go to sleep, they had to rest completely. Even looking at stamps was forbidden. To signal the end of this first rest period, the nurses monitored everybody's pulse rate. However, patients had to take their own temperatures.

The morning finished with the midday meal. In the afternoon visitors might arrive, or time could be spent in doing occupational therapy. Making baskets, scarves, leather wallets, rugs and photo albums kept some busy. Others read books selected from the weekly library trolley. Then, later in the afternoon, came the second rest hour of the day, followed by the evening meal, which might be something like stuffed marrow. After this some patients played games, such as cards, chess or Monopoly, while others chose to go into the rest room for a game of bridge. One patient had his own projector on West Block and, as the walls were cream-coloured, they provided a good film screen. Everybody else made a small donation, thus enabling him to hire silent films such as the *Keystone Cops*. Eventually, the day drew to a close with the last milk drink and then lights-out at around 10 p.m.

On some days there were extra attractions, such as going to the recreation hall to see a film. Patients would try to arrange their day, perhaps by staying in bed in the afternoon, so they could go to the film show in the evening. Occasionally, concerts, plays or handbell ringers from the surrounding area provided entertainment in the hall for those on bed ordinary and above. However, almost everybody attended the Christmas concert and the pantomime performed by the locals each New Year. Christmas was remembered by Philip Lyndon in glowing terms, at least for the fitter patients.

It was fantastic really, you'd get dressed and you were up all day. And you could wander around, see other people, do what you liked. You would have Christmas dinner in your own ward, the turkey carved in one ward on the block by the superintendent.

In the evening the recreation hall was packed for the concert performed by the doctors and nurses with topical songs and sketches made relevant to the sanatorium.

Treatment

Tuberculosis was treated in various ways. The mainstay therapy throughout the whole life of the sanatorium came in the form of lots of bed rest and good food in a healthy environment with as much fresh air as possible. Common practice involved sleeping out on the verandah or by large open windows. At breakfast time it was not unknown for cornflakes to be blowing around the ward or out onto the lawn when the weather was windy! Food, much of it grown in the grounds, in general appears to have always been plentiful, and the usual three cooked meals a day meant many experienced a gain in weight. Patients were kept away from their families and friends for probably 6 months or more and, although men and women lived in separate wards, sometimes romance began to blossom. Towards the end of their treatment, when they were allowed up and encouraged to take walks outside, patients would often take the path at the back of the hospital together, which led up towards the reservoir at Trenchford - this was one of the most private places they could go. Unofficially, this lane had the highly unglamorous name of 'Sputum Hill'.

More invasive treatment was also needed in the fight again tuberculosis. One longstanding method of actively intervening to stop the progress of the disease was to administer an artificial pneumothorax. Dr Midgeley reports that, in May 1938, a total of 36 patients were receiving this form of treatment. For this procedure air was injected into the pleural cavity between the chest wall and the lung, so deflating the lung. If the treatment was given to the left side then the patient laid on the right for several weeks. Usually the amount of air outside of the lung would have to be topped up since the injected air tended to work its way out. For the first three weeks the patient had to remain in bed at all times and would even be fed by the nurses. After that they could get up once a day. Resting the lower region of the lung involved a pneumo-peritoneum, a temporary treatment whereby the phrenic nerve was crushed causing the diaphragm to be paralysed. Air was then injected to push up the diaphragm. The problem once more was that the introduced air tended to escape, causing the lung to re-inflate. Therefore every week or fortnight more air had to be added. The patient had to sleep sitting upright in bed for months when this technique was used.

Surgical intervention intended to contain the spread of disease might be more radical. The most invasive procedure was the thoraco-plasty, which involved removing a small section of ribs, thus making that side very much smaller and guaranteeing a permanent collapse in the corresponding section of the lung. From 1938 'operations for phrenic evulsion' were discussed, involving the removal of the phrenic nerve whereby the lower lung stayed immobile forever. Other more major operations were connected with complications following artificial pneumothorax treatment. Patients had to reach a level of fitness before these operations were performed and, at the initial stages, the main form of care was to rest and build up the body's own resistance to the disease. Occasionally, in order to improve the patients' chances of recovery, they would be sent to a house at Widecombe-in-the-Moor called Windwhistle, which was run by a retired matron from a former sanatorium at Torquay. After a few months they returned to Hawkmoor ready for the more radical treatment. However, at least in the late 1940s, this house only catered for two people. Despite the time taken to build up the patient, surgical intervention usually significantly shortened the patients' subsequent stay in hospital.

The arrival of antibiotics heralded the most dramatic upturn in the rate of cure for tuberculosis. The first major antibiotic came in the form of streptomycin which, after its introduction in 1948, halved the number of deaths. There were, however, problems in that sensitivity to this new wonder drug could build up very quickly, and for an unfortunate few it had the side effect of causing deafness. The advent of a combination of different antibiotics allowed more effective treatment. As a result, patients tended not to stay at Hawkmoor for as long as hitherto and could go home the moment it was decided that they had ceased to be infectious. The usual way of ascertaining if the tuberculosis had completely cleared up involved taking a test sample of sputum, or the patient might have a 'gastric lavage'.

In the late 1950s another innovation came in the form of widespread screening of the population using x-rays. Mass radiography service and the chest x-ray initiative found patients in the very initial stages of tuberculosis. Early detection, when combined with the availability of new antibiotics, meant that the spread of the disease declined dramatically. The demand for beds fell and, for those patients who were admitted during the 1960s, the length of stay varied from three to six months with a total recovery the norm. In the quest to conquer tuberculosis, the staff had accumulated a high degree of knowledge and expertise and, as far back as 1945, the Ministry of Health had reported that 'besides the usual minor surgery undertaken in sanatoria, major operations are also carried out at Hawkmoor'. In an attempt to continue using this high level of surgical expertise, during 1959 tremendous efforts were made by senior medical, nursing and administrative staff to persuade the South West Regional Hospital Board to give approval for open-heart surgery at Hawkmoor. As a thoracic hospital, the doctors would treat anything in the thoracic cavity such as heart conditions, hiatus hernias or lung cancers. Major items of medical equipment, including a heart/lung machine, had already been purchased and, during these latter years, Dr Trowbridge in the physiology department campaigned tirelessly for the hospital to become a specialist chest and cardiac unit when the demand for tuberculosis care halted. But, perhaps because of the hospital's isolated position and the attending problems with specialist staff and support services, the necessary permission was refused.

In the early 1970s the growing use of the facilities for patients with learning disabilities heralded a new direction and, in March 1975, Hawkmoor's function as a chest hospital finally terminated as all its thoracic patients were sent to hospitals in Exeter and Torbay. During the 1990s the hospital was demolished to make way for a new housing development. Only the chapel, the house used by Dr Midgeley and the cottages have survived.

Acknowledgements

Oral histories, particularly from P. Lyndon, J. Bessell, M. Treeby, P. Kemble, B. Smalley. At Bovey Tracey Heritage Centre.

Bibliography

DCC/155/2/9/1-7. Public Health Sub-Committee's Minute Book. At the Devon Record Office.
Bessell, B.R.C. *Hawkmoor 1913-17* (A three-page history unpublished, 1975). At Bovey Tracey Heritage Centre.
Smith, F. *The Retreat of Tuberculosis 1850-1950* (London, 1988)
Midgeley, R. L. *'Management of Chest Disease'*. Nursing Mirror (2nd August 1957) pp. 7-10.

✶ ✶ ✶ ✶ ✶

The Parish Council: Its First 50 Years

by Gordon Haigh

While I was clerk to the town council for five years I often looked at the old photographs of former Bovey Tracey parish councillors and wondered how much life in the council chamber had changed from their day to ours. To satisfy my curiosity I decided to explore the dusty, old parish council minute books that were hidden away on a shelf in a virtually forgotten cupboard in the town clerk's office. These books date back from the years immediately following the Second World War to the latter part of the 19th century. Although the minutes are tantalisingly brief, they do reveal fascinating glimpses into the workings of the parish council during the first 50 years of its life.

In the 1820s local government was incompetent and corrupt, and in Arnold-Baker's words 'became notorious half a century later for inefficiency and complication'. The government made efforts to resolve this through legislation, and, in 1894, the Local Government Act created the new style civil parish councils to replace the former ecclesiastical bodies. The legislation required that the parish councils should consist of a chairman and councillors, and that the parochial electors should elect the appropriate number of councillors at an annual parish meeting. Following the election, the parish council would elect a chairman at the annual meeting.

Bovey Tracey council meetings were held in the town hall which, before 1894, was called the vestry rooms. The building was constructed in 1865 on the site of the former village green. New vestry rooms had become necessary because, in 1864, it had been forbidden to hold vestry or other meetings in churches. The churchwardens and overseers bought the land on which the market cross and two cottages stood. The cross was moved, the cottages demolished, and the new building was erected at a cost of £800, raised by loans which had to be repaid out of the rates.

Two hundred parishioners attended the inaugural parish meeting held in the Bovey Tracey town hall on 4th December 1894, the main purpose of which was to elect the 14 councillors for the new parish of Bovey Tracey. Although four candidates withdrew before the vote, 33 remained from which the 14 were elected. William R. Hole was subsequently elected as the first chairman of the council.

There was much local interest in the parish council and, from 1894 to the start of the First World War, the average attendance at the parish meetings was about 150, and there were always about 30 people contesting the 14 seats. This interest continued for most years, although, in 1937, there were expressions of concern at a national level about the way in which parish councils were elected. In 1948 the clerk reported that, in future, the method of show of hands would be suspended and future council elections would be by nomination and ballot.

The council's minutes indicate that it operated through a committee structure with committees dealing with matters such as the management, leasing and maintenance of the town hall, the cemetery, the fire brigade, the recreation ground, footpaths, allotments and finance. In addition, there were ad hoc committees for special events. The problems of local housing, the maintenance of roads and flooding matters also concerned the parish council. The committees concentrated on much of the detail work and reported to the council at the monthly meetings. The clerk of the council, in addition to administering the meetings, also presented the monthly expenditure.

In 1974, following the reorganisation of local government, the parish council became known as a town council. Based on the information contained in the minute books, what follows are some of the more interesting items that the council had to deal with in its first half century, including its interest in national events.

The First World War obviously had a major impact on the council. The roll of names of Bovey Tracey men serving their King and country was the first recorded matter. At the parish council meeting on 5th October 1914 a letter was read from Lord Fortescue, Lord Lieutenant of the county, with the following resolution:

That it be desirable there should be obtained from every City, Borough, and Parish in the County a return showing the number of men belonging to it who were servicing in the Navy, the Army or the Territorial Force on the outbreak of the War, and the number of those called up for Service as reservists in the Navy, Army and National Reserve and the number who have enlisted in any branch of the Navy, Army or Territorials between that date and the 1st October. That the Lord Lieutenant be requested to take the steps necessary to obtain such returns.

The council 'unanimously agreed that a list be sent up as requested'.

At the parish council meeting on 2nd November 1914 the clerk reported that he had not sent the list of men serving their country as requested by the Lord Lieutenant 'as it was a most responsible thing and to make sure that no names were left out it was necessary that every house should be visited'. It was 'unanimously agreed that each councillor take a section of the parish to make sure every house should be visited'.

On the anniversary of the declaration of war the council, at its meeting in August 1915, unanimously agreed that:

We wish to put on record our appreciation to the Grand Services of our Army and Navy in the protection of our beloved country and that we now stand in silence in respect of those who have given their lives for our safety, and we further wish for our Army and Navy a speedy and successful ending of the present war, and we intend to do all we can to further that end. GOD SAVE THE KING.

During the war the council became involved in the 'national egg collection' scheme, which involved organising a collection of eggs for wounded soldiers in hospitals. The chairman of the council was able to announce that after the first week over 30 dozen eggs had been collected and sent to headquarters. This collection went on all through the war, and at the parish meeting in March 1918 it was 'unanimously agreed that it be recorded that the school children still keep up their collection of eggs for the wounded'. One girl had collected 4,000 eggs.

In 1915 the National Registration Act was introduced in which all the parishes in England and Wales were required to prepare a register of everyone between the ages of 15 and 65. Bovey Tracey was divided into eight enumeration districts and councillors volunteered to act as enumerators.

Also in 1915 a 'forget-me-not-day' was considered by the council. Mr Pascoe received a letter from the Mayoress of Exeter asking the council to organise a 'forget-me-not day' in aid of the Mayoress' Fund to provide refreshments for soldiers passing through Exeter. By September 1915 Councillor Wallen was able to report that it had been a great success and they had collected about £27.

In October 1918 a display of women's war work banners was considered at a council meeting. Councillor Mardon asked council's permission to fasten three to the town hall. This was unanimously granted.

Following the end of the war, the provision of a war memorial was considered at the meeting on 7th March 1921. A letter was read from the Bovey Tracey War Memorial Committee reporting that the plans of Messrs Wippell & Co. for eight tablets to fix around the faces of the town cross had been accepted. The time for completion was given as from four to six months at a cost of £225. H.A. Bentinck formally handed over the memorial to the custody of the parish council at the unveiling ceremony on 11th September 1921. It cost, in total, £350 10s. 0d. The chairman mentioned that the parish was indebted to Mr and Mrs Bentinck for providing, over the past three or four years, the temporary tablets with the names of the fallen inscribed on them until the permanent memorial was fixed. These temporary tablets were then to be displayed in the council chamber.

On 13th May 1935 Mr Dart drew attention to the fact that the war memorial required cleaning and the rails repainting. 'The matter was referred to the town hall committee for consideration.'

Preparations for the Second World War started as early as 1936. The matter of air raid and gas attack precautions was regularly considered by the parish council. In June 1936 it was reported that a circular had been received from Newton Abbot Rural District Council respecting precautions to be taken locally in the event of an air raid by aircraft using gas and incendiary bombs. On 13th

August 1936 it was reported that the Newton Abbot RDC had written respecting the air raid precautions for the parish asking that a parish meeting be called to discuss the forming of an air raid precautionary corps.

Mr Stephens suggested that Chief Officer L.S. Mardon should be the air raid precaution corps officer. It was then proposed that:

the Town Hall, Riverside Assembly Rooms and Dolphin Assembly Rooms should be used as the headquarters of the Corps for use as dressing stations for the injured etc. and that the same should be distinctly marked with the Red Cross and in such a manner as to be easily discernible from the air.

Dr T.F. Arnott suggested deferring the calling of the public meeting and also the forming of any scheme until after the British Red Cross Society's anti-gas lectures had been held.

Over the next few months there was much discussion about the anti-gas lectures and particularly the cost of them. At the beginning of 1938 the council received a letter saying that Messrs Boots & Co. were exhibiting models of full-size air raid refuge rooms and were organising a display in Newton Abbot, which they hoped local officials would attend.

In April 1938 it was agreed that Captain A.C. Curtis should be asked to accept the office of voluntary parish organiser under the air raid precaution scheme, and a meeting was arranged at the Dolphin Assembly Rooms. In May, Captain Curtis asked that a room in the town hall should be provided as a depot 'in time of emergency'. A month later he asked for a telephone to be installed, and for the room to be wired with a wall plug. Then, in April 1939, Captain Curtis wrote to the council saying he felt that a younger man should be appointed in his place 'as he felt he could not act in the case of an emergency'. It was agreed that Mr Mardon should interview Captain Curtis on the matter, and at the end of April he was able to announce that a compromise had been agreed. Captain Curtis would continue, but Mr Carpenter would be the deputy organiser. In December Captain Curtis finally resigned and Mr R.C. Aiers was appointed as his successor. Sadly, in October 1940, Mr Aiers died and Mr Carpenter was appointed as voluntary air raid precaution officer.

Sandbags and stirrup pumps were also considered by the council. A house-to-house canvas for subscribers for new stirrup pumps was organised and deemed 'highly satisfactory'. In February 1941 the chairman of the council gave permission to Mr J.H. Waugh to hold a demonstration of stirrup pumps in the recreation ground.

The problems associated with the black-out demanded attention from the councillors. At the meeting in December 1939 anxieties were expressed about pedestrians during the black-out, and it was agreed that

Mr Powlesland be asked to place a pole across the entrance to the river and have the same painted white and that the wall which protruded a trifle above Mr Tolley's shop should be marked with white lines.

In January 1941 a letter was read complaining that lights had been displayed at Devon House during black-out time and it was suggested that a deputation should visit the Brigadier-in-Charge.

The need for temporary accommodation for local residents was included in the agenda of the meeting in October 1940. Newton Abbot RDC sent a circular asking the council to 'compile a list of householders prepared to temporarily accommodate any residents of the district who might be rendered homeless as a result of an air-attack'. It was agreed that the clerk should make a list of available homes. In November he reported back that he had received only two offers, so it was decided to ask all the local clergy and ministers to make an appeal from the pulpit on Armistice Sunday. As a result of this, the clerk was able to report in December that eight householders had responded to the appeal.

The war continued with the council having to deal with issues as they arose. In December 1944 Mr Stephens reported on the recent fighting between troops in the town. He proposed that a letter be sent to the Chief Constable asking for an immediate inquiry in the hope that this would stop any further disturbance.

When the war finally ended the meetings considered how that should be celebrated. Celebrations were arranged for VE Day and then, again, for VJ Day. It was decided that the British Legion should light the bonfire, that children's sports should be held on the cricket field, that bell-ringers should be asked to ring the bells and that a dance should be held at the Dolphin Hotel.

One of the council's next tasks was to update the war memorial. Discussions took place throughout 1947 about the form it should take and the cost of it. By December of that year the council had reached the point of seeing a stonemason, who suggested cutting out a portion of the existing stone and inserting a fresh piece to take the names of the fallen. 'It was agreed to await his estimate of the price.'

The parish council always paid due respect to events connected to the royal family. Following the death of King Edward VII on 10th May 1910, the minutes record that a special meeting was held a week later and a resolution of condolence passed whilst members stood in silence.

From 1910 until the Second World War, the parish council had to consider the coronation of George V, his silver jubilee celebrations and then his death, the coronation of Edward VIII, although this never happened, and then the coronation of George VI. All the celebrations followed much the same pattern and were taken very seriously, although it is interesting to note that there appears to be rather less enthusiasm for George VI's coronation than for earlier events.

At the coronation of George V it was resolved that

the perambulation of the Bounds of the Parish so happily begun last year be continued this year on the day (not the Coronation Day) to be appointed by the Authority as a public holiday before or after the Coronation Day.

(The minutes of the parish council until 1947 indicate that the beating of the bounds took place annually from 1910 to 1915, again from 1922 to 1924 and then in 1947.)

By considering in some detail the celebrations for the 1935 silver jubilee of King George V and Queen Mary, we can see how the parish council approached each occasion. On 28th January 1935 the parish council met to discuss what form the celebrations should take and, at once, anxieties were raised about how they would be funded. Mr Stephens explained that the Ministry had sanctioned a grant to be made to local authorities and that the celebrations could be paid for by the levy of a rate or by voluntary subscriptions. Mr Godsland proposed that all the children of the parish should be given a free tea and that they should be presented with souvenir mugs made by the Bovey Pottery Company. Reg Mardon proposed that a dinner, the cost of which should not exceed 2/6d. per head, should be given to all old-age pensioners and other 'necessitous' people. Mr Carpenter proposed that a free dance should take place in the evening. It was then agreed that all the clergy of the town should be invited to organise a united service of thanksgiving. Then Miss Tolley moved, as a lasting memorial of the jubilee year, that provision should be made for a local swimming pool. Mr Mardon concluded the meeting by moving that May 6th should be observed locally as a public holiday and that all shopkeepers should close their premises all day and that local employers should see their way not to deduct a day's money from their employees' wages.

Meetings of the committee were then held regularly until May. At the second meeting it was suggested that a permanent memorial be provided in the form of a maternity and children's ward at Bovey Tracey Hospital. Dr Arnott said there would be 'certain inconveniences' if a children's and maternity ward were made as one. He wanted to see the erection of a children's ward at the hospital as the permanent memorial, and he thought this proposition would appeal to the public and be greatly appreciated.

At the third meeting it was decided that the refreshments should consist of sandwiches and soft drinks. The band would be required from 10 a.m. until 7 p.m. All householders were to be asked to decorate and illuminate as much as possible and a door-to-door collection was to be made for contributions to the permanent memorial.

At the next meeting the committee heard that the Dartmoor Hotel was prepared to let its room for 12/6d., and would charge 3d. for each sandwich and 2d. for the coffee. The Dolphin Hotel was

The start of the beating of the bounds in 1911 (B.T. Heritage Trust)

George V coronation celebrations in 1911 (B.T. Heritage Trust)

asking £1 1s. 0d. for its room and 3d. for coffee and 3d. each for sandwiches and sausage rolls. It was thought that these prices were rather 'heavy' and that the parties should be asked to come down in price. The committee decided to employ a band at the Dolphin, which would play modern dance music. Old-time dances would be held at the Dartmoor Hotel. Mr Aggett said that he had a 'radio-gram' which could be used.

In March the committee heard that £100 had been raised towards the children's ward. There was some discussion about whether it would be better to have a cricket match or adult sports, and in the end they decided to have obstacle and comic races. It was estimated that the cost of the celebrations would come to £123. They then decided to have a beacon. Henry Heath agreed to provide 400 faggots from timber he was cutting in Furzeleigh Copse, and to convey and stack them on the site for £5 10s. The scoutmaster, Mr Pascoe, suggested that some scouts should camp on the site for a night or two to prevent any damage being done to the beacon. The scoutmaster also offered to decorate the town hall and the Temperance Hall.

The discussions at the final meeting after the celebrations had taken place were about the enjoyable day everyone had had and the cost – £120. Teignmouth Electric Company had provided electricity for an extra one and a half hours at the cost of one shilling. All the residents had contributed with 'their splendid illuminations'.

Following the death of King George V, a special meeting of the parish council was held on 21st January 1936 for the purpose of sending a message of condolence to the royal family. A vote of condolence was passed, the members standing in silence, and a telegram of sympathy was sent to King Edward VIII from 'parishioners and Parish Council of Bovey Tracey'. Convened by the chairman, a meeting of the local tradesmen and shopkeepers was held in the council chamber on 25th January 1936 to decide the hours of closing of local business premises on the day of the royal funeral. It was unanimously agreed that all shops and other businesses should be closed on 28th January from 1.00 p.m. to 2.30 p.m. The chairman authorised the chief officer, L.S. Mardon, to discharge the fire maroon at 1.00 p.m. to signal the commencement of the two minutes silence. To prevent overlapping, the chairman said he would notify Messrs Candy & Co., the Bovey Pottery Co. and the stationmaster that the maroon would be regarded as the official signal, locally, for the silence.

The foregoing are just a few of the activities of the parish council of Bovey Tracey during its first 50 years. Thanks to the present town council, the minute books of the former parish council have been deposited at the Heritage Centre. They are available there for examination and provide a revealing account of life in Bovey Tracey within the historical setting of the times.

Bibliography
Arnold-Baker, C. *Local Council Administration* 5th ed. Butterworths, 1997

❋ ❋ ❋ ❋ ❋

Sport

Sport has always been an important way of binding, and occasionally dividing, communities and Bovey is no exception. There has been an enormous commitment to providing facilities for and supporting particular activities. Some of these sports, such as cycle speedway and the Vespa Club, have disappeared as fashions have changed, but others have gone from strength to strength as shown in the sections below.

Cricket
by Victor Coombes

In the middle of the 19th century, outside the small market town of Bovey Tracey, an area of land covered with gorse, bracken, silver birch and fir trees was known as Bovey Heath. It was here, in 1850, that a small band of men cut out a cricket pitch and formed the Bovey Tracey Cricket Club. Bovey Tracey, at that time, had a population of less than 2,000 and no houses would have been visible from this new cricket ground; the nearest dwelling would have been Indio House, which housed a pottery in its grounds.

The first recorded match was a game in 1848 between the married and single men of the Bovey Pottery. The weather was fine and it is, perhaps, surprising to read that the Bovey Tracey Band played during the match. It is assumed that the pottery workers would have had contacts in other parts of the country where cricket was already well established. The players in this game were probably the men who, on 15th August 1850, played Isca (Exeter) as the newly-formed Bovey Tracey Cricket Club.

In the 1860s the present pavilion was built. At first it was a single-roomed thatched building but, later, changing rooms and an equipment store were added. It is interesting to note that, like most pavilions at this time, it faces north as Victorians were not sun worshippers and preferred sitting in the shade. The pavilion was heated by an open fire, which was in use up until the 1930s. This was probably the cause of the fire which, in the 1870s, destroyed the thatched roof and led to the construction of a higher, slated roof. Fortunately, the club has in its possession several cups and plates showing the lovely old thatched pavilion and also the original copper plate on which these pictures were etched for transfer to the pottery at the Bovey potteries.

In 1866, upon the enclosure of Bovey Heathfield, the owner of Indio House, Mr C.A. Bentinck, was awarded the stewardship of the ground on condition that he preserved the surface in good condition and permitted it to be used as a place of exercise and recreation for the inhabitants of the parish. He also had the right of pasturing sheep there and took on the responsibility of maintaining the fences. This arrangement continued until 1921, when Mr Bentinck considered that it had become too expensive and passed control to the parish council.

The club has many framed team photographs, the earliest dating from 1885. This shows that 'whites' were becoming cricket team wear and also that the turf was not so immaculately cut as in later years. The photograph of the 1908 team also illustrates the strides made in the intervening years. The players are dressed much as they are in the present day, the umpire is dressed in a white coat and a scorer is included. The decision to buy two white umpires' coats was taken in 1899 at the AGM in the Dolphin Hotel, when it was also decided to buy a collecting box.

The club closed down during the First World War because so many young men went away to war, many never to return. At the end of the war the club was restarted with just £1 5s. 5d. in the bank. Nevertheless, by 1923 the players were being paid a proportion of their travelling expenses and, in 1926, they were being urged to purchase the new club caps in yellow and green. It was around this time that the first evening matches were organised, and bats costing £2 were presented at the end of each season to the player heading the averages.

The first half of the century produced many fine cricketers. Two, in particular, appear in the 1908 photograph mentioned above. The first was Lew Stevens who was, without doubt, the best batsman of the first half of the 20th century. He was elected onto the committee in 1909 and was captain of the first team from 1914 until he retired in 1949 - a record that is unlikely to be equalled. He was an excellent bat and a very good bowler, topping the bowling and batting averages many times between the wars. In 1926 he was awarded 15 shillings by the committee for his feat of scoring two centuries in the previous season, a wonderful performance at that time.

The second was George Rowe, known as 'Old Georgie' to distinguish him from his son who was also a fine bowler. 'Old Georgie' is first mentioned in 1907 and during the next 30 years took thousands of wickets. He was considered by many to be the best spin bowler in the county for many years. With long powerful fingers, strengthened by his work in the potteries, he could 'pitch the ball on a sixpence'. His contemporaries would say that the ball could be heard humming in the air before turning sharply either way. Even as late as the 1940s, when he was almost 60, he was still a fine bowler and headed the averages in 1946 with 56 wickets at an average of 7. 06.

The club is fortunate to have most of the scorebooks from 1927 to the present day, including one with the cover embroidered by Mrs G. Sharp in 1929. In this year it is interesting to see that the 59 vice-presidents contributed £50 and that they included 7 retired army majors, 4 captains, 4 doctors and 3 reverends. Collections on the ground exceeded £20 for the season for the first time.

The cricket team in 1908. Back row, left to right: F. Turner, G. Black, ? Willcocks, L. Stevens and J. Steer. Middle row, left to right: B. Waldron, L. Coish, B. Pascoe, V. Fry and J. Conian. Front, left to right: A. Mountford, W. Bond and H. Mountford (Geoff Coish)

The 1st XI in 1921. Back row, left to right: B. Fry (scorer), L. Coish, A. Mountford, L. Mardon, H. Mountford and W. Pascoe (umpire). Middle row, left to right: A. Pascoe, L. Stevens (captain), A. Courtier, W. Waldron and G. Rowe. Front, left to right: J. Heath and F. Waldron (Geoff Coish)

In the early 1930s the club became the fifth club in the county to employ a professional. This was L.V. Vaughan, who was employed for a wage of £2 a week for three evenings, coaching and playing in all matches. He was also paid his bus fare from Torquay, which amounted to an additional 2s. 9d. per week. He was an excellent slow bowler and took over 100 wickets in each of seasons 1931 and 1932, but was so enraged at being given out lbw by the Chudleigh umpire that he refused to leave the wicket. The club had to apologise and the minute book simply reports that, despite a most contrite letter to the committee, he was not engaged for another season.

There was considerable enthusiasm in the club during the 1930s, with a rise in support and a big improvement in the playing standard. The first 10-wicket haul by a club bowler occurred in 1936 when W. (Bill) Mountford, a fast bowler and hard-hitting batsman, took all 10 wickets against Tiverton Heathcot at Tiverton. After water had been taken to the square in 1924, the pitches had gradually improved in the next decade and a new grass cutter costing £9 19s. 0d. was purchased. This mower served well for five years, after which the club wrote to Miss V.E. Wills (Dame Violet) asking for a donation towards a new motor Atco costing £34. The committee was overjoyed to receive a note from her the following day enclosing a cheque for the full amount which, today, would be equivalent to a donation of over £2,000. A few years later, in 1934, a major project was undertaken when extensive returfing was done on the square: a total of 540 turfs, each 3 feet by 1 foot, were laid at a cost of £20.

The club kept going during the Second World War and played several matches each season against local opposition and army regiments stationed in the area – despite the fact that in 1940 only ten players paid their subscriptions. In that year a match between the Old Boys and the Young Boys raised £30 for the Spitfire Fund. A letter was received from the Teignmouth Lighting Co. to say that as the pavilion was important to the war effort they would install in the pavilion five lighting points and one power point. The troops billeted locally were given permission to use the grounds on Sundays, but there was 'much dissatisfaction' in 1943 when the American troops were allowed to use the ground for baseball.

Thanks to the dedication of a few men the ground was in good condition at the end of the war and a second team was formed in 1946, when the playing support rose to forty. Support was strong as can be seen from the number (200 – all male) who attended the annual dinner at the Dartmoor Hotel that year.

For many years the playing strength was not strong and the club relied heavily upon a few good players, notably Stuart Mountford, who was club captain and played for Devon as wicket-keeper/batsman for many years: he was still playing well when he retired in the 1970s. Many innovations occurred in the 1950s: the first Sunday matches took place; a motorised roller was purchased for £70 and has been in constant use since; the old method of scoring with 'tins' was replaced by rollers operated from within the scorebox; and, against strong opposition, a bar was installed in the pavilion. In 1951 showers were built, paid for by the parents of a young, 21-year-old, fast bowler, John Crossley, who died within a few days of being taken ill.

The 1970s also saw a considerable improvement in the fortunes of the club, both financially and on the playing field, where many good players were coming through. The income in 1971 rose to £405 and the first ride-on mower was bought from Stanley West for £200. The number of matches played had gradually increased since the beginning of the century, when each eleven played only a dozen or so matches. In 1977 this number had risen to 38 for the first eleven, 34 for the second, 11 evening matches and 18 games for the Colts.

Until 1980 the club had been known as the Bovey Tracey Cricket and Bowling Club, but the bowlers decided to go their own way and their name was deleted from the title. The departure of the bowlers allowed their rooms to be converted into a much-improved kitchen and an umpires' changing room and store. The pavilion was, by now, over 100 years old and becoming very expensive to maintain. In 1978 over £2,000 was spent on the balcony, which faces north and is open to the elements the whole year round. Shutters were made to keep out the worst of the weather. Just a few years later the roof was re-slated at a cost of £4,000, financed by members who bought £10 'tiles' on the basis that the money would be repaid over the following eight years.

Practice pitches had always been a problem and various pitches had been laid over the years. In the 1930s a rota of players erected nets three times a week on the outfield. In 1938 two concrete wickets had been laid. These were dug up after the war and two more laid on what is now the car park. However, they were not satisfactory, as players would not carry gear over to the nets and during the evening the setting sun shone directly into the batsman's eyes. As a result, they were quickly abandoned and dug up, and another was laid in the early 1990s parallel to the new road behind the pavilion. Later, two more were added beside the pavilion, with the run-ups on the outfield.

Such has been the improvement on the ground over the years that the club was selected to stage its first Minor Counties match, Devon v Cornwall, on 26th and 27th August 1980. The club's efforts were singled out for praise in the Devon secretary's report to the AGM of the Devon Cricket Club and in the minutes of the Minor Counties Cricket Association AGM at Lords. That first match set a high standard for others to follow and every year since then the organisation could hardly be bettered. The pitch and the organisation invariably receive high praise from the players and the hundreds of spectators who support these matches each year.

The first Colts team was formed in the early 1950s and produced several good players who played for the club for many years. Probably the best player to emerge was Lewis Gibbs, who was to prove the scourge of many teams for years to come. As probably the best fast bowler in Devon for many years, he was unfortunate not to have played for the county. Many times he took 6, 7 and 8 wickets in an innings, but his best performance was to take all 10 wickets against Barton in 1975 with figures of 16. 1 overs, 40 runs, 10 wickets - all the more remarkable for a fast bowler when it is seen that 9 of his victims were clean bowled. In all, he took nearly 2,000 wickets at just over 13 and scored 10,000 runs, including a century in 75 minutes. When the Colts system was re-established in the 1980s one of its many products was Barry Shaw, who dominated the batting throughout that decade. He opened the batting and was the mainstay of the first team for 13 years, when he was never out of the first three in the averages and headed the averages in 6 out of the next 10 years. In most seasons he amassed over 1,000 runs, scoring 1,603 in 1989. His career in cricket ended when he injured his knee playing hockey in 1991.

Until 1974 all games had been 'friendlies' and only players from the immediate area were considered for selection. However, in that year, the club was selected to play in the 'B' division of the newly-formed Devon League and it soon became clear that this policy could not be adhered to. This became even more evident when, amidst great celebration, promotion to the 'A' Division was achieved in 1984. In 1992 the club was invited to be a founder member of the new Premier Division and now play the best clubs in the county. In the years after 1998 the club finished third, seventh, third, third and finally, after a great season in 2002, became Premier Division champions.

Swimming
by David Iley

For many years the people of Bovey wanted a swimming pool. At the time of King George V's silver jubilee and again at King George VI's coronation, it was suggested that a swimming pool could be built as a permanent memorial to these events, but nothing came of these ideas.

Then, in 1964, a public meeting was convened by Mr E.R. Vinnicombe, the headmaster at Bovey Tracey Primary School, to explore ways of providing a small pool for the school. A rousing call to action by Mrs Sylvia Smith created a surge of enthusiasm and determination to build a larger pool for the town as a whole, to which the school could have access. The Bovey Tracey Swimming Pool Association (BTSPA) was formed.

A committee, embracing a wide range of relevant interests and expertise, was formed on the spot under the chairmanship of Ron Harris. It immediately set to work investigating possible sites, planning requirements, pool contractors, fund-raising activities and sources of grants. A constitution setting out the aims and objectives of the association was drawn up under the guidance of committee member David Jervois, a local solicitor, who also attended to all matters requiring a legal input during the formative years before and after the pool was built.

The parish council kindly agreed in May 1965 to grant a 60-year lease of the site on the recreation ground for a nominal rent. This enabled all the other activities to proceed. Gilliam and Company of Purley was selected as our main contractor and, after much consultation between Sidney Mountford, his brother, Walter, and Bob Moore, our building and surveying experts, and Dudley Rogers, Gilliam's local agent, a basic design for a 25-metre pool, its surrounds and associated buildings was agreed.

A tender for £12,755 was eventually received in February 1968, which was reduced to £11,184 after the association decided to carry out, or sub-contract, some of the less specialised work itself. For example, Sidney Mountford and Bob Moore constructed all the shelving systems in the kiosk over two weekends in August 1968; these are still going strong today (2003). The grants sub-committee had conducted negotiations for a major grant for some time and the Department of Education and Science offered us a provisional 50% grant of £5,572 on 7th May 1968.

Site work started on 13th June 1968 and, amazingly, the pool opened to the public on 24th August 1968. The opening ceremony started with a life-saving demonstration by a local police team, followed by ceremonial lengths of the pool swum by Tony Gaton, Michael Steer, Eugenie Clifford and Sarah Mann. At last Ron Harris, our chairman, declared the pool OPEN and, with an enormous cheer and splash, most of the children of Bovey Tracey, who had waited patiently round the sides, launched themselves into the water, followed by showers of coins and notes hurled after them by the adults - a sight to be remembered and savoured.

At this stage only the basic facilities were in place, that is the pool itself, two rows of surrounding slabs, the kiosk, changing rooms, toilets and filter room (all the wooden buildings were supplied by 'Devon Lady' of Honiton and are still in good order 34 years on), and the wooden fence. The month of operation in 1968 was extremely valuable in giving us experience in operating the pool and in exposing a number of teething problems. The following year, 1969, was our first full season and further improvements were introduced over the next few years, such as the heating system in 1970, spectator terraces and reformite boundary wall in 1971 and an improved surface drainage in 1974. Since then many more facilities have been added (hot showers, office and storerooms, insulating covers, toddlers' pool and so on).

None of this would have happened, of course, without the necessary funding and, right from the start, a tremendous amount of enthusiasm, imagination and energy was expended in raising our half of the cost in order to qualify for a government grant. It must be remembered that, in 1964-68, £6,000 could buy three houses, and the population was considerably lower and less well off than now. That our target was achieved was largely due to the very active support and interest of the community of Bovey Tracey as a whole. It was this which encouraged and sustained the committee in its work. Membership of the BTSPA and the conferring of voting rights at the AGM was open to all on payment of an annual subscription of half a crown, and this gave us an early financial base.

Many local people, businesses and organisations made donations to start us off; annual grants were made by the carnival committee and the parish council; Ashburton County Secondary School (precursor of South Dartmoor College) contributed; our own primary school children raised money selling foreign stamps; and the people of Bovey, in general, contributed in many ways. The

The swimming pool opened on 24th August 1968. Back row, left to right: ?, ?, ?, ?, James Brown, Sam Fogwill, Jack Collier, Mrs Collier, Doreen Jackson, Sheila Iley, David Iley, Ann Crosby, Claude Steer, Bob Moore, Sydney Mountford, Ginge Spence, ?, Ron Vinnicombe, ?, Betty Clifford, ? and Derek Hart. Behind the table, from the left: Chairman of TDC, Mrs Bond and Bert Bond. To the far right, at the end of the row: Keith Bruce (H.R. Rivers, courtesy of Lil Moore)

committee also organised several major fund-raising events, notably a Caledonian market held in Wyatt and Bruce's premises in the old pottery buildings - now the House of Marbles. An art show and sale in the Dolphin Hotel also generated a lot of interest and support. Dances and draws were held regularly.

Once the pool was open, fund-raising still continued apace to pay for the improvements and to underwrite running costs when necessary. Mr Alfred (Ginge) Spence played a major part as the driving force behind many money-raising schemes, such as the 'buy a brick' badges for the wall fund, balloon races, guess the time the watch stopped, smash the crockery stalls (misshapes and miscolours donated by our local pottery, now defunct), sponsored swims and summer fairs. Perhaps the most eye-catching idea was the 'Dunk-a-Belle' stall in which a bikini-clad young lady was tipped into a tank of water if a ball, bought and thrown by a competitor, rang a bell at the bull's-eye of a large target. Ginge and David Iley and the girls took the stall to various events in Devon and gained useful publicity as well as raising money. Our gallant and beautiful girls were all local and included Sarah Mann and Jackie Phillips.

The biggest and most consistent money-spinner, however, was the weekly lottery conducted every Wednesday evening, mostly in the Old People's Rest Room - now occupied by the police (2003) - at the town hall. This was a real community effort first suggested and promoted by Brian Beeney but soon taken over by David Iley when Brian left the area a few months after the first draw on 20th January 1965.

The promoter collected the takings from the collectors, conducted and oversaw the weekly draw, returned prize cheques to the appropriate collectors to give to the winners and maintained all the records of payments and receipts to satisfy the auditors and the requirements of the Lotteries Act. Results were printed and duplicated on the spot, each collector received a copy and other copies were posted on noticeboards in the town. Membership quickly rose to around one thousand, varying from week to week as new collectors and members were added and old ones left. This raised approximately £50 per week, which had to be allocated strictly according to the provisions of the Lotteries Act. Quite often the winners did not cash their cheques as a form of donation! The rest of the takings went to funds contributing around £1,000 a year in the early years. David Iley and James H. Brown supervised the proceedings, nearly always accompanied by Mrs Lil Moore, Sidney Weeks, Mrs I. Brown, Liz Steer, Sam Wilson with Cindy, his smiling Labrador, Joyce Tregoning and anyone else who cared to drop in to see that fair play was maintained. This continued, without break, for 22 years until late 1987, when the old firm retired and the lottery was relaunched by Janet Walling.

The committee breathed a collective sigh of relief when the pool opened, prematurely, as it turned out, since fund-raising had to be maintained and the greater burden and responsibility of running the pool had to be shouldered. As ever, numerous volunteers came forward to man (or mainly woman!) the kiosk in the season. This was also when a succession of organisers such as Doreen Jackson, Betty Clifford, Pam Spence, Joyce Tregoning and many more came into their own. School bookings in the morning sessions were arranged and matters concerned with safety, swimming classes, supervision of pool attendants and so on were dealt with expertly and efficiently by Brenda Morgan.

David Iley became the voluntary pool supervisor responsible for water quality and treatment, day to day supervision of the use and maintenance of filtration, chlorination and heating equipment, instructing the pool attendants on the technical part of their duties and commissioning and closing down the pool each season. There were many, many problems in the early years, especially with the supply and delivery of pool chemicals. On one remarkable occasion David complained vigorously to the suppliers when their lorry driver dumped dangerous chemicals over the bank surrounding the recreation ground when delivering well before the time agreed for reception. On the following, timely, delivery the driver and David Iley exchanged remarks which escalated into blows until an attendant, alerted by the noise, arrived and intervened and, honour being satisfied, handshakes were exchanged and normal relations resumed.

We were not always able to find pool attendants with all the desirable qualifications and expertise, although they always had life-saving certificates and skills. One notable example was a personable young man who managed to close all the valves in the circulatory system when the pumps and boilers were going full blast, which resulted in the 'springing' of most of the joints in the system and closure of the pool for several days. This was Peter Richardson who, not long after, found fame as a television and film actor and producer.

Many people have been involved in the story of Bovey Tracey's swimming pool. Ron Harris, our first chairman, guided us through the formative years, metaphorically twisting arms and smoothing feathers through many meetings, in addition to contributing his knowledge of things electrical. He was followed by a succession of hard-working chairmen who built on and developed the foundations which he had laid - Douglas Piedot, John Griffiths, Malcolm Billings and Martin Brealey. Doreen Jackson was our secretary from the beginning; she burned the midnight oil and kept the telephone lines busy in promoting and co-ordinating our activities for many years. The good work continued for another lengthy period in the hard-working and capable hands of Ann Crosby. The success of our enterprise depended largely on good financial management. Brian Beeney was our first treasurer. He was followed by Sheila Iley. She kept the records during the early fund-raising years and presided over all the intricacies of wages, national insurance and PAYE once we became employers. Mr Arthur Stone, Brenda Morgan's father, kept us all in order in the period of expansion. Their able successors included Mr Lowndes, Mr West and John Hughes.

Many people, including Lil Moore, Mollie Sheffield, Claude and Margaret Steer, James and Irene Brown, Mrs Cann, Sam Wilson, Barb Yeo, Betty Brealey, Ann Crosby, Joyce Tregoning and the publican at the Bell Inn, collected faithfully for the lottery right from the start and went on doing so for over 20 years. The kiosk has always been looked after on a voluntary basis by many Bovey and Heathfield worthies.

The pool is now in its 35th year and each summer provides pleasure and relaxation for the people of Bovey and the surrounding area.

It is hoped that a collection of letters, minutes, financial records, lottery records and other ephemera from the early years of the BTSPA will be lodged in the archives of the Bovey Tracey Heritage Trust for safe-keeping and for further study by anyone who may be so inclined.

Bovey Tracey Bowling Club
by Joan Thompson, with information from Jack Stoneman and Victor Coombes

In 1904, at a meeting of the cricket club, it was proposed that a piece of ground be specially prepared for a bowling green. Men who were employed at the Bovey Pottery subsequently carried out the work. Trees and bracken were cut down and roots dug up, and a level base was made with cinders and ashes from the pottery. Moorland turf brought down from Holne by horse and cart was used to lay three rinks.

There is no record of any activity until 1911, when the first bowling committee was formed with W.H. Ley, J.D. Dannell, G. Black, W. Sampson, J. Wilcox and A. Pascoe as members. The club was a founder member of the Mid Devon League.

In the 1930s the groundsman was paid 11/3d. a week. The field belonged to Henry Bentinck, who closed the green once a year to claim his rights. At about this time the trees that covered the back of the green from Newton Road to the railway line were cut down, and the roots dug up to provide the town's refuse tip. This was later levelled off and seeded, and is now the site of the tennis courts. In 1939 water was taken to the bowling green, and wire netting was obtained to keep the rabbits out.

The club closed when the Second World War began but, in 1941, there was a request to turn the bowling green into tennis courts. This galvanised members into quickly meeting to restart the club. Playing did not take place, but the green was prepared ready and, in 1945, the secretary, Mr Webber, reported that, although the green was not perfect, many pleasant evenings were spent there. In 1946 a fourth rink was constructed to conform to league rules. This cost £4 and was paid for by Mr A.B. Dahl, the president of the club.

The bowls club on VE Day 1945. Back row, left to right: Ted Larcombe, Tom Tolley, H. Davey, L. Smith, Walter Kendall and Harry Tregoning. Front row, left to right: Fred Cox, Pinder Davey, B. Wyatt, Jim Webber and Alan Martin (B.T. Heritage Trust)

In 1955 W. Brealey, the secretary, reported that in order to retain league status overdue improvements had to be made to the rinks. It was agreed that up to £20 could be spent.

Up until the mid-1970s the bowlers and cricketers had shared the pavilion, but now the bowlers decided that they should try to have a pavilion of their own. Planning permission was granted and ways and means were discussed until, at a meeting, it was resolved to obtain the money from personal loans from the members. A target of £1,000 was set through raising interest-free loans on a ten-year repayment, and this figure was guaranteed the same night. As a result, a second-hand prefabricated pavilion was purchased, and this was later installed with the help of the members after they had first cleared the site of rocks and a hedge. Laurie Lawrence did the stonework and also attended to work needed at the front of the building.

In 1980 the bowlers officially broke away from the cricket club. Then, in 1981/2, the green was reconstructed. The turf was removed, the playing area enlarged, levelled and redrained, and new turfs were bought, all under the skilful eye of H. Cook.

In 1985 ladies joined the Devon County Ladies Bowling Association and started to play in competitions, and have since had some very good results.

Improvements continued to take place and new cups given. There are now 60 members, and the club continues to thrive.

Bovey Tracey Lawn Tennis Club
Information from Fran Brealey

Tennis was a popular sport at the beginning of the 20th century, usually played on courts belonging to private houses. Bovey had a private tennis club in the 1930s run by the Misses Gurney. In 1937 public tennis courts were suggested and the council set up a sub-committee to look into the matter. They contacted interested players to raise funds and draft rules for a tennis club, but war intervened.

It was not until 1958 that a meeting of all those people interested in starting a tennis club was called. Around thirty people turned up and resulted in the Bovey Tracey Lawn Tennis Club being formed. The first chairman was Mr Vinnicombe and the president was Dr Midgley.

Fund-raising had already begun, and a series of dances and other events raised £300. The club received £231 4s. 4d. from the Festival of Britain Committee, and a grant of £260 was promised from the National Playing Fields Association towards the cost of the courts.

Until the courts were built members played at Whitstone for the first year and then, for the following three years, Colonel Bacon let them play at Ashwell. In 1962 Sam Wilson became secretary, and he and the committee decided that they must provide two courts as the nearest tennis club with its own courts was in Newton Abbot. The parish council leased the site for the courts at a peppercorn rent, and the club was granted a loan from the Devon Playing Fields Association of £500. To receive this loan, fifty people each had to stand as guarantor for £10. They also received a grant of £300 from the local council and, finally, in 1963, they had two courts completed at a cost of just under £1,300.

In 1963 the club became the Bovey Tracey Lawn Tennis and Badminton Club, which it remained until 1976, when the badminton section broke away again. During that time badminton was played in the town hall, and joint memberships were in operation.

In 1966 a cedar wood pavilion was bought, and put up by the members. Then, in 1975, a third court was added as the club grew, and a request to play on Sundays was granted – but only after 2 p.m. The third court was finished just after Christmas, and the first game played on it in January. In 1976 lights to the clubhouse and an extra court were put in. During the period from 1970 to 1976 the coach was Joan Sydney-Turner.

Improvements have continued to take place and now there is a thriving club with three courts (two lit), a practice wall and a clubhouse with all facilities.

Cycle Speedway
Information from Geoff Wills and John Small

In the early 1950s, when cycling was very popular, a group of young men decided to create a cycle speedway. They approached the council who let them have a piece of ground in the recreation field, where the tennis courts are now. Their first match was against Heathfield and, because the Bovey boys were only using ordinary bikes, they were pulverised, as John Small described it. They then started to modify their bikes and became more successful, becoming joint second in the South Devon League in 1953. The team was known as the Bovey Spurs, and they wore cockerels on their shirts. John Wills, son of Geoff Wills, and later a parish councillor and mayor, was their mascot. At the time it was very popular, and crowds of people came to cheer the team. Michael Steer remembers as a boy of 15, 'gaping at the races open-mouthed. As the bikes and riders lay in dusty mangled heaps on the first bend, Charlie Parker, standing next to me, said, "I love they tanglements".' Gradually interest was lost in the sport, and the club folded in the late 1950s.

Vespa Club
Information from Christine Gale

Ken Harris, son of Alder Harris who made and sold shoes in Bovey, set up the Vespa Club in 1955. The club met once a week for a social evening, and went on a club run on Sundays. Members came from Newton Abbot, Exeter, Crediton, Kenn and Plymouth. Amongst the Bovey members were Jean Gilpin (née Harris), Bill Gale and Noreen Battershall. Members took part in the San Remo Trial in 1955, the Paris Gymkhana in 1955, the Menton Rally in 1956 and the Munich Rally in 1957 as well as the Isle of Man scooter rally every year. Christine Gale, Ken Harris' daughter, remembers passing her scooter test on the Isle of Man at the age of 16.

During the summer months club members attended fetes to give displays and went to carnivals to act as escorts to the carnival queen. The club folded in 1965 when 'mods' and 'rockers' started causing serious trouble, particularly at seaside towns, thus making it more difficult for reputable clubs to flourish.

The opening of Bovey Tracey tennis courts on 13th July 1963. From the left: Ted Vinnicombe, Mrs Copp, Mr Dyer, Mr Copp, Mrs Wilson, Mr Wilson, Mrs Dyer, Anne Cook, Mrs Midgely, Anne Hebditch, Mrs Klinkenberg and Dr Midgely (Fran Brealey)

Above left: Bovey Spurs cycle speedway 1952. Back row, left to right: Alec Small, Andrew Waldron, Bill Holden, Denny Ball, John Small, Leonard Webber, Geoff Wills, Roy Black, Terry Wills, Bert Bond, Dennis Southwick, Jimmy Netley and Bert Maunder. Front row, left to right: Bert Powlesland, Dave Manley, Les Harris, Freddy White, Roy Small and John (Jack) Smith (H.R. Rivers, courtesy of Geoff Wills)

Above right: Ken Harris (on the left) and Don Hassall of the South Devon Vespa Club in Orchard Way. Both men made a 1,000-mile trip to the French Riviera and are shown with their winning trophy (The Torquay Times, courtesy of Christine Gale)

Football
by Nigel Call

Although football has been played in Bovey since the late 1890s, the present club was formed in about 1950 by the merger of Bovey Town, who played on the Co-op fields (proposed community centre site), and Bovey St John's, who played at the recreation ground. This merger owed much to the work of Frank French who was, at the time, the local policeman.

The earliest documented game was on 11th November 1899, when Bovey entertained Torquay United for a friendly in what was Torquay's first season. The game was refereed by a local man who, apparently, made a series of debatable decisions in Bovey's favour. Bovey took the lead from a dubious penalty and, when Torquay equalised a minute from the end, the referee promptly

Bovey Tracey AFC's victory in the Herald Cup 1961. From the left: Ken Northcott and Derek Hart (committee), Barry Henley, John Slocombe, Ian Hydon, John Smith, David Holcombe (captain), John Small, Lewis Gibbs, Ian Rowe, Alan Dawe, Norman Fone, Dennis Ward, Jack Stoneman and Sam Fogwill (committee). Bovey was the last team to receive the cup from the stand in the Newton Abbot recreation ground as it was knocked down soon after (Derek Hart)

Facing page:–

Top: Pottery United football team, 1921–2. Standing, left to right: Les Brealey, Herbie Rowe, ? Hannaford, Wallace Steer, ?, Jack Bartlett and Jack Wills. Seated, left to right: Bill Paddon, 'Esher' Steer and ? Black. Front row, left to right: Henry Wonnacot, 'Nattie' Bray, Harold Winkle, Bill Brealey and Nick Brealey (A.P. Steer, courtesy of Geoff Wills)

Lower: Football players and officials in 1957–8. Back row, left to right: Walter Kendal, Bob Barrett, PC French, Don Welsh, Ken Northcott, Eric Newbury, Fred Waldron and Mark Skelly. Middle row, left to right: Jack Stoneman (trainer), Colin Snell, Colin Maddicott, Alan Dawe, Michael Snell, Derek Stevens, Pat Mountford, John Heale, Andrew Waldron, 'Nimmy' Maunder, Ian Male, Tom Herniman and Sam Fogwill (reporter). Front row, left to right: David Holcombe, Cyril Small, Peter Beer, John Small, Les Harris (captain), John Smith, Peter Wright, David Wedden and Cecil Brealey (H.R. Rivers, courtesy of Derek Hart) played 20 minutes of injury time, then awarded another controversial penalty, and blew the final whistle as soon as Bovey had scored.

The Bovey captain apologised to his opposite number, admitting that Torquay had been the better team. The Torquay secretary took the remarks literally, recording the match as a 1-0 win to Torquay.

Don Welsh, ex-England, Torquay United and Charlton Athletic wing half, at that time landlord of the Union, took over the management of the team in 1957. In the 1957/8 season, under his guidance, Bovey had unprecedented success, coming top of the First and Second Division in the South Devon League and winning the Les Bishop Cup. Les Harris, who had started playing for Bovey in 1947, was captain of the first team from 1955 to 1959.

During this period one of the local referees was Jack Wills, who, now aged 98, remembers being a referee in Burma and India during the Second World War. He always had a reputation for being very fair, even when his own son was playing. In 1948 he was the referee for the final of the Herald Cup, played between Buckfastleigh and Babbacombe. One story he tells is of refereeing a match at Teign Village, where he sent a player off. The other members of the man's team all threatened him, saying they would get him after the match. As the game went on, Jack gradually edged his way towards the exit gate, blew the final whistle, rushed out to his bike and cycled back to Bovey Tracey as quickly as he could.

In 1961, on Good Friday, Bovey Tracey won the Herald Cup by beating Totnes, who were cup holders, in a surprise victory of 3 goals to 1. Bovey have also appeared in this final on two other occasions, in 1931/2 and 1993/4, both ending in defeat.

In 1979 the football club made its biggest purchase to date when it bought land at Mill Marsh Park. In 1984 part of this land was sold under a compulsory purchase order to assist in the construction of the Bovey bypass.

More recent times have seen the promotion of the senior side back to the Devon premier division for the 2003/4 season after a period of absence following their relegation back in 1994/5. The 2003/4 season sees the club host a total of nine sides, two senior, two youth and five junior.

The Building of the Football Clubhouse
Information from John Small and Derek and Joan Hart

The original clubhouse with its first annex built on (Derek Hart)

After the Second World War, until the 1960s, the football team used an old Nissen hut, half of which was still the town morgue, as changing rooms. Club meetings were held at the Bell Inn. This was clearly unsatisfactory, so John Small, who was chairman of the football club for about ten years, and his committee, including Derek and Joan Hart, whose connection with the club lasted for 30 years, decided to raise funds for a new clubhouse. As well as holding fund-raising events, such as bingo and jumble sales at the Bell, they made the decision in 1962 to reactivate Bovey carnival, which had been moribund for several years. Dr Jack Harrisson was asked to judge the carnival queen and, because of his connections, was able to introduce the committee to several celebrities to add to the carnival's appeal. In the first year Charlie Drake opened the carnival, and brought along Jackie Rae and Janette Scott, who were both performing in the same summer show in Torquay as he was. The committee hired a barrel organ from Torquay for four guineas and drove around all Bovey's outlying villages advertising the carnival. Most of the profit at the beginning was for the building fund but, as time went on, more money was distributed to other town organisations. The carnival committee accounts of the time give a fascinating insight into its organisation. In 1967 the football club stopped organising the carnival and a cross-organisational committee took over.

The club found a hotel in Torquay which was prepared to give it a wooden chalet on condition that the club removed it, so Ted Butt brought it back on a Harris and Miner's lorry on top of 22 tons of clay! A year later, as money was raised, showers were installed, and then an extension was built on to use as changing rooms and a committee room. Derek Hart emphasised the amazing help given by local traders and residents who, with their work, made it all possible. Eventually, they were able to install a licensed bar. Mrs Beer officially opened the new clubhouse in June 1972.

Dart team (the Red and Greens) in 1957. Back row, left to right: Dave Gardner, Philip Cleave, Mike Snell, Bob Cooper, Fred Easterbrook and Peter Wright. Front row, left to right: Alan Raisey, Cyril Small, Derek Northcott, John Small and Derek Wyatt (Alan Raisey)

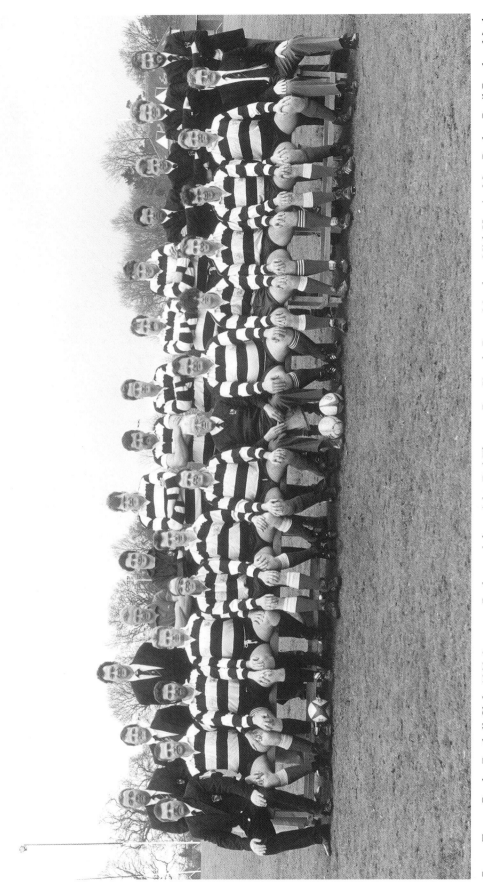

Bovey Tracey Rugby Football Club, 1992-3 season. Back row, left to right: Dyl Thomas, Ben Knock, Bruce Meechan, Nick Harris, Max Bayles, Basil Brealey, Mark Baker, Paul Nosworthy, Gerald Starling, Mark Bullock, Jonathan Baker, Cliff Paddon, Barry Hingston and Allen Malpass. Front row, left to right: Mike Steer, Steve Smith, Andy Wakefield, Mark Wavish, Paul Smith, Andy Breeze, Trevor Jackson, Toby Finch, Leroy Devonshire, Ben Metheringham, Shaun Hottot, Hugh Bayles, Nigel Lang and Steve Leigh (Dyl Thomas)

After a gap of many decades, BTRFC was reformed following England's world cup win at Twickenham in 1991. The club, which reached Devon Division II, was extremely well supported in its eight years but collapsed, like many small clubs, due to the lack of new players. Toby Finch, who is 80 in the photo, was club president. He brought with him many years of rugby experience, having played for Newton Abbot, Totnes and Devon.

Public Houses, Inns and Hotels

Information from Gladys Butler, Lynda Horrell, Bill Noon, Arthur Pritchard, Norah Davis, Barbara Carpenter, Elizabeth Hebditch, Pat Day and the regulars

There used to be a saying that Bovey had seven pubs and six and a half churches, which shows a fine balance between the sacred and the secular. Interestingly, there would have, at one time, been no such division because many public houses, or inns, were established by monks near churches to cater for pilgrims. In Bovey Tracey the earliest recorded brew houses, or apple-pounds, were situated in the Church House, where cider and ale were brewed and sold for the benefit of the church. Only later did the churches come to frown on 'the demon drink'.

In any town or village, and Bovey is no exception, both pubs and churches are always felt to be the heart of the community. But, whereas it is comparatively easy to research the history of the churches, it is much more difficult to follow the story of the pubs. Inns and pubs have always had to move with the times, so are constantly changing; rooms are altered and names are changed for all sorts of reasons. Perhaps the pub has acquired a bad name and a new landlord wants to make a fresh start; perhaps there are political reasons, as we see with the King of Prussia. Hotels come and go and, as in the case of the Riverside, change from being a private house to a hotel to a pub. Some landlords stay for years; others leave after a short time and, because they have no local roots, disappear forever.

The various directories for Devon, as well as Bovey Tracey's own town guides, tell us the names of particular landlords and, perhaps, some speciality they want to advertise, but not every pub advertised. Most of what is written below comes from local anecdote.

Pub stories are noted for being inaccurate, bawdy and possibly libellous so, sadly, some of the best stories have been left out.

The **King of Prussia** was, according to Armitage Hargreaves, named after John Carter, the famous smuggler of Prussia Cove, in Cornwall. The story is that when John Carter was a boy he heard about Frederick the Great and, for some unknown reason, decided to nickname himself after him. Later in life he built a house partly kept as an inn, which he called King of Prussia. It is suggested that, as there had possibly been evasion of excise duty in Bovey, this might have been why the inn was named after John Carter. It is said that during the First World War people, including troops stationed in the town, objected so strongly to its name that it was renamed the Heavitree Arms. It was known as this until after the Second World War, when it went back to its original name.

From the 1881 census we can see that a 51-year-old widow from Inwardleigh, Elizabeth Lavis, was the innkeeper here. At the time of the census she had three sons and a daughter, all of whom had been born in Bovey. Jack Lavis, her son, took over from her. His son, Frank, was born in the pub but was teetotal all his life. Both Noel Lavis, Frank's son, and Rita Hearder (née Lavis), Elizabeth's great granddaughter, still live in Bovey.

Claude Prowse, 'a discharged soldier', was granted the licence for the King of Prussia in October 1917. He remained landlord for over 30 years. He used to keep pigs in an orchard by the Old Manor House and paid local boys sixpence for a bucketful of acorns for his pigs. Dave Lewis remembers collecting two buckets from the oak trees on Stattons Hill and earning a shilling, of which he used 5d. to go to the pictures, 3d. for fish, 2d. for chips and 2d. to take home to his mother.

While Claude Prowse was landlord, during some building works, a mummified cat was discovered. Someone has suggested that certain items, including cats, were buried in the foundations during building to ward off bad spirits. Claude Prowse, according to Dave Lewis, kept the cat behind the bar and used it as a way to frighten troublesome customers. It became one of the pub's traditions that it was unlucky to move it, so it was passed on from landlord to landlord and is still kept on the premises.

Ted and Trixie Ingham were the next landlords, followed by Tony Kirby who was known for keeping a strict pub and for having a fantastic memory. Holidaymakers returning another year to the pub would often be surprised to hear themselves greeted by name. He was a large man who played cricket to a very high standard. His wife, Monica, was the daughter of a farmer from Moretonhampstead and well liked. A standing joke amongst locals was Tony's attitude to his fire. Whenever anyone wanted to tease him, they would poke his fire to liven it up. Tony would at once appear and roar out, 'Don't you know the price of coal?'

Gladys Davey took over from Tony Kirby, and was there from 1983 to 1989. She says that she believes there was a ghost in the pub because they could hear it moaning at night. She remembers her years there as being very happy, particularly as she met her husband, Frank Butler, when she was working there. Other landlords include Jim Coffey and Sean and Meryl Duff, who were there for about five years until early in 1997. The pub was closed for ten months for refurbishment, and then Lynda Horrell, who was born in Bovey Tracey, took over and is still there.

The **Old Thatched Inn** and the **Dolphin Hotel** are linked in an unusual way. Richard Keverne in *Tales of Old Inns*, published in 1939, says:

> *The Dolphin is worth a visit because it is an example of an old inn that deserted its original premises, took its sign to a new-built house and left the old one still standing*

The house that bore the Dolphin sign was an old thatched building, thought to date back to 1649: it was a busy place, but subject to sudden floods. Often the water came so unexpectedly into the tap room that all the customers had to rush out of it. This factor certainly influenced John Joll, its landlord, to build a new house in the 1880s. The new Dolphin Hotel was built with a traditional long room on the first floor front above the front door. Extensive stables were built around the yard. John Joll also owned the Moorland at Haytor and the coming of the railway to Bovey enabled him to arrange trips from Bovey onto Dartmoor. At Haytor the horses were changed and one route was taken down to the Golden Lion in Ashburton and the other to the Plume of Feathers in Princetown. The timetables at Paddington included these destinations.

Sometime in the 1920s Trust House Forte took over the Dolphin. It was then sold, in 1967, to Captain Blandford, who also owned the Riverside. However, he only had it for a year, during which time he closed down the kitchens.

In 1968 cousins Terry Thompson and Bill Noon, with their wives, bought the Dolphin and they stayed until 1980, putting a lot of capital into refurbishing the ballroom, installing heating, and making other improvements. Bill and Terry always wore black jackets and pinstriped trousers, and the women who worked there wore black and white uniforms. They employed their own dance band, the Dolphins, and put on cabarets at dinner dances in which guest stars from Torquay shows appeared. Bill's mother, Maisie, was in charge of the kitchen and remained so at the age of 74. Between them, they organised 120 large functions a year in the ballroom, and employed 52 members of staff at weekends.

Since retiring from the Dolphin, Bill has run other businesses, was a volunteer for the CAB for 7 years and helped start the Shopmobility, Ring and Ride and Community Transport schemes in Newton Abbot.

What had originally been the Dolphin closed as a pub and became a series of shops. For many years it was Harris', a grocery which sold everything, including coal. Later it became Parson's Dairy, and, at some stage, the Invertere Clothes Company turned it into a showroom for their goods but never used it as such. In the 1970s, as the Old Dolphin, it was a restaurant and tearooms. It was later renamed the Old Thatched Inn and, once again, became a pub.

The **Dartmoor Hotel**, across Dolphin Square, was built by J.G. Beer in the 1860s to support the newly-built railway line and was originally known as the Railway Hotel. In 1898, when Bovey Tracey experienced one of its worst floods ever and horses were unable to get through the water to

The Heavitree Arms (King of Prussia) after the First World War. The man with the bicycle is Charlie Dart, dairyman (Stan Dart)

Dolphin Square, showing the Dolphin and the Railway hotels (May Moir)

The Dolphin at night in the 1970s (Pauline Noon)

Eileen Thompson, Bill Noon, Pauline Noon and Terry Thompson (from left to right) at the Dolphin in the 1970s (Royalton Photography, courtesy of Pauline Noon)

Harris' shop (now the Old Thatched Inn) under water in 1930 (Pat Tregoning)

The Dartmoor Hotel in the 1940s. In the bus are the Leicester Nomads, a cricket team which was staying at the hotel (Arthur Pritchard)

bring home employees at the pottery, the Dartmoor Hotel opened its doors to them and other stranded people.

In the inter-war years it played an important part in Bovey's life; dances were held there regularly in its ballroom, and it was known as the place for all the young people of Bovey to go.

In 1942 Bert Pritchard, who worked as Escott in the music hall duo of Angus and Escott, bought the Dartmoor. His son, Arthur, was in the RAF, having been a court hairdresser before the war, but his wife, Sylvia, and her mother, Mrs Archer, came to run the Dartmoor, with Arthur joining them when he could. Joice Darke was a barmaid there at that time, and met her future husband, Murray Coombes, there. Arthur remembers that the American soldiers hired the ballroom as an office but, after a knife fight between black and white soldiers in which Moses Small had to intervene, the use of the office was strictly segregated. Arthur also remembers the garden at the back of the Dartmoor with its fruit trees, vegetables and chickens, all providing fresh food for the customers. During his seven years there, Arthur believed that the Dartmoor was known as the best hotel in town. (The Pritchards then moved away to other pubs but, after Sylvia died, Arthur returned to Bovey and bought Moir and Davie's garage. From there he often drove the town ambulance.)

Other memories of the Dartmoor include Cyril Small's of the large gathering of gypsies there at Christmas time. Michael Caunter remembers the fun he and some friends had there. One night, they took a sheep up to the bedrooms and let it loose. He records that the landlord was not very pleased, but there is no record of what the guests said!

Now (late 2003) the Dartmoor is boarded up and is in the process of being developed into flats or houses.

The **Riverside Inn** was originally a gentleman's private house called Bridge House and was where John Divett lived. John Divett, born in 1810 and educated at Eton and Cambridge, played an important part in Victorian Bovey. He married Henrietta Buller and, in 1843, became a partner with his brother-in-law, Captain Wentworth Buller, in the Bovey Pottery. As part of a company, he was instrumental in having a branch line of the railway brought to Bovey. When he died in 1885 his obituary said he

combined great powers of mind and memory with unswerving rectitude of purpose; he was universally respected.

He possessed his own water-cart to lay the dust outside his house, and this may have been the reason for the existence of the water tower above the old stables. The waterwheel drew water from the river up to a tank in the tower, providing enough pressure to send the water around the building for the horses and over to the main house. It was probably the first house in Bovey Tracey to have running water. The wheel was last seen working for this purpose in the 1920s.

The building which served as the stables has had a variety of owners, including the Co-op bakery, Standard Telephone and Cables, Invertere Clothing Company and, now, the Devon Guild of Craftsmen. The Bovey Band used to practise there when it was the Co-op bakery. One of the conductors was Ernie Smithers, who had played with the Black Dyke Band. The band won several cups, including first prize in Bristol in the 1950s.

After John Divett died his daughter lived at Bridge House (later Riverside House) and was there until at least 1910. She left the house to a relation, Ralegh Buller Phillpotts. He moved from Whimple to live in Bovey Tracey, bringing with him his servants who included Ivy Youlden and James Conway, his groom/chauffeur. In 1925 Ivy married Reginald Godfrey and settled in Bovey, while James Conway married Beatrice Black: the latter couple had no children but brought up Beatrice's niece, Eileen Black, now Harvey. After the First World War the Phillpotts moved to Rora House, Liverton.

Riverside House eventually became a hotel. An early undated postcard describes it as the Riverside Private Hotel owned by Mr and Mrs Nicholas Hellens. In the mid-1960s Captain R.S. Blandford, as resident proprietor, advertised the Riverside as having fifteen large bedrooms with lovely views, extensive lawns in a secluded and interesting riverside garden with rare shady trees and its own stretch of salmon and trout fishing. Sometime in the 1970s it applied for a licence and became the inn it is now.

Riverside House (Courtesy of Dave Lewis)

The **Cromwell Arms** was built as a row of tenements, including an apple-pound, brew house and apple yard. As an inn, the building was first known as the Lamb and records of it date back to 1777. In 1817 the Lamb became the Union Hotel, when Robert Hole sold the land to Thomas Loveys for £650. From White's 1850 *Directory of Devonshire* we learn that the landlady then was Eleanor Loveys.

In the 1880s the Wolfindens came to the Union Hotel. Thomas Wolfinden had ten children, one of whom, Sarah, married John Mann, Arthur Mann's grandfather. In the 1890s Mr Wolfinden began excursions to Dartmoor with a second-hand coach named the 'Vivid' and four horses. A trip to the moor was offered with a rest for luncheon and then high tea back at the Union. The drives were personally conducted by Mr Wolfinden and became very popular. Together with the Dolphin and

The Union Hotel in the early years of the 20th century (May Moir)

Railway Hotel, there were soon over 100 horses engaged on the tours during the summer months. For the first part of the 20th century these outings were for men only, and it wasn't until the late 1920s that women were included.

Dave Lewis remembers 'Hell's kitchen', a room at the back, where no ladies were allowed. He says that all the older men, including his father, Fred, used to drink cider there. One evening Alfie Davey, who only had two teeth, complained of toothache. The landlady's wife applied oil of cloves with no success so Harry Tickle, who drove a lorry for Moir and Davie's, took a pair of pliers and pulled Alfie's teeth out. Another regular was Dicky Aggett, the mole catcher who lived under a bit of galvanised iron covered with gorse beside the road to Lustleigh but later moved into Bovey to lodge with Sam Wills. Many of the older men of Bovey talk about the cider drinkers of Hell's kitchen, of how the men would queue up waiting for opening time, and of the state the men would be in after a few pints of cider. Joseph Butler remembers when dog club meetings were held in the room that had been Hell's kitchen. Henry Raisey says he remembers this bar being called thieves' kitchen, so called because if anyone wanted a salmon, trout, hare or pheasant they would go there and get it.

Henry also remembers hearing how his grandfather, keeper at Parke, supplemented his income in the hard times of the 1920s and 1930s. If he caught a good-sized badger he would boil it, then smear it with honeycomb, and sell the hams to the pubs who fed it to customers as genuine ham.

Dick Markham, an ex-navy man, was landlord after the Second World War and when he died in 1949 his wife took over. In the late 1950s the landlord was John Plenty. Norah Davis worked as a barmaid for him, and remembers him well. Peter and Tina Dewhurst, from Leicestershire, took over from him. Tina owned the boutique next door.

An interesting landlord was Don Welsh, who played for Charlton and England in the late 1930s and was at the Union in the late 1960s. He had come from managing Liverpool Football Club and was here for a few years before leaving to manage Bournemouth. Tom Booker, who lives in Cromwell's Way, and his wife, Joan, stood in for him for a few months while he made the transition

Men ready for a pub outing from The Union in the 1930s. Back row, left to right: 'Malta' Godsland (baker), 'Josh' Conian, Organ Edworthy, ?, ?, Charlie Collier, ?, Mr Rich, Jim Payne (blacksmith), Mr Brealey, Lou Steer, Bill Brealey and Charlie Amiss. Front row, left to right: ?, Charlie Hyden, A. Steer, Joe Conian, Sid Hawkes and Charlie Phillpotts (Nick Evans)

to Bournemouth. Tom was also a taxi driver for Moir and Davie's at that time. He describes Don Welsh as a real character who used to shout at the locals.

Football produced another landlord, Ted Head. He had previously been chairman of Wembley Football Club, and spent a lot on alterations in the pub, building on new kitchens and a function room. He was also supportive of local sport and gave two cups, one to the football club and one to the cricket club, for club person of the year.

At some time the Union changed its name to the Cromwell Arms, connecting it to the nearby remaining arch of the 1170 priory and known as Cromwell's Arch.

In 1997 many people in the town were upset when plans were released to turn the Cromwell into houses, and to use the car park for more building. Landlords Dorothy and John Tibble had wanted to develop the pub for their retirement. Petitions were got up and luckily the pub was sold to Phillip and Louise King. Nick Evans worked for them, and a couple of years ago took it over, thus preserving this historic pub.

The **Bell** is listed in White's Devon directory of 1850 as having George Endacott as the landlord but, unfortunately, Heavitree Breweries were unable to provide any more details about its early history. From 1929 to 1966 H.J. (Jimmy) Netley and his wife, Flo, owned and ran the Bell. Jimmy had volunteered for service in the First World War at the age of 16 by lying about his age. He had been a trumpeter in the army, spending most of the war in India. After the war he was a member of Bovey's town band, and became involved in restarting the Bovey St John's Football Club. He himself played soccer for Bovey, Heathfield and Moretonhampstead at different times, and he remained a very keen supporter of Bovey's football team, allowing the players to come to the Bell for their baths after matches.

For a few years after acquiring the Bell, Jimmy continued working at Candy's to help pay for it. At the weekends Flo cooked a copper full of pigs' trotters and sold them on Saturday evenings on a piece of bread for 3d. At that time beer cost 5d., 6d. and 7d., and cider straight from the farm cost 3d. a pint. Jimmy's daughter, Barbara, now Carpenter, remembers days out when they went to various farms to taste the cider and select it. During the war they were only able to get one barrel of beer a week, so it had to be eked out. To encourage the customers to try something else, Jimmy devised Devonshire cocktails which consisted of rough cider with a dash of gin.

Flo, as well as running the pub, was the first woman member of Bovey Tracey Parish Council and, later, was the first woman chair.

Jimmy hated giving up the Bell and, in his later years, he was often seen sitting on the seat opposite the Bell, staring mournfully at it.

The couple who took over from the Netleys only stayed a year, and then Norah and Gordon Davis took over in 1966, and stayed there for 18 years. Norah was the daughter of Louis Steer, the well-known postman, and Dorothy Thompson, whose father had a cycle shop in Bovey. Norah was brought up in the first council house built in Bovey – at Brimley – which, in 1922, had no electricity and, although it had a bathroom upstairs, only cold water. Gordon, from Leicester, had been stationed here during the war and had met and married Norah. Norah remembers lots of laughter as a landlady, but also found her role as agony aunt very demanding. She joined the Licensed Victuallers and became its chairman for three years. When Gordon and Norah left the pub their daughter, Lorraine Turner, took over and stayed there for about ten years. Norah is now caretaker for the Tracey Almshouses.

The Buffs (The Royal Antediluvian Order of Buffaloes) had their lodge in a room built onto the Bell. Louis Steer, Norah's father, was one of the founding members in the 1920s. As well as being a social organisation, it had a philanthropic purpose, particularly in supporting widows and orphans. It also had convalescent homes in Harrogate and Weston-super-Mare for members and one, in Southport, 'for the wife or other female relatives solely dependent on the member'. Norah remembers the secrecy and how the Buffs had to come through her kitchen to avoid being seen, and how they would knock three times on the door. In 1984, when Norah left the Bell, there were only six Buffs left, so they disbanded and joined the group in Moretonhampstead.

A view of Bovey showing the Bell, circa 1900 (Dave Lewis)

Jimmy and Flo Netley at the Bell (Barbara Carpenter)

Norah and Gordon Davis at the Bell (Norah Davis)

Coombe Cross Hotel in the 1960s (Elizabeth Hebditch)

Hotels have come and gone in Bovey as elsewhere. A hotel which no longer exists is the **Marlborough Hotel**. From the town guide of 1927 we read that the Marlborough Hotel was situated in the building which had been the old hospital in Marlborough Terrace. It had electric light in all its rooms, constant hot water and good bathrooms. It claimed to be patronised by leading families and said it was situated facing the proposed golf course, a proposal that never happened.

Coombe Cross was a large family house, constructed of brick with part rough cast exterior and a slated roof in about 1911. In 1952 the Misses Elizabeth and Anne Hebditch bought the house to turn it into a hotel, and it soon became a successful and well-run venture. In the late 1960s Elizabeth and Anne Hebditch pioneered specialist out-of-season holidays, which began with garden holidays but which went on to include holidays for studying local churches, birds, wild flowers, antiques and bridge. As Elizabeth Hebditch said, 'the times we wish to encourage guests to visit is obviously the time of their greatest resistance, so it's a running battle to encourage trade, keep prices competitive but make a little profit'.

In 1974 the hotel was awarded the British Tourist Authority's coveted commendation for its quality of service, food and accommodation and value for money, and, although the Misses Hebditch sold the hotel in 1984, it still flourishes today.

The **Edgemoor Hotel** had been the town grammar school until 1908. It was then known as the Edge Hill Private Hotel and officers were billeted there during the First World War. It was advertised in the Bovey Tracey town guide in 1927 as standing in its own grounds of three acres, as having electric light throughout and serving meals at separate tables. By the 1970s the town guide was advertising it as the Edgemoor, and central heating was a selling point. Rod and Pat Day took it over in 1990 and stayed there until June 2003. During their time there they employed about twenty members of staff, and, in 2001, won the West Country Cooking award for the best hotel in Devon as well as being runners-up to the best hotel in the West Country. They championed local food and always served a West Country cheeseboard. It now continues to be a successful hotel in new hands.

Bibliography

Keverne, Richard. *Tales of Old Inns*. Collins, 1939

Edge Hill Hotel (once the town's grammar school, now the Edgemoor Hotel (Dennis's Aqua-Gravure Series, courtesy of Pat Day)

Organisations

The list of clubs and societies published in *The Cottage* gives some idea of the richness and diversity of Bovey's social life today. Below is the story of some of these organisations.

The Bovey Tracey Heritage Trust
Why and How it Happened
by Nick Harman

On a cold Friday evening on 10th November 1995, in Bovey Tracey Town Hall, a small and slightly nervous band of inexperienced enthusiasts faced 106 members of the public who had come to hear why it was so important to get them out on a cold winter's evening.

Addressing the meeting were myself as chairman, Paul Williams, Brian Brett, Mavis Smith, Ronnie Elphick, Ian Carveth and John Wills. We put to the meeting our two main objectives:

1. To preserve the evidence of the past by having a system for people to donate important documents, photos and artefacts to the trust and to find a building in which to archive the material and offer it for public use.
2. To create a permanent exhibition of history open to the public.

An hour and a half later, with the formal speeches and questions from the floor answered, the hall was buzzing with chatter over coffee and biscuits. The Bovey Tracey Heritage Trust had been born. There were discussions about old houses, family characters and old property deeds as well as many a 'Did you know…' and 'I've got this amazing old photo…' An elderly, seasoned committee-type lady warned me, 'you can't be too frivolous with other people's money you know!' Little did we know then, that it would take eight years before success could be claimed.

Over the previous year or so, the local bookshop had become a meeting place for a handful of people who would chat about the remarkable state of preservation that Bovey enjoyed. The age and grandness of its old buildings, so many of them unspoilt, was apparently ignored. What was, to us, fascinating information about the old industries such as pottery, mining, agriculture, quarrying and railways needed to be shown in the context of Bovey Tracey. The list seemed endless; Saxon origins, manorial rights, church, civil war and legends all formed a rich backdrop. Many ancient features had been undisturbed by new development, making history seem very close to the surface and almost alive in the Bovey Tracey of the 1990s. Was it also the random collection of anecdotal local knowledge that made it feel this way?

Uppermost in our minds was that Bovey was on the verge of a massive change in its environment and its population. New housing was being built, and the population would grow. What would happen when the indigenous population, who have passed down memories and history by word of mouth, are outnumbered by a new wave of people who mainly have no interest in the roots of the town? How would they be educated into understanding the town's origins, to respect and preserve its ancient environment and achieve a sense of belonging? When the children of the older generation have moved away, and the old photographs, artefacts, records, dialect and memories have left for good, where would evidence of a past be then? These are the things that inspired the founding members.

Heritage Centre opened
Within weeks of its formation, the trust was offered the Old Bakery, a dilapidated building owned by Kevin Wakefield of Thomas' Bakery in Station Road. It was resolved that if the trust refurbished the building into habitable premises then it could be used, rent-free, for five years. This was no easy

path to success, however; a key founder member resigned in disagreement, but the majority were convinced that a small start was better than no start; and so it proved to be. With funds from the Rural Development Commission and a local charity, the interior was reconstructed on a small budget of about £8,000, thanks largely to a local builder, Les Black.

In 1998 the Bovey Tracey Heritage Centre was opened to the public, with a permanent exhibition of Bovey's history and a fully-indexed archives room. However, the future of the trust depended on finding a new home by the end of 2002, when the lease ran out on the Old Bakery. The Old Bakery gave the trust a start that was to pay off when the opportunity of a permanent home, combined with the chance to save an important historical building, came to pass.

Railway Station saved

The old railway station building in 2003 being prepared as the new heritage centre (Nick Harman)

The Victorian granite-built, grade II listed railway station had been derelict since the closure of the railway. It had been part of the Newton Abbot to Moretonhampstead branch line opened in 1866. In May 1999 there began speculation that the disused 'Bibby's Mill' site, which included the railway station, was to be sold for a housing development. Since the demolition of the mill buildings in 1996, no commercial interest was shown in its industrial use, so it was inevitable that pressure for housing would ensue, given the demands of the time. The trust decided to approach the owner of the site with the idea to preserve the station building - but to no avail - and sure enough, late in 1999, a planning application was received by Teignbridge District Council to build 25 houses, including the conversion of the railway station to a bungalow.

Could this be the only chance to secure the future of the heritage centre and save the railway station for the community at the same time? We had to move fast and intervene. A proposal was quickly written by myself, together with sketches from local architect Peter Hall, describing the potential use of the building as a heritage centre, railway museum and tourist attraction. Copies were sent to the chief planning officer and the town council. The town council responded quickly and, led by Councillor Anna Klinkenberg, proposed to the developer that they should donate the station building to the council for community use, and they would then lease it to the trust at a peppercorn rent. It transpired that this enabled the district council to allow a change of use to the remainder of the site for housing, and the developers naturally found that acceptable.

It took the Heritage Trust a further two years of patience to raise the £100,000 needed for the work. Funds were mostly raised from The Heritage Lottery Fund, Viridor Landfill Waste Management, and a well-known local charity. Local architect Peter Hall, of Van der Steen & Hall, steered the trustees through the design and building issues, mostly voluntarily. Local builder Bryan Cowell was contracted in May 2003 and the work was completed the following August.

The original objectives that eight years before had been placed before the public had now been finally realised. Its own building, safely in trust for the town and with a tourist income, would guarantee the existence of the heritage centre for future generations providing people wanted it, resulting in an education of the town's ancient roots and its people. It would encourage preservation of Bovey's environment and signal to those who would ride roughshod over its ancient landscape that it should not be messed with in its proud and rightful place in this beautiful corner of Devon.

Horticultural Society

A cutting from the *Mid Devon Advertiser* tells us that the Horticultural Society, then known as Bovey Tracey and District Produce Association, was established in 1863. Another cutting describes a flower show held at Indio in 1898. There were three marquees on the ground, one for vegetables and two for flowers, as well as a stall which contained useful and fancy articles, presided over by Mrs Bentinck. The proceeds were devoted to the Beneficient Society. The Bovey Tracey Band, under Mr Mountford, was in attendance.

The society was affiliated to the National Allotment and Garden Association and, in 1959, we read in the minutes of the society that the affiliation fee was increased from 6d. to 9d. per member. After some discussion it was decided to keep the member subscription at one shilling. In 1965 the society changed its name to the Bovey Tracey Horticultural Society and then, in 1968, it withdrew completely from the National Gardens and Allotment Association as it was realised that only two members had allotments.

Until 1975 the society sold fertiliser and seeds to its members, but it was a constant worry finding a storage place and then ensuring that everything was sold, so it was then decided to discontinue this service.

As well as providing series of lectures for the members on garden topics, the society holds an annual show in the summer, although it has experimented with shows at other times of the year. The summer show was, and still is, the major focus of the gardening year and creates a great deal of work for the committee. Phil Waldron, who was show manager from 1965 for 30 years, said that his main tasks were to arrange the judges for the following year's event, to organise the schedule, sort out the sponsorship, prepare the prize cards and then hope for a good season. The weather, inevitably, had a major effect on the success of the show. Inclement growing conditions in the spring could seriously affect the range and quality of items shown in the summer. Every year the committee has tried to think up new classes for the show to involve more people. The inclusion of babies and dogs in 1963 for the first time was a great success with the public, but the judges began to hate going into Bovey after the results had been declared!

In 1992, after having done all the usual work to prepare the show, Phil was woken at 2 a.m. by the police to hear that arsonists had burnt down the £40,000 marquee in which the flower show was to be held on the following day. The committee met at 6 a.m., decided that cancelling the show was out of the question and put a message out on local radio saying what had happened and asking for donations for a bring-and-buy sale. Scouts from Bovey Tracey Scout Group arrived at the site and erected four tents and tables. Many local shopkeepers produced food or gifts, the public poured in and, instead of the disaster everyone feared, it became one of the most successful shows ever. Elizabeth Hebditch, who was president at the time, said she was 'proud to belong to such a caring community who were determined not to allow an act of mindless vandalism destroy one of our outstanding local events'.

The society continues today, and the August show remains a major event in Bovey Tracey's social calendar.

The remains of the Horticultural Society's marquee after the fire in 1992 (Phil Waldron)

The Bovey Tracey Activities Trust
by Margaret Wade

The trust was formed in 1984 as a self-supporting totally independent group, assisting other local charities. The primary aim of the group is to enable those who have retired, or who are approaching retirement, to continue to lead a physically and mentally active life. This is achieved by members participating in the many activities and events organised by the trust, which is a self-help group and which pools its talents to provide classes on many different subjects. The class leaders/organisers are drawn from the membership, and the activities provided range from art, bridge, calligraphy, computer training, darts and gardening through to spinning and weaving, table tennis, whist and yoga.

The Phoenix Project began in May 1998 with an idea put forward by the then secretary of B.T.A.T., Margaret Wade. The suggestion was to apply to the National Lottery for funding towards the rebuilding of the Phoenix Hall. The old hall was in need of a new roof, was draughty and expensive to maintain; it had poor amenities and the lack of space precluded any expansion of activities to meet the needs of the trust's members. The decision was made to begin the enquiries which eventually led, in June 2001, to the award of a £180,000 National Lottery grant and the raising of a further £260,000 from trusts, foundations and the membership on behalf of the Phoenix Appeal.

A widespread search for alternative sites within or around Bovey Tracey drew a blank. Architectural plans were then drawn up to illustrate the proposed redevelopment, together with initial costs. The membership voted unanimously to remain independent and redevelop on the Phoenix site in St John's Lane, which was already owned freehold by the trust.

Margaret invited Paddy Pollock to join her on the project as chairman of the Fund-Raising Appeal, whilst she became Appeal Secretary. Poppie Lucking joined them to assist with the background work and Bernard Wade to assist with the planning permission and, later, as Project Liaison Officer. When grants started to come in Lynne Rose joined the team as Appeal Treasurer. Planning permission was eventually granted in June 2000.

Help the Aged agreed to provide advice on the way forward, but the small team, which became known as the 'Phoenix Team', had to do the actual fund-raising work and project management - and so the long job began. A feasibility study was completed in June 2000 and the business plan produced two months later. The application to the National Lottery took some six months to perfect and was submitted in October 2000. The work continued tirelessly to produce over 700 grant applications, update letters, write re-applications, make decisions and solve all the problems which arose. A success rate of 8% of actual applications resulting in grants was achieved, which is 3% above the national average (source HTA figs). All of the work was done voluntarily and for less than £2,500, a brilliant result by any standards.

Margaret Wade was elected as chairman of the trust in 2001 and immediately proposed a monitoring system that the executive committee approved and was then put into place. The initial results were staggering, showing that in the year 2000 over 9,000 visits to the old Phoenix Hall were made. In 2001, after some local promotions and the enthusiasm created by the success of the Phoenix Project, over 10,000 visits were made. In 2002, despite the trust using temporary premises whilst the construction went ahead, attendances did not decline and, in fact, were a 1,000 more than in the previous year. This proved beyond doubt the increasing need for the trust's services.

As the construction phase commenced Bernard Wade, as Project Liaison Officer, became the link between the architect (as team leader) and B.T.A.T. As with any project of this size problems arose along the way and he dealt with these, consulting with colleagues and professionals alike, with the efficient manner learned from his 40-year record in the building industry.

Fund-raising, with the help of the membership, continued throughout the project period and many events took place; craft sales, auctions, dinners, lunches, quizzes, spring and summer fairs, and evenings with a theme to dress up, with much fun being had by all. In addition to the money raised, the free reserves of the trust were pledged, which, with the internal fund-raising, gave a total of £25,000 and demonstrated the commitment, support and dedication of members past and present.

Members were consulted about the type of new classes/activities/social events they wanted to see in the new Phoenix Hall. This resulted in no less than 90 people registering an interest in computer training, many of whom would be first-time users. In addition, a further 14 subjects and activities were suggested, including short mat bowls, table tennis, local history, singing for pleasure, film nights, woodwork, creative writing, calligraphy and others. One of the objectives was to deliver what the members would support and provide the environment for continued success.

The Phoenix Project was never just about creating the bricks and mortar, but about the opportunities that the building would offer to members through a programme of self-help, independence and delivering services through volunteering. The chairman and committee stuck to these principles throughout and encouraged all members to find the level at which they were happy to volunteer. Whether that was leading a class or activity group, or making the coffee at a Wednesday meeting, members found a way to become involved, which was what the project intended.

On 18th November 2002 the new Phoenix Hall was ready. Four hundred people attended two 'open days' and were amazed at what had been achieved in what was locally a fairly low-key fund-raising campaign. As at March 2003 membership, Wednesday attendance, class attendance and class/activities on offer all stand at record levels.

Since the grand opening, Margaret and Paddy have also raised the funds to equip and install the hardware for the I.T. suite and sufficient to keep it going for at least one year at no cost to the trust. Margaret has also taken on the job of co-ordinator for the facility and recruited a small band of volunteer members to help deliver computer training to members, and a professional trainer to help 'train the trainers'. In April 2003 all nine courses on offer were fully booked. A waiting list was immediately started, and the next phase is being planned.

Although the Phoenix Project will not be finalised until the end of 2003, it is already a magnificent tribute to the Phoenix fund-raising and project management team who brought the construction to completion within budget, and to specification. It has been a triumph of perseverance over adversity - a lasting, tangible inheritance for members present and future and insurance that the charitable work of the Bovey Tracey Activities Trust can continue.

The old Phoenix Hall in 2001 (Margaret Wade)

The new Phoenix Hall in 2003 (Margaret Wade)

A Brief History of the Bovey Tracey Players
by Anne Broom

*'Suit the action to the word, the word to the action…
the purpose of playing…was and is to hold, as 'twere,
the mirror up to nature'. Hamlet, III.2.17-22*

Like the drama it stages, The Bovey Tracey Players can trace its inception to the Church. Historically, drama has its roots in religion. From the late 10th century, Mystery and Miracle plays performed around the country in churches and, later, in city streets brought the Bible alive. On Good Friday, 9th April 1971, a simple presentation for Passiontide and Easter entitled *In Three Days* was performed in Bovey Tracey's Parish Church of St Peter, St Paul and St Thomas of Canterbury. The cast included Arthur Mann, electrician Larry Copp, local potter Jeremy Leach, Barbara Weeks and Mary Leathlean. That October a constitution was drawn up and The Bovey Tracey Players was officially formed.

On 20th and 21st December the society staged its first Nativity, *A Miracle Play.* With basic costumes and props, a small cast acted out the Christmas story. Lighting technician Michael Hynd enthralled the audience by projecting a star high on the church's magnificent barrel roof, while Benjamin Cartwright, as the Archangel Gabriel, made a spectacular entrance over the choir stalls. Directed by founder member Joan Bailey, the cast included Nancy Collins, Marjorie Milne and Sam Wilson, with Sheila Iley as prompt. It was stage-managed by James Brown, the society's first chairman, a position that he held for many years. Eventually elected The Players' first president, James re-mained actively involved with the society throughout his life. A society stalwart and churchwarden, he was indefatigable, building sturdy portable staging and, despite his small stature, moving the sets with incredible energy. He worked hard to raise funds. Whether selling tickets or promoting the society's shows, none could refuse James's persuasive salesmanship.

With a growing and enthusiastic membership, the society elected to put on a programme of one-act plays at the Wickham Hall. Entrance on 8th August 1972 was by programme/ticket costing 15p, with coffee and soft drinks on sale in the anteroom during the second interval. Three contrasting plays were

The shepherd pipes his tune. David Iley in 'A Folksong Nativity' at Bovey Tracey's Parish Church of St Peter, St Paul and St Thomas of Canterbury, December 1986 (Anne Broom)

Pantomime glamour in 'Robinson Crusoe' at the town hall in February 1996. From left to right: Louise Goodbody (Queen Jingo), Annette Vaitkus (Robinson Crusoe) and Norman Broom (Dame Amelia Crusoe) (Anne Broom)

chosen. In J.B. Priestley's whimsical *The Rose and Crown*, directed by Marjorie Milne, the cast included Anne Broom as The Stranger, with Gillian Harwood as Ma Peck. *The Dear Departed*, a play by Stanley Houghton, was produced by Val Nickless with a six-strong cast, including Jeremy Nickless, James Brown and Beryl Baber, while the comedy *Waiting at the Church* by L. du Garde Peach was performed by the town's Women's Institute's drama group under Joan Bailey's direction. That autumn, The Players took a major step forward with its first three-act play. *Breath of Spring*, a comedy by Peter Coke, was directed by Joan Bailey, with Benjamin Cartwright as the Brigadier and Audreay Harrisson, wife of retired local doctor Jack Harrisson, as Lily the Maid. A hit with audiences, its success encouraged the society to move forward in new directions.

Costumes were begged, borrowed and made over, jumble sales being a fruitful source of suitable material. With slim finances, funds were raised by every possible means, from selling scrap metal, newspaper and cardboard, to in-house entertainment. Performance royalties and room hire represented a major outlay, and additional income from raffles manned by the chairman's wife, Irene Brown, also a founder member, helped offset expenses.

Following the drama *A Letter from the General* staged in June 1973, the society branched out into variety shows. Directed by Audreay Harrisson, with Sidney Weeks as pianist and Geoff Wills on drums, *The Good Old Bad Old Days* (August) and *Christmas Pie* (December) attracted many new members. The summer carnival was an opportunity to take The Players into the community. With a borrowed tractor and trailer, hospitality from David and Elizabeth Weddon, several straw bales, a piano with Sidney Weeks at the keyboard and a flagon of cider, a colourfully-dressed crowd sang its way around the town to entertain the crowds. Autumn 1974's production was a major challenge with the choice of Jean Anouilh's *Ring Round the Moon*. Directed by Elizabeth Lycett Steele, the cast included Michael North in the dual role of identical twin brothers, local schoolteacher Travis Billington, and Angela Browning, who, in later years, entered Parliament as Conservative MP for Tiverton and Honiton. That Christmas *A Dickensian Evening* in the parish church continued the Nativity tradition.

Looking to encompass more sophisticated staging with larger performance and audience space, the society moved to the town hall in spring 1978, where Patricia Berry directed Coward's comedy *Nude with Violin*. Renting storage space in the bay next to the old fire station for The Players' props, costumes and lighting was to prove fortuitous. On a night when storms threw the town into total darkness, in the best theatrical traditions the show went on. Actors continued their performance of the farce *Rookery Nook* on a stage lit by the fire brigade's two powerful searchlights.

In January 1980 the society was ready for a new challenge. Putting immense energy into its first pantomime, *Robin Hood,* directed by John Wills, it had a huge cast. Its writer, Patsy Wills, was principal boy. News reached television's TSW, who sent a camera crew and reporter to film part of the dress rehearsal. The Players' pantomimes became huge successes, with photographer Bim Bolland writing, directing and acting in several clever and sophisticated productions. For *Dracula and the Magic Lamp* (1998), The Players gained an Arts Lottery award to fund professional scenic design, music and dance.

As members of the South Devon Drama Federation the society has won many awards competing against other societies throughout the area in the annual drama festival. From their first major award of Best Overall Production in March 1977, with Enid Bagnold's *The Chalk Garden* directed by Patricia Berry, they have gained numerous nominations, certificates and trophies. More recently, there have been successes in Teignmouth's drama festival, with society veteran David Iley adjudged Best Actor in 2003.

The society, actively involved in community events where possible, finds that a traditional Christmas Mummers' Play scripted and directed by Anne Broom remains popular, the story of St George and the Turkish Knight retold through lively street theatre. Over the years the society has presented plays by a wide range of dramatists, including Chekhov, Moliere, W. Somerset Maugham, Agatha Christie, Aykbourne, Stoppard and Ben Elton.

The Nativity Play remains a tradition of The Players. With its candlelit procession and seasonal music, this biennial presentation in the town's ancient church is a unique experience for both actor and audience. Each production is a new challenge. For every member of The Players there is hard work, a few tears and a great deal of laughter.

Bovey Tracey Women's Institute
by Rosemary Barker

Bovey Tracey WI was formed in October 1947 in the Temperance Hall, with Mrs Beryl Tanner as president. It was proposed that they move to the Baptist room 'as it had china', but this proved too small so they then moved to the Wickham Memorial Hall, where they still meet on the second Monday of the month. The original rent was ten shillings.

At the first meetings, eight members 'taken alphabetically from the register should be in charge of teas' and 'all should bring their own eatables'. Now three members bring cakes and help serve tea each month.

In August 1950 the WI wrote to the Devon General Bus Company asking 'if a service could be arranged from Bovey Tracey to Exeter, or the Plymouth to Exeter bus could come through Bovey Tracey'. We have no record of the bus company's reply, but a bus does now come from Plymouth to Exeter through Bovey Tracey, so perhaps the WI letter had some effect.

At this time 'fruit canning arranged for the first week in July after school hours' was offered, presumably to help people who had a surplus of fruit but no traditional skills to provide for the coming winter.

In April 1953, to commemorate Queen Elizabeth II's coronation, it was suggested a flowering shrub should be planted in the cemetery, but members felt a seat would be more useful, so council permission was sought for a seat at Mount Pleasant. The seat cost £7 plus £2 10s. for the plaque and was presented to the town council on 30th April 1954. The seat was restored with a new plaque to celebrate the Bovey Tracey's WI's golden jubilee in 1997 at a cost of over £100.

In 1999 it was felt there was a need for an evening WI, attracting members not free during the day. Parke WI was formed in September 1999, meeting on the first Thursday evening of the month, initially at the Phoenix Hall and subsequently at the Wolleigh Golf Club.

In 2003 both WIs are still providing friendship, education and entertainment and are actively involved in local events, either singly or together.

The presentation of the coronation seat by Bovey Tracey WI to Bovey Tracey Town Council on 30th April 1954. Seated, left to right: Mrs F. Rice (WI treasurer), Mrs B. Upham (WI secretary), Mrs G. Rogers (WI president) and Major General D.T. Cowan (council chairman) (H.R. Rivers, courtesy of Rosemary Barker)

Bovey Tracey Amenities Society
by Tony Kightley

The society seems to have been started by Francis D'Ath in the late 1970s with Don Higgin, of Ashwell in East Street, who was associated with it from the beginning. In 1980 Don took over as chairman and, within a short time, it was a thriving organisation with membership approaching 200 at one point in the late 1980s. There was a committee of around 12, and Dorreen Black was its secretary for many years. As now, it combined monthly open meetings of general interest with committee and special meetings which dealt with matters of concern about planning and other matters in the town. Letters were sent quite often to the town council and to Teignbridge District Council concerning matters which the society thought needed attention. In fact, the society got a reputation for being rather a 'thorn in the flesh' to the town council. At one point, after a meeting with the chief planning officer for T.D.C., the society even considered making a planning application for a multi-purpose meeting hall in Mill Marsh Park. As this park is 'sacred ground' to the town council, this did not go down very well!

The society could certainly not be criticised for being inactive during this period of its existence, for it also put a float in the annual carnival procession for several years. Meetings were held in the Cromwell Arms for some time and then in the hall attached to the Catholic Church until this was damaged by fire. After that the society met in the Dolphin Hotel for a while, but now meets in the Methodist Church Hall.

Don Higgin was chairman for 11 years and then, in 1991, John Wigney took over. He soon became very active on the society's behalf, to the extent of representing the society - together with Maurice Simmons on many occasions - at meetings of the Devon Alliance of Amenity Societies and Devon Conservation Forum in Exeter, and further afield at seminars on planning matters, for example. About this time the committee was much smaller than previously, and the society became more co-operative with the town council rather than critical of it.

In 1992, following a recommendation by the Civic Trust, the society changed its name to Bovey Tracey and District Society, the intention being to broaden its influence. The committee dwindled in numbers and John ran the society almost single-handedly, with Colleen Loughton as secretary. When, in accordance with the constitution, he had to resign at the 1994 AGM after 3 years in office no-one was forthcoming to take his place. However, several people new to the town were persuaded to join the committee and, one of these, Peter Hall, became the chairman. John Wigney gradually withdrew from an active role in the society and Peter and Paul Beecher have continued to be either chairman or vice-chairman ever since. When, in 1995, Colleen became ill, Phyllis Crouch took over as secretary and, a few years later, Tony Kightley took over from Phyllis, who became speakers' secretary. This latter office was recently taken on by John Richards. The treasurers over the years have been David Anderson, Mary Wigney, Peter Taylor and Tony Kightley. The society changed its name back to the original one in 1996.

Throughout its life the society has kept an eye on local affairs and when, on two occasions, there was a possibility of a supermarket being built in the town, it canvassed local opinion and sent the results to the town council. Recently the threat of clay extraction on the edge of the town spurred the society to get the inhabitants to write letters of protest. Very many other matters of lesser importance have been aired and commented upon, where necessary, over the years. The society has been in close contact with the town council on many matters, and a committee member reckoned to attend each full town council meeting. For the last few years Tony Kightley has obliged and a report of the meeting appears in *The Cottage*. Also, it is now an annual custom for councillors to come to talk to the members about council affairs. Several committee members have been involved in local forums and similar ventures over the years.

The Devon Guild of Craftsmen
Information from Christine Halstead

Today one of Bovey's best-known attractions for visitors is the Riverside Mill, home of the nationally-renowned Devon Guild of Craftsmen. This was founded in 1955 by a group of makers who were enthusiastic about the idea of promoting the best in regional craftwork. From 1956 until 1986 they had an annual exhibition in venues in South Devon, and, although these were very well received, there was always the idea that it would be beneficial to have a permanent home of their own.

In 1986 Michael Skipwith saw that the Riverside Mill in Bovey Tracey was for sale, and somehow the money was raised from loans and grants to buy it. The mill was opened with a summer exhibition and a small shop. Soon afterwards the cafe was opened, and then the upstairs gallery.

Later, the guild became a charity with broadly educational aims. Its Big Hand, Little Hand scheme, for instance, takes craftspeople into schools for varying lengths of time to work with the children.

Exciting refurbishment is due to take place in 2004, when a new gallery will be built and the cafe moved upstairs, where, it is hoped, it will remain the centre of much of Bovey's social life.

Overleaf: The Riverside Mill, home of the Devon Guild of Craftsmen (Robert Hesketh)

Bovey People

History books have traditionally focused on royalty, politicians and industrialists – the people who have shaped society – but, in this section, we have included some people who are well known as well as others who may not be known outside Bovey and yet, together with their families, have played an integral part in creating its rich diversity. Bovey families not written about here have, in most cases, been mentioned elsewhere in this book.

Canon Courtenay
by Joan Robertson

Canon Courtenay (B.T. Heritage Trust)

The Reverend Honourable Charles Leslie Courtenay was a towering figure in Victorian Bovey, and his legacy can be seen in almost all that survives of that period. He was born in 1816, the youngest son of the 10th Earl of Devon and the brother of William and Henry, who were destined to become the 11th Earl of Devon and 13th Earl of Devon respectively during his lifetime: he also had an older sister named Harriet. After being educated at Christ Church, Oxford, where he was a contemporary of Keble, Pusey and Newman, founders of the Oxford Movement and Catholic revival, he became, in 1842, domestic chaplain to Queen Victoria. He was a great favourite of the queen, who admired 'his subdued temper, his sensitiveness and his studious character'. He married her lady-in-waiting, Caroline Somers-Cocks, in June 1849, and a month later he was presented to the living of Bovey Tracey. He was appointed Canon of Windsor in 1859, with the precentorship of St George's Chapel, Windsor.

When he arrived at the Parish Church of Ss Peter, Paul & Thomas he found matters not to his liking. Holy Communion was celebrated only five times a year, the vicarage was in a state of disrepair, and there were many aspects of the church that needed reforming. Very soon after he arrived he decided to build St John's Church at his own expense. It was suggested that he went to St John's to preach 'Romanism' and then went back to the Parish Church of Ss Peter, Paul & Thomas to preach 'Non-Conformism'. His reply to that charge was 'as a matter of fact I preached the same sermon in both Churches'.

He founded the Devon House of Mercy, built the National School and set up the Mission House (now named Courtenay House) to care for the sick of the parish under the administration of the Clewer Sisters. He organised an evening school, which provided adult classes, a lending library and a Sunday School clothing club. Books, mainly bibles and prayer books, could be bought at a discounted price and paid for by instalments at the vicarage. He also said, 'Any respectable married women making application at the Vicarage a month before she is likely to want them can have the loan of baby linen and things necessary together with a packet of groats and half a pound of soap'. He was responsible for restoring the parish church largely at his own expense and also rebuilt the vicarage, now known as Grey Gables.

He died in October 1894 aged 78 years and, after the service of 'vespers of the dead' in the parish church, his body was taken to St John's, where it remained throughout the night at the chancel steps, attended by devoted friends. On the following day six Masses were celebrated before a Requiem Mass took place, which was attended by his widow, other relatives, including Lord and Lady Halifax, and a large number of his parishioners. In accordance with his wishes, Canon Courtenay was laid in an ordinary earth grave, which was lined with ivy and chrysanthemums and situated in front of the east window of the chancel. On the announcement of his death, Queen Victoria sent a telegram and personal letter of condolence to his widow. A bell was tolled from the Curfew Tower at Windsor Castle and a memorial service was held at St George's Chapel, Windsor, at the same time as the funeral was being held at St John's Church.

The biography of Earl Somers records that Canon Courtenay lived in an impressive style with innumerable servants and drove in a carriage between the two churches preceded by an outrider sounding a horn. From Canon Courtenay's will, we learn that the gross value of his personal estate was £2,498 11s. 4d.

His wife, Caroline, cared greatly for the welfare of her husband's parishioners, especially in teaching the girls at the pottery how to read and write and providing them with clothing. She was of a delicate disposition and only went out in a conveyance on fine days. She died two weeks after her husband, having, it is believed, caught a cold at her husband's funeral. Although she went to the funeral in an enclosed bath-chair, she stepped from it to drop a bunch of violets into the grave. Pleurisy developed and this was followed by pneumonia, which proved fatal.

The *Western Morning News* of 16th November 1894 stated that

... a heavy gloom hangs over Bovey and the sorrow is general, as the Vicarage has been for nigh half a century a centre of help and sympathy for all...whoever is appointed will be a poor successor to the good departed vicar and his lamented lady, unless he is fond of hard work, has great tact, a long purse and a heart full of sympathy.

They had no children, but Canon Courtenay's memory lives on today in Bovey Tracey through the buildings in the town and the memorials erected to him.

The Black Family and their association with Bovey Pottery
by Andrea Herat

In 1874 Dinah Black gave birth to her thirteenth and last child, Ellen. All of her surviving children were given Dinah's maiden name, Loveys, as their middle name. Dinah and her husband, John, lived in Chudleigh Knighton and Halford (Liverton) before moving to Higher Mill, Bovey Pottery, and settling at Pottery Cottages. Higher Mill housed machinery for making the pottery slip in a huge vat, with circulating paddles to keep the slip mixture smooth. If this machine stopped working during the night, it was John's job to ensure that it started working again.

By the age of 16, Ellen was already employed as a biscuit painter at the Bovey Pottery Company Limited. The pottery had employed her father, John, and a number of her brothers, John (labourer), James (printer), George, Albert and Henry (potters).

Albert had started work at the pottery at the age of 12 and almost certainly met his future wife there. Emma Cooper had relocated from Burslem, Stoke on Trent, to assist in teaching hand-painting skills. They married at Newton Abbot Registry Office in 1892. During their married life Albert and Emma lived at Belle Vue, Liverton, and Albert walked to work every day. Belle Vue had been built by the Divett family, who also owned the pottery, and housed the workers from Staffordshire when they first moved to the area. Albert spent all his working life at the pottery, finally retiring at the age of 72.

Albert's siblings all married into local families, including Loveys, Pinsent, Webber and Tolley, living in and around Bovey Tracey.

Not surprisingly, it would seem that James also met his wife at the pottery. She was Elizabeth Coysh Lethbridge, who worked as a transfer printer. They married in 1885. Five years later James was widowed when Elizabeth died, probably giving birth to their fourth child. Elizabeth was the first person to be buried in the Bovey Tracey Cemetery on 8th June 1890. By the time Christmas arrived around twenty individuals in the town had been buried there. Four of these were members of the Black family. They included James' daughter, Elizabeth Evela, aged 5 months, and his brother, John, aged 36. With three young daughters under the age of 5, life for James was certainly not easy. Help arrived in the form of Elizabeth's cousin, Lucy Paddon, who James later married in 1894. They had a further ten children, a number of whose descendents are still living locally today.

James Loveys Black was one of the founder members of the Bovey Tracey Co-operative Society, serving on the board and as president. He was also chairman of the local Rational Friendly Society. A well-known member of the Plymouth Brethren for over 60 years, James worshipped at the Gospel Hall in Mary Street and often conducted the services. He lived to the age of 85, and is also buried in the Bovey Tracey Cemetery.

The Black family had a long association with the Bovey Tracey Pottery Co. The pottery had opened in 1843, and, from circa 1880 until its closure in 1956, four generations of the family had worked there. The pottery had been the largest employer in the town, and many local families will, no doubt, identify with this example of a family whose lives were inextricably linked with its employment.

James Loveys Black (Andrea Herat)

The Steer Family
by Michael Steer

It is entirely possible for a visitor to ask several of the many Steers in Bovey whether or not they are related to certain other Steers in the town, and discover, with surprise, that they believe they are not related. In many instances their belief is the result of so many of the family having resided in Bovey for well over 500 years. The surname itself is Anglo-Saxon in origin and derives from Sture or Stiur, meaning a young ox. In Devon the name is fairly common in the South Hams, in and around Crediton, west through South Tawton, South Zeal and Okehampton, and is found in the early records of several North Devon parishes. The very earliest record of the name was as Ster, Stur or Stir in the Domesday Book in a number of places throughout northern and southern England, although not in Devon. The earliest recorded Steers in Bovey were Robert Stuer, or Steere, alias Clarke (born about 1520) and his wife, Tomsyn or Thomasin, and Joanna Sture (also recorded as Steere) alias Clarke, who married John Frenche in 1557. Robert and Tamsyn are named in the 1541 Lay Subsidy Roll for the parish, and in 1544 Robert paid a property tax of £2. They seemed to have lived either at Crownley or at a place in the parish then called Stantor. He and Tamsyn had eight children whose surnames were recorded in the parish registers as Sture, Stewer, Steur and Steere, the spelling in those days being phonetic and varying at the whim of the priest or clerk who was the recorder. Over the next several centuries the name underwent several changes until it became standardised by about the 1720s as Steer throughout Devon.

The Steer family photographed in 1915. Back row, left to right: Cecil Ewart b 1897, Rosaline Norah b 1890, Edward Louis b 1892, Salome Winifred b 1888 and Walter Roland b 1896. Front row, left to right: Sidney Horace b 1894, Edwin b 1853, Linna (née Seller) b 1863 and Arthur Percy b 1899 (Norah Davis)

In 1642 the Protestation Returns for Bovey indicate that there were at that time nine male Steeres listed as heads of households. In 1861 and 1891 there were 10 Steer heads of households, many with very large families by today's standards. The 1901 census for Bovey reveals 32 male and 18 female Steers, with clusters of the family at Newton Abbot, Plymouth and in the surrounding parishes. Little wonder then that there should be confusion about relationships between members of its many branches.

Census data indicate that the majority of Bovey Steers were either agricultural labourers or tradesmen; carpenters, tailors and stonemasons. With the advent of the potteries, several found employment as potters, kiln men and printers. The Public Records Office has preserved a copy of the 1845 will of Grace Steer of Indeo and the 1851 will of Thomas Steer, Blacksmith, of Bovey Tracey. They both seem to have been relatively well off.

Perhaps the jewel in the family crown and its black sheep was Joseph Steer (1776-1856) who, with his brother, Thomas (mentioned in Lyson's *Magna Britannia*), were proprietors of the old Bovey Pottery at Indio. Initially the Bailiff (or Steward) of Wifford, Joseph was, by 1826, an Overseer of the Poor for the parish and, by 1832, had styled himself Gentleman. He had, in 1814 and 1817, been required to pay £2 18s. 0d., and maintenance of 2/6d. a week as 'father of Elizabeth Rich's female bastard child'. In his will (also preserved at the PRO) he left Bridge End Cottage in Bovey to Jane Ann Mead, daughter of his servant, Elizabeth Pinsent, and 'born before her mother's marriage' with the provision that her mother 'shall be entitled to reside, occupie [sic] or let and take the rent of the above house until Jane Ann Mead shall attain the age of 21 years'.

Over the centuries few Steers seem willingly to have left the town. Among the several who did, Joseph Steer was, in 1869, a Trinity House Lighthouse keeper in Guernsey. In 1871 he, with his large family, was at the Start Lighthouse, and in 1881 at the Menai Lighthouse off Anglesey.

The Bovey marriage registers link the Steer family over the centuries with White, Taylor, Langworthy, Rackwood, Denley, Heward, Rowland, Satterley, French, Tapper, Cruse, Wills, Coniam, Tapley, Gribble, Stonelake, Smale, Brown, Curnow, Manley, Christopher, Carpenter, Frost, Clampitt, Smith, Hart, Leaman, Yard, Lamble, Creed, Lavers, Sellers, Slee, Weeks, Caunter, Holmes, Davis, Coombes, Ridd and many more old Devon family names.

Michael Steer, son of Ron and Cora Steer, was born in Bovey, but now lives in Australia.

Edwin Steer - Parish Water Bailiff
by John Parnell

Edwin Steer, the illegitimate son of Sarah, was born in Hind Street on 1st February 1853. When the census was taken in March 1861, Edwin was staying in Fore Street with his grandparents, Joseph and Mary.

Joseph and his father, also named Joseph, earned their living as carpenters. Edwin, however, wanted to be a policeman, and in 1881 he was a member of the Metropolitan Force living in Middlesex. Unfortunately for Edwin, ill health meant an early retirement and he returned to Bovey. There he started to court Linna Seller, who was a lady's maid at Parke. They were married in 1887 in the Honiton area but made their home in Bovey, in Mary Street, convenient for Edwin's work as a potter.

Edwin and Linna raised two girls and five boys, the oldest three boys all serving in the Devonshire Regiment during the First World War. The family group photograph was taken during 1915 at the rear of The Retreat, 8 Abbey Road.

Edwin Steer was a devoted Baptist, and a story exists in the family that when his son, Sidney, died in 1915 at the early age of 21 he wept for weeks afterwards. His diary contains several poems written in a beautiful copperplate hand, one of which refers to the death of a son.

In addition to his duties as water bailiff to Bovey parish, Edwin was retained as a road worker by Newton Abbot Rural District Council. These positions he held for over 20 years. Edwin served with the Bovey Tracey Fire Brigade for many years and possessed the Long Service Medal. He was made an honorary member on his retirement.

Edwin Steer died at his home in Abbey Road on 15th February 1927. He was 74 years old and had maintained an active life almost to the end. A widow and grown-up family were left to mourn his passing. The long-time servant to his local community was widely missed, and Edwin was fittingly given full fire brigade honours at his funeral.

The funeral of Edwin Steer in 1927, showing the cortege passing the Union Hotel (now the Cromwell Arms) (Norah Davis)

Dame Violet Wills
Information from Mary Twist and Gwen Leamon

Although not strictly a Bovey person, Dame Violet Wills was such a benefactor to the town that she has to be included in this section. She was the daughter of Edward Payson Wills, a director of Imperial Tobacco, and brother to Sir Ernest Salter Wills, 'the tobacco magnate'. There is an unsubstantiated story that, in her earlier years, Violet Wills had fallen in love with the son of a well-known Devon landowner who belonged to a Roman Catholic family. The Wills family put pressure on her, and she is said to have given him up, living the life of a recluse thereafter. Many older residents in Bovey have described her in these terms, saying she was rarely seen out. In 1923 she moved to Torquay to live with her widowed sister, Ella Rowcroft, and, in 1926, she moved to Bel Alp, near Haytor, with its stunningly beautiful views. This had been built in 1906, but Violet had it extensively altered before moving in. As well as Bel Alp, Violet bought the houses around her and rented them out to friends or members of staff. Her sister bought nearby Blueburn, although she continued to give her address in Torquay. Violet Wills also owned houses in Torquay, run on Christian lines, to which she sent clergymen and missionaries of all denominations for rest, as well as those in need of a holiday home when on furlough.

The whole Wills family were noted benefactors, endowing Bristol University among other acts. Ella Rowcroft gave £135,000 to make the building of Torbay Hospital possible, and, of course, was responsible for the setting-up of the Rowcroft Hospice. In the coronation honours of 1937 Violet Wills was created dame. Among her gifts to the West Country were a first-aid ship to the National Mission to Deep Sea Fishermen, named and dedicated in Brixham, and big donations to the Maynard School and St Luke's College in Exeter. Specific gifts to Bovey Tracey included money for the district hospital, the new fire engine, a mowing machine for the cricket club, and a new chapel for Hawkmoor. The *Western Morning News* of 11th May 1937 described her as 'the lady bountiful of the Westcountry'.

An interesting glimpse of a more personally generous side is given by Gwen Harwood (now Leamon) who lives in Tracey Vale. In 1937, at the age of 17, she went in service to the three Worsfold sisters who rented Older Town Shotts from Dame Violet, and were friends of hers. Gwen stayed there 25 years. She remembers getting a very bad attack of quinsy and Dame Violet sending beef tea round for her. Because she took some time to recover, Dame Violet sent her down to Rowcroft in Torquay to recuperate, and that year gave Gwen a pair of fur gloves for Christmas. Gwen was very friendly with Audrey Barnes, Dame Violet's kitchen maid, and one day they were late back from walking on the moor so started running. They met Dame Violet and Princess Marie Louise, Queen Victoria's granddaughter, who used to come and stay with Dame Violet, and were chided for being unladylike. Gwen said, 'You always had to be prim and proper'. Whenever Gwen called on her friend at Bel Alp they both had to go and see Dame Violet and have a chat with her.

Gwen Leaman (née Harwood) in her uniform (Gwen Leaman)

Dame Violet was known for two idiosyncrasies. In spite of her great wealth coming from tobacco, she was vehemently opposed to smoking and forbade anyone who worked for her to smoke. Gwen remembers that as soon as Dame Violet left the premises, the gardeners would start smoking. She was also the owner of a blue Rolls-Royce, bought in 1929 and mentioned by the people of Bovey. It was one of only a handful of its kind in the country, built during a transitional period between the phasing out of one model and the introduction of another.

After the war it became more and more difficult to get staff, so houses on the estate were gradually sold off and Dame Violet moved to Clevedon. She died in October 1964. Bel Alp was sold and is now a flourishing country hotel.

David Leach

David Leach, recognised as one of the most important potters in the 20th century, was born in 1911 in Tokyo, the eldest son of Bernard Leach. He lived in Japan until he was nine, when the family returned to Britain. David intended to be a doctor but, in 1930, he started working with his father at the St Ives pottery and then took over the management of the pottery in 1937. He worked in partnership with his father from 1946 until 1956. At this time he decided he needed to develop creatively away from his father's influence so moved to Lowerdown Pottery in Bovey Tracey with his wife, Elizabeth, and his sons, John, Jeremy and newly-born Simon. The house had previously belonged to the Ehlers. Lily Ehlers was a potter who had earlier worked with Lucie Rie making buttons, so the house already had a pottery studio complete with an electric kiln. David quickly turned to the making of electrically-fired slipware and tin-glazed ware, with the intention of doing this until he built a stoneware kiln, a task which was completed in 1961.

When the boys left home the original house seemed too large, so the Leaches commissioned the architect Ann Horlock Stringer to design a spacious modern house to be built in the grounds. At the pottery is a showroom from which at least a quarter of what is made is sold direct to the public.

David has always been involved in education. He was instrumental in starting the Dartington Pottery Training Workshop and became involved in the establishment of the Devon Guild of

Craftsmen in 1955. He played a major part in helping it find its permanent home in the Riverside Mill in 1986. He was a visiting lecturer at many art schools as well as helping individuals develop their own skills when working with him. He has a strong belief in the apprenticeship system, and has had many potters working with him at his studio. Some have stayed for a couple of weeks; others, such as Richard Brooks, an Australian potter, came as a 19-year-old from Sidney and stayed for two years.

His philosophy as a potter is always to look 'for the whole integrated pot'. He believes in 'good design, simple, direct, but skilled making, complementary glaze and decoration. No virtuosity or unintegrated eyecatching deviations'. A pot should have 'something of the identity and integrity of its maker'.

In 2003 a major retrospective exhibition of his work took place at the Devon Guild of Craftsmen and then went on tour around Britain and on to two venues in Japan. This contemporary and historical work by David Leach celebrated his importance and the lasting contribution he has made to the world of pottery over the past 70 years.

David Leach in his studio, June 2003 (John Adey)

Dr Frank Arnott
Information from Robert Arnott

Over and over again Dr Arnott has been described as an 'old-fashioned family doctor' who made his patients feel better just by visiting them. Frank Arnott was born in Scotland and, at the age of 17, enlisted for service in the First World War. He fought in Gallipoli and was evacuated to Malta. After the war was over he finished his medical studies at Glasgow University and then came to Bovey Tracey as partner to Dr Andrews. He met and married Catherine Farquarson, whose family lived at Whitstone. The couple bought Moorlands in East Street, eventually having three children.

As well as being in general practice, Dr Arnott became involved in the setting up of the new Bovey Tracey Hospital in the early 1930s.

He served in the Territorial Army and volunteered for full-time service on the day the Second World War was declared, becoming attached to the Armoured Brigade. Later, as a colonel, he set up a field hospital in Normandy. He was then sent to Singapore, where he ran a 1,000-bed hospital. He was Deputy Director Medical Services to Admiral Mountbatten, and was present at the signing of the surrender

Catherine and Frank Arnott (Robert Arnott)

of the Japanese in Singapore on 12th September 1946, being then placed in charge of the release of all the prisoners of war from the Japanese. He ended the war as a brigadier and was made an OBE. On his return to Bovey he rarely talked about his war years.

Back in Bovey, he was in partnership with Dr J.M. Harrisson and Dr T. Healey in Chudleigh. Dr Arnott was an enormously respected and hard-working doctor. He had a great interest in all his patients and believed that he should 'treat a patient's house as my own'. He always took his outer coat off when he went to see a patient. Many of his surviving patients talk of his 'wonderful bed-side manner' and the way he was involved in helping them improve their lives. Robert remembers that every morning he went through his list of patients and decided which ones needed checking on before they even asked for a visit. One year he walked to Manaton in the snow to see a patient when the roads were impassable.

Right up until his last illnesses and his death at the age of 72 he played a full part in the affairs of the town.

The Mann Family
Information from Arthur and Helen Mann

Arthur and James Mann (John Adey)

In 1829 William Mann opened a butchery in Fore Street, opposite to what is now Mann's. His sons, John, who married Sarah Wolfinden from the Union Hotel, and Alfred, ran the business and farm. The present shop was created out of three cottages which were converted into a shop but had buildings behind for the slaughterhouse and stabling for the horses. In 1914 John's son, William, joined the armed forces and in 1916 the slaughterman, Arthur Mitchell, was called up to fight in the First World War. John could no longer operate as a butcher so he began to sell milk and dairy produce. In 1919, when William returned from the war, one of his jobs was to walk around Bovey delivering milk. A pony and trap was bought in the early 1930s to make life easier.

Many people in Bovey remember the sight of Mann's cows walking up Fore Street from their field to the milking shed behind the shop. They were well known by the greengrocer at the bottom of the town, who always had his vegetables out on display. The cows were particularly fond of taking the cabbages as they went past. Anne Broom remembers the day when one of the cows put its head through the plate-glass window of the garage she and her husband owned.

William's son, Arthur, came into the business and carried on milking the cows and delivering milk until 1979. He married Helen Bath, whose parents owned Brookside tearooms, and she helped him turn Mann's into the delicatessen it is now, selling as much local produce as possible. Helen is a well-known local artist and was a founder member of Bovey Tracey Society of Artists: she is now its honorary president.

Arthur has always been involved in Bovey life, playing football for the local team and being a parish councillor. When he was aged 34 he was Bovey's youngest chairman of the council. He was a founder member of the Chamber of Trade, was chairman of the Carnival Committee and was involved in the twinning with Le Molay Littry. He is also chairman of the trustees of the Tracey Almshouses and was chosen to be Bovey Tracey's first modern lord of the manor.

Arthur's son, James, worked with his father and took over completely when Arthur retired. Carrying on the tradition of public service, he was elected Bovey's youngest mayor at the age of 33.

The Coombes Family
Information from Victor, Geoffrey and Murray Coombes

In the late 19th century Albert Coombes, from Trusham, married Norah Steer, a member of a family who had lived in Bovey for generations, and moved to Bovey. They had four children – Roy, Leonard, Renee and Linna – before Albert spent four years in the Royal Engineers during the First World War. After leaving the army he borrowed £3 from his grandmother to buy a wheelbarrow and a ladder to start a building business. The business began to prosper and he and Norah had five more children – Rodney, Geoffrey, Murray, Victor and Austin. It was a blow to the family when Linna, who was a bright, energetic girl, died after an accidental fall.

Austin (left) and Victor (right) Coombes in the 1920s (Victor Coombes)

As well as starting the building firm, Albert followed his father-in-law into the local voluntary fire service. Later, he was to be followed by four of his sons and a grandson until, by the end of the 20th century, the family had given over 100 years of continuous and unbroken service to the Bovey Fire Brigade. Sadly, Roy, one of the sons, was to die when fighting a fire in Brimley in 1964.

The family first spent a few happy years crowded into a small terrace house until moving into a large house in Fore Street in 1927. At the rear of the house was a big workshop which was needed for the growing firm. In the 1930s the firm employed over 40 men building new houses and doing general repairs. They also built the present Bovey hospital, which had an up-to-date operating theatre and where the first patient was the young son, Austin: he had appendicitis and would have died if he had not been operated on quickly by Dr Harrisson.

All the older boys were in the St John's Church choir. Every year all the choir boys had to go to Pring's, the local tailor, to be fitted for a new suit for Easter Sunday. They were given a shilling to spend on the annual church outing to Totnes for a trip down the River Dart and then on to Torquay regatta.

By the end of the 1930s all the sons had entered the thriving building business except for Rodney, who was a great car enthusiast and went to work in a garage, Victor, who went into a surveyor's office, and Austin, who went into banking.

During the Second World War all seven sons were in the forces, two in the army and five in the RAF, a unique occurrence according to the War Office. Albert managed to keep the business going as well as he could with the help of young men not yet called up, but he and Norah were devastated when Rodney was killed in 1941. He is still remembered for his beautiful voice and for the duets he sang with Jim Stoneman.

After the war the returning sons, except Victor, who became a teacher, went back into the firm, but in 1950 their father died having never really recovered from the death of his son. Sadly, their beloved mother died ten years later. After the death of their father, the building firm was carried on by Roy and Geoffrey (painters), Leonard (a carpenter), Murray (a mason) and Austin (in the office). The undertaking side was expanded and headed by Austin. Many people still remember the sympathetic and understanding care he gave during the sad times in their lives. In 1985, when Murray retired, the family decided to sell the business. Austin stayed on with the new owners for a couple of years until he, too, retired. However, the name of the company has been retained.

Renee, their sister, died after a long illness, but all the brothers, except Leonard, retired to live in Bovey Tracey, where they take great pleasure in watching their families grow and reminiscing about the wonderful variety of jobs they have tackled over the years, the interesting people they have worked for and the eccentric vicars they have met.

The Weeks Family
Information from Arthur, Esther, Sidney and Barbara Weeks

The Weeks family in 1941. Back row, left to right: Henry, Sidney and Arthur.
Front row, left to right: Barbara, William and Susan (Arthur Weeks)

William Weeks was born in Bovey Tracey and worked for the Co-op in Bovey and Lustleigh for 50 years. In his early years there, he was expected to walk to Haytor, Liverton, and Chudleigh Knighton, whatever the weather, to take orders. He and his wife, Susan, whose father was a saddler and bootmaker in Bovey, had four children, three of whom still live in Bovey.

Arthur, when he left school, first worked with his father at the Co-op, but then joined the army in 1939, adding an extra year to his age so he could join at 16. He spent four years in Kenya training Africans to use anti-tank guns. After the war he returned to the Co-op for a year and then went to work for Devon General buses. In the 1950s he worked as transport manager for Wyatt and Bruce, where he was responsible for maintaining up to 43 vehicles and organising all the deliveries to the various farms. In 1959 and 1960 Arthur won the lorry driver of the year competition, in which he had to display his skills as a driver as well as answer questions on the Highway Code.

He married Esther Clark, daughter of Elizabeth Warren who had been born in Bovey but had left for the bright lights of London. Esther was evacuated to Bovey to live with her grandmother and aunt when war broke out. In 1942 she was taken on at the pottery as a 'dogsbody'. Her skills were soon recognised and she started working with Joseph Nekola and Florrie Woollacott in the Wemyss shop. Joseph Nekola had moved from Fife to work at the Bovey Pottery in 1929, bringing with him many of the Wemyss Ware moulds in the form of blocks and cases as well as his unique expertise. He taught Esther the secrets of his work and, as a young apprentice, she worked with him on a large dinner, tea and coffee service with cabbage roses and burnished gold edge for the US president, Franklin D. Roosevelt. Esther succeeded Joseph as head of the Wemyss Decorating Shop in 1952, and continued in that capacity until the pottery closed in 1957. She stayed on for about two years finishing orders and then went to work for the Devonshire Pottery and stayed there until 1973. Wemyss Ware was strangely neglected for many years, but a recent revival of interest in it has meant that Esther is often called upon to demonstrate her skills. She painted a cup for the Queen Mother's 80th birthday and again for her 100th birthday. Griselda Hill, of Ceres in Fifeshire, has restarted making Wemyss Ware, and, for the last ten years, Esther has been teaching her potters the secrets of her skill.

Sidney and Barbara, the youngest Weeks, are twins. Sidney was born weighing only one and three-quarters of a pound. There were no incubators in those days and his mother managed to keep him alive by feeding him through a fountain pen feeder and wrapping him entirely in cotton wool.

Esther Weeks (John Adey)

He was unable to walk until he was 5 years old and was of such a nervous disposition that Dr Arnott suggested that a piano should be bought and Sidney taught to play it. Barbara also learnt, and in later years they often played duets at local functions. Arthur played the double bass in the local band and became its deputy conductor. All three were choristers for the parish church.

Sidney worked at the Devonmoor Art Pottery Company at Liverton as an office clerk from 1936 until 1980, with five years in the Royal Air Force during the Second World War, where he spent time in Belgium, France and Kowloon. Barbara went to work at Bovey Pottery as a fettler, and during the war worked in munitions. After the war, with Lance Tregoning, his sister Barbara and Leslie Steer, Sidney helped set up the Bovey Parish Church Social Service Club which aimed to raise funds for the church and provide young people with a social life. Michael Steer described it 'as the only show in town' and so it was immensely important for young people in the town. In 1946 Sidney became musical director for the Brownies and Guides when they formed the Bovey Pantomime Company under Marie Goss. Rehearsals began in September and performances took place for a week in January at the Wickham Hall. They then went on tour on Fridays and Saturdays to outlying villages for about six weeks. Sidney also played all the incidental music for the Candy drama group.

In 1959 Sidney was asked to play the parish church organ for the midnight service and then deputise until a permanent organist could be found. By 1972, after 13 years of deputising, it was decided that Sidney should be offered a permanent position. Sidney accepted and carried on as church organist until 2001, when he retired at the age of 79.

Lance and Pat Tregoning
Information from Pat and Minola Tregoning

Lance Tregoning and Pat Tregoning, with Snooker on his lap, in 1946
(Pat Tregoning)

Harry Tregoning worked for the Co-op in Bodmin and was moved to Bovey Tracey just before the First World War. In 1916 he married Florentia Farnes, daughter of Kate Farnes who was a midwife and ran a lodging house at Summerfields in East Street. Lance was born there in 1917. His brother, Pat, was born in 1923. Harry left the Co-op and opened his own grocery shop in Town Hall Square, which Lance joined as soon as he left school. The business later moved to the corner of Orchard Terrace. Pat always knew he did not want to work as a grocer, but during the depression in the 1930s his parents were no longer able to employ two assistants so Pat, at the age of 14, had to join the family business. Lance was called up in 1940, and Pat then joined the Home Guard until he was called up. Pat remembers this as being a particularly difficult time in the grocery business; rationing had been introduced and it was impossible to please their customers. Lance was in the Artillery and went across on the D-day landings through France, Belgium, Holland and Germany.

Minola Snow, who was brought up in Exeter, often came to stay with relations in Bovey as a child and had met Lance then. During the war she joined the Land Army and worked on the same farm as Joyce Pettet, whom she introduced to Pat Tregoning after the war. For Pat it was love at first sight and for eight months they wrote to each other every day until they could be married. They had five children, two of whom still live in Bovey. Minola married Lance and they lived over the shop until their twins were born. The family business closed in 1963 when Harry Tregoning died. Lance had already left to become a travelling salesman. He later worked in the office of Wyatt and Bruce until he had a heart attack and took early retirement.

After the war Pat joined C.J. Ellis, where he worked as an electrician for four years until he moved to working with radios. In 1969 Pat decided to work for himself and had his own workshop, repairing televisions and radios.

Both Lance and Pat were brought up to be involved in the church. Their father was a bell-ringer and sidesman for the church. They both attended Sunday School, and then had to go to church after that and sit through Reverend Howell's sermons, which lasted at least three quarters of an hour. Pat went into the choir when he was aged 9 and left when he was 24. He remembers singing in the choir on Christmas Day evening to a congregation of two people and Reverend Howell still giving a sermon for at least half an hour. Lance was a churchwarden for 28 years. After the war he started a youth club at the church, which lasted for many years.

Lance had always been interested in local history and photography, and after his early retirement he put his knowledge to good use and produced *Bovey Tracey: An Ancient Town* in 1983 and *Bovey Tracey in Bygone Days* in 1989. He died in 1991 and new approach steps to the south door of the parish church were dedicated to him in 1992.

The Gribble Family
by George Gribble

Vera Gribble with Pauline (now Waller) on her lap and George by her side in 1942 (George Gribble)

When Bovey Tracey Town Council secured the purchase, by public subscription, of the title deeds of the 'Lordship of the Manor of Bovey Tracey' an exhibition of old deeds and tithe maps was held in the town hall. Amongst the long-standing names were the Gribbles. They were shown as having rented land in the parish in 1642.

By and large the Gribbles formerly resided in the Mary Street area, living in, amongst other properties, Revelstoke, which had once been the local hospital.

Joseph Gribble, born in 1830, had three children, including a son, Joseph, born in 1865. The latter had nine children and, as his father had before him, worked at the potteries. When he retired he could be seen around the town selling turnips, swedes and other vegetables. One of his sons, Charles, was a sawyer who worked for many years at Heath's timber yard. His youngest son, Samuel (1909-69), was apprenticed as a stonemason at Candy's and, later, became resident mason at Hawkmoor Hospital. Samuel's youngest sister, Rosena, died of consumption at an early age. She spent much time in a nursing home in Exmouth, where Sam met his future wife, Vera, who was working there as a nurse.

Samuel and his brother, Joe, both turned out for the local football teams and cricket club, Samuel playing regularly for the first XI. Although his bowling was good enough for minor county cricket, he could not afford the time from work to play at that level.

Sam had three children – George, Pauline and Susan. George, after attending the local primary and Torquay Technical schools, served five years apprenticeship as an electrical engineer before joining the merchant navy, where he reached the rank of Chief Electrical Officer. He left in 1972 and returned to Bovey. He married Faye Manley, a member of an old Bovey Tracey family, and had two sons, Mark and Adam.

George rode for Bovey Tracey Spurs at cycle speedway and played football and cricket for Bovey Tracey. He joined the town council in 1973 and first became mayor in 1981, since which time he has had the honour of serving as town mayor on six occasions. He was mayor when Bovey Tracey received its coat of arms, and welcomed Diana, Princess of Wales, and the Duchess of Kent on their visits to Bovey Tracey.

George's family connection with cricket continued as his two sons became colts with BTCC. George became chairman of BTCC, an office he held for ten years, finally standing down in 2003 after the club had won the Devon County League premiership for the first time in its history in 2002, with Mark Gribble as captain and Adam in the team.

The Small Family
Information from Reuben, Cyril and John Small

Moses Small was a horse dealer who lived in Exeter at the end of the 19th century and supplied horses for the Boer War and to the council. He travelled to all the fairs in the West Country with his large family, staying on Bovey Moor and near the Traveller's Rest on their way through Devon. One of Moses' grandsons, Joshua Reuben (always known as Reuben), was born in a wagon in Newton Square, Newton Abbot. During the First World War Reuben took part in the Battle of Ypres, where he was wounded. He then went to Gallipolli, where he was so badly wounded that, from then until 1939, he had to have twenty-seven operations on his leg, the last one taking place in a tent on his land on Newton Road. He was so weak that the surgeon came from Exeter to do the operation.

Despite his injuries, Reuben continued travelling when he returned from the war, but he decided he wanted a more permanent base. He and his brother, John, bought some land from Les Manley on Newton Road and settled there with their wagons and tents. He remained a horse dealer in the inter-war years, but, during the Second World War, he kept about 500 pigs, feeding them on the swill collected by him and his sons from the army camps at Heathfield, Stover, Chudleigh and Haytor. Reuben had eight children, but lost two in infancy, and another, Moses, was killed on the Newton Road at the age of 19.

Moses, one of Reuben's brothers, was a carpet dealer but was unable to trade during the war because of the shortage of petrol. He also settled in Bovey Tracey and kept pigs, some at Brimley Gardens and some at Indio. At night, to make extra money, Moses' and Reuben's sons walked to Lustleigh, Manaton and Ashburton to collect rabbit skins. Rabbits were eaten extensively during the war, and their skins were sold to make fur for flying helmets and gloves. Reuben's wife, Rebecca, and her sister, Eliza, both had the gift of fortune-telling and they used these powers to make money for the war effort by setting up in the Toc H building adjoining St Mary's to tell fortunes.

During the war Moses' children all served in different ways. Two sons, Reuben Junior and Alec, joined the army, one daughter, May, worked at the pottery and another daughter, Genty, worked for the Forestry Commission, helping to prepare trees to be sent to the coal mines. After the war Reuben and Alec joined their father in the business of selling imported carpets. Later, they moved into recycling clothes. Reuben married Britty in 1945, and they have settled in Bovey Tracey, although, as Reuben says, 'travelling is always in the blood'.

John Edward Small, who had bought land on Newton Road with his brother, Reuben, was shot in Barnstaple in 1934, and his wife was left to bring up five children. Their son, John, who had been born in a tent on Bovey Heath, was only 3 years old when his father died. This event, combined with the onset of the war, caused Reuben more or less to give up travelling. He wanted to keep an

Lila, Moses and Cyril (on the horse) Small in 1938 (Cyril Small)

Cyril Small with his first lorry in the late 1950s (Cyril Small)

Reuben Small in 2003 (John Adey)

eye on his fatherless nieces and nephews, so all John's and Reuben's younger children went to Bovey schools.

One of Reuben's sons, Cyril, who was born in 1936, and his cousin, John, are both well known in Bovey for their sporting prowess. Cyril had a slightly chequered career at school. He was brilliant at mental arithmetic but remembers being one of the naughty boys. Once, when out on a cross-country run, he caught the bus back rather than finish the run. Other children in his class remember more stories, and they must have contributed to the headmaster telling him he would 'never make anything in life'.

Cyril, starting when he was aged 14, and John both played football for Bovey. John was chairman of the football club for about ten years and, during that time, the football club was transformed. This story is told in the section on the football club. John was also involved in the cycle speedway and was a singer with the Smokey Mountain Boys, which included Les Harris, Roy Small, Alec Small and Bert Maunder.

Cyril began playing darts at the Bell at the age of 15 and later won the Bovey individual and pairs darts. His team, the Red and Greens, moved to play at the Dartmoor, and were then invited by Colonel Beer to play at the Conservative Club, where they won numerous cups.

Latterly, enormous changes have taken place in the way Gypsies live. Once travelling was an intrinsic part of their life. They left their winter base in March each year in their wagons and came back in October, attending large Gypsy gatherings such as Barnstaple, Bampton and Princetown fairs, and were often involved in horse dealing. Every year there was a great gathering of Gypsies from all over the country at Epsom on Derby Day, and it was here that Cyril met his wife, Olive. When Reuben Small first bought his land on Newton Road he kept a wagon and tent on it. Then he built a wooden hut, and in the 1950s electricity was installed. In the 1960s Reuben's house had its own water supply, having had to share a communal tap in the yard until then, and, finally, in 1970 it was connected to the town sewage system. When Cyril was a child Romany, based on ancient Hindi, was spoken widely, but now that so many people have settled and married into non-Gypsy families it is dying out. Only a few words have been retained. Gypsy culture has been diluted, but the Smalls are still proud to be called Gypsies, with their traditions reaching back to India, from where they had been driven in the 11th century.

Jeremy Leach

Jeremy is a familiar sight in Bovey as he cycles through town on his way from Devon House to Lowerdown Pottery. He is the second son of David Leach and was born in 1941 at St Ives, Cornwall. When he was in his teens, his family moved to Bovey. His initial pottery training was at Lowerdown Pottery, where he trained with his father, and then at the Central School and Camberwell Schools of Art and Craft. After living in Oxford and travelling extensively he returned to Bovey, where he continues to work from Lowerdown Pottery making his own stoneware and porcelain pots, both functional and individual pieces. He has exhibited extensively in the UK and abroad.

Justin Knowles

Justin Knowles was born in Exeter in 1935 and went to school in Tavistock. He had no formal art training and, after national service in the army, he worked in advertising. During this time he spent two years in Africa and became interested in African dance, dress and sculpture, which has had a life-long impact on his work. In 1965 he became a professional artist and was one of the artists of 'The New Generation 1966' (Whitechapel Gallery, London).

He was living in a chapel at Ideford in the 1970s when a devastating fire destroyed nearly ten years of work as well as work in progress. He moved to Bovey Tracey, where he lives looking across at Dartmoor, which he loves.

Although Justin didn't exhibit for many years, Mel Gooding describes his work as having 'a most remarkable intellectual and artistic consistency'. His 1997 exhibition at Exeter Museum and Art Gallery relaunched his career in terms of public exposition, and since then he has had exhibitions in London, Prague and, in 2003, in Plymouth. In recent years he has constructed three remarkable sculptures from found granite blocks, industrially cut and dressed from Dartmoor stone, one of which stands at Forde House, Newton Abbot. His work is represented in seventeen public collections, including the Tate Gallery. He has a commission at Exeter Cathedral.

A digital archive of Justin Knowles' work is now being compiled by the University of Plymouth.

Justin Knowles (Justin Knowles)

Some of the well-known people of Bovey photographed in 2003
photographs by John Adey

Above: Robert Arnott
Right: Jim Ayres

Dorothy Beer

Bert Bowden

Above: Derek and Henry Bowden
Right: Cecil Brealey

Linda Caunter (née Steer)

Michael Caunter

Joyce Collins (née Harris)

Murray Coombes

Stan Dart

Norah Davis (née Steer)

Eric Godfrey

Les Harris

Fernley Holmes

Christine Holmes (née Steer)

Dave Lewis

Hughie Mann

Walter Mountford

Anthony Porter

Alan Raisey

Brian Steer

Michael Steer

Pat Tregoning

Phil Waldron and, right, Winifred Waldron (née Davey)

Len Webber

Arthur Weeks

Barbara Weeks

Sidney Weeks

Geoff Wills

Jack Wills

Bovey Heath and Yarner Wood

We live in one of the most beautiful parts of England and, while most of us take the scenery and wildlife for granted, the two sections below both introduce us to some of the unique features of the landscape around us, and show us that maintaining them calls for constant vigilance.

Roundheads and Narrow-heads on Bovey Heath
by Stephen Carroll

Tchak tchak tchak. On Bovey Heath the distinctive call of a stonechat challenges my intrusion. It's an encounter that could have been played out at any time over the last 4,000 years, for the history of Bovey Heath and the local communities of Bovey Tracey and Heathfield are as intertwined as the heather and gorse on which the bird perches.

Originating from the farming activities of Bronze Age settlers before 2000 BC, archaeological evidence suggests subsequent periods of Roman occupation and medieval industry on the ancient heath. And, as every local schoolchild knows, Bovey Heath was also the site of an important Civil War battle in 1646, which decided the outcome of the conflict in the South West. Finally, in the last century, the heath was used for military exercises during the time of the Second World War.

So Bovey Heath has close links to the local community, its origins and its history. More recently, though, a visitor has been more likely to stumble over discarded oil cans, tyres or smashed glass instead of Bronze Age arrowheads or Civil War musket shot. For the last 20 years the heath has suffered from pernicious car dumping, flytipping, malicious fires, illegal off-road scrambling, vandalism, and, unsurprisingly, a desperately poor image. Perception of the area as an unofficial motorbiking venue has become as deeply ingrained as the extensive ruts and tracks now scarring the landscape. Such abuses have persisted despite protection as a designated Site of Special Scientific Interest (SSSI) and Scheduled Ancient Monument (SAM).

Unfortunately, this is not so exceptional. Lowland heathland has declined massively in the last 50 years. Nationally, and in Europe, over 90% of heaths have been lost - victims of 20th century agri-chemical cultivation, conifer plantation, industry, housing, roads and neglect. Heathland habitats and their special wildlife are becoming increasingly rare, and hence valuable. The south-west of England is now the stronghold for this unique habitat in Europe - and the world. Bovey Heath might be one of the last few remaining examples of Devon heathland, but is the wildlife still there? It has certainly declined drastically over the last 10 years, with protected birds like Dartford warbler and nightjar, and butterflies like the silver-studded blue, barely hanging on by their wingtips. There is also the perilously endangered narrow-headed ant *Formica exsecta* which exists at only one other site in the country; by the end of the 1990s just two colonies were left on the site.

Grasping the gorse bush
After years of stalled attempts to deal with the site's problems, a change in the law enabled wildlife conservation charity Devon Wildlife Trust (DWT) to assume ownership of Bovey Heath in September 2002. But it was clear that finding a cure for Bovey Heath's various ills would require much more than a straightforward land purchase and reintroduction of traditional heathland management. Taking on such a troubled site after so many years of mistreatment is a new type of venture for DWT, very much a case of grasping the nettle - or gorse bush. A different approach was needed, not only to restore the heathland, but also to involve the local community in the future management of the site and re-establishing the bond between Bovey people and Bovey Heath, an area that has had such an influence on the historical development of the local town. Active participation is to be encouraged through a strong focus on community-based activities: programmes of site events, a children's nature study group, volunteer wardens' team and the

'Friends of Bovey Heathfield', and working closely with local societies, schools, businesses and individuals to promote the area as an educational and recreational resource.

Coming soon to a heath near you

A walk on the open heath among the irate stonechats should be a rewarding, wildlife-rich experience. First though, throughout spring 2003, with the invaluable help of local volunteers, DWT cleared some 49 wrecked cars, 100 tyres and 32 tons of assorted rubbish, including a kitchen sink. Heather mowings were spread on the bare eroded tracks, encroaching pine saplings were felled and ponds were relieved of their toxic litter. These represented small, but significant, ant-like steps on the path to the heath's recovery. More importantly, as the noxious layers of 20 years' worth of tipping and detritus were removed, it became possible to glimpse underneath what Bovey Heath once was - and can be again.

Above left: Moving the rubbish from Bovey Heath in April 2003 (Stephen Carroll, Devon Wildlife Trust)
Above right: Turf relocation on Bovey Heath in 2003 (Stephen Carroll, Devon Wildlife Trust)

Ling, bell heather and cross-leaved heath, common gorse and low growing Western gorse promise a landscape of purples, pinks and yellows, studded by the deep blue flowers of milkwort. The bleached acid white sandy soil (called a 'podsol' after the Russian for 'ash'), leached of its nutrients by precipitation, is characteristic of heathland; these extremely acidic, low nutrient conditions are the key to the heath's rare wildlife, giving a habitat in which only a few specially adapted plants and animals can thrive. The dearth of nutrients means that many species survive through supplementing their diets - by eating each other. Plants such as dodder and lousewort parasitise other plants, while insectivorous sundews entrap midges in their sticky clasp. Not much can grow taller than the heather canopy, but, unlike upland moors, at lower altitudes the microclimate under the heathery blanket is hot, dry and humid. This encourages a superabundance of insect life.

In high summer the heath should be a purple jungle full of voracious predators, albeit on a small scale. One might encounter bright green tiger beetles, 22 different dragonflies (of 38 species breeding nationally), half of the UK's 650 sorts of spiders and some 20 types of ant - not forgetting Bovey's famous narrow-headed ant. Bovey Heath boasts records for 56 nationally rare, protected and county notable invertebrate species, embracing *Adrena* solitary bees, moths, butterflies and unusual solitary wasps. Further up the food chain, it's possible to see overhead birds such as linnets, tree pipits, and species like yellowhammer and skylark that have suffered recent national declines. Alongside these, stealth and luck permitting, might be spotted the clockwork, tail-flicking motions of the Dartford warbler, foraging amongst the gorse tops. In the 1960s UK numbers of this rare heathland specialist plummeted to just 11 pairs. And one shouldn't read about heathlands without a mention that this is the prime habitat for Britain's native reptiles, though all a visitor may know of this is a sudden rustling at the path edge as a lizard or snake scuttles or glides away, back into the wilds of the heather.

The heath can recover. Things are stirring on Bovey Heath: the roots of the heathland plants are re-turning to life, plants whose provenance leads back to the prehistoric roots of the local community. People can once more look forward to admiring unbroken panoramic views across the heather to Haytor, Shaptor and the rest of the Bovey Basin, just as Bronze Age, Roman, Medieval, Roundhead and modern-day Bovonians, and the stonechats, must have done down through the centuries.

DWT's Bovey Heathfield Community Project is supported by English Nature Wildspace! (through the New Opportunities Fund), Bovey Tracey Town Council and Teignbridge District Council.

Stephen Carroll is Bovey Heathfield Community Officer for Devon Wildlife Trust.

Yarner Wood
by Phil Page

Where certain high-climbing hills take leave of the lowlands, there spread, beneath the eastern frontiers of Dartmoor, extended ranges of forest…lies Yarner - a fair kingdom, peopled by many myriads of the unconscious.

So wrote Eden Phillpotts of Yarner Wood in his novel, *The Forest on the Hill*, in 1912. Forty years later, on 19th May 1952, his Forest on the Hill became one of the first six national nature reserves to be declared in England. The others were Kingley Vale in West Sussex, Ham Street Woods in Kent, Cavenham Heath in Suffolk, Holme Fen in Cambs. and Moor House in Cumbria.

Up until 1951, when it was sold to the Nature Conservancy, Yarner Wood had been part of the Yarner Estate. Access to the woodland was prohibited to the general public and this strictly enforced seclusion is used to good effect in Phillpotts' novel. We know very little about Yarner Wood from the period following Phillpotts' novel up until the 1920s. According to the former woodman of the estate, a rabbit catcher (but no keeper) was employed by Sir Harry Eve, who owned the Yarner Estate from 1902 until 1919, and it appears that there may have been no gamekeeper in the wood when Phillpotts wrote his novel. The new owner in 1919 was R.H. Lee, who may have decided to employ a gamekeeper and, fortuitously, records of Leonard Evans, who became the estate gamekeeper soon after 1919, were provided by his widow and grandson, Jack.

In September 1922 after her wedding to gamekeeper Leonard Evans, Mabel Evans (nee Ridgway) the keeper's bride, came to live in her new home at Yarner Wood. Her husband had promised that there was a bathroom in the cottage (a most unusual feature in rural houses in those times). After searching the house following her arrival she failed to find one and upon enquiring with her husband was taken outside to the stew pond opposite. 'There's yer bathroom!' was his retort.

This account came from David Rogers after a conversation with Mabel Evans when she visited the wood in the 1980s. The very same stew-pond is mentioned in the second paragraph of Phillpotts' novel!

Len Evans was an impressive and memorable character - his great grandfather was Charles Pinkerton, founder of the famous detective agency. Unusually for someone in his position he was also a socialist and considered to be a man with ideas above his station. On one occasion he was dismissed for having the audacity to purchase a small horse-drawn gig for himself and his wife.

During the 1920s and 1930s Yarner Wood was managed as a seasonal shooting venue for the gentry, with pheasants, partridge and even black grouse (now a nationally rare species) being found in the immediate vicinity. The keeper was also required to supply pigeons, rabbits and wildfowl for the estate table all the year round.

Len and Mabel Evans left Yarner in either 1925 or 1926. Len finished his days in Bishopsteignton - during the war he was a particularly officious special constable! He died in 1965 aged 65 years, but Mabel survived him by 31 years, having spent the latter part of her life in Newton Abbot.

Fred Toby was the Yarner Estate gamekeeper in 1950 and had a life tenancy for the same cottage that had been lived in by Len Evans and which was the fictional home of Timothy Snow, the hero of *The Forest on the Hill*. There is no record of when Fred Toby first came to work in Yarner Wood, but it was probably in the late 1920s or early 1930s. He had worked for Major Hole on the Parke Estate, on the edge of Bovey Tracey. By virtue of his existing incumbency Fred Toby thus became the first 'warden' of Yarner Wood.

In 1960 a Land Rover was finally allocated to the reserve – despite the comments included in an official letter written some two years earlier, which stated that: 'it is highly unlikely that Yarner will have a vehicle to itself in the foreseeable future...'. Up until then only a horse was available. Meanwhile, although he had no wish to retire from his position at Yarner Wood, Fred Toby was finding it increasingly difficult to carry out the often physically strenuous activities associated with his job, because of advancing years. As a result, in November 1963 he eventually opted to become a part-timer, and continued on that basis until he died on 25th June 1965, just nine months after the death of his wife, Lily.

The passing of Fred Toby was the end of an era - not only had he worked at Yarner Wood before and after it became a national nature reserve, but he had also witnessed the changeover from handtools to the power tools of the modern era. A further significant change was the transition of the site from part of a closed private estate to the gradual opening up of the wood to the general public following National Nature Week in 1963.

Public access and visitors

There was no tradition of public access to Yarner Wood. When it became a national nature reserve it was felt that visitors would interfere with the various research programmes and so access was provided only by permits issued upon written request (only 36 permits were issued in 1962).

The reserve was opened to the public for the first time in 1963 during National Nature Week, but only eight people took advantage of this 'special offer'. In 1965 an 'educational trail' with exhibits was established in association with the Devon Education Authority's Schools Museum Service, and this aroused considerable interest amongst teachers.

From 1965 public interest in the reserve increased, although access was still by permit only. In 1972 a second, longer trail, the woodland walk, was created and in 1973, 70 school parties and 823 individuals visited the reserve. From 1973 the public were finally able to use both these trails without a permit.

Yarner Wood is now part of the 365-hectare East Dartmoor Woods & Heaths National Nature Reserve, which also includes the adjoining Trendlebere Down and Bovey Valley Woodlands sites. The whole reserve has 'Spotlight' status, which means that there is an emphasis on providing information and interpretation for visitors. In 2001 a new reserve base was completed at Yarner Wood with new interpretive displays and a redesigned nature trail leaflet.

Woodland Management - Past and Present

The first known reference to Yarner Wood is in an inventory of the King's forests in the reign of Edward VI (1547-1553) and it is, therefore, certainly 'ancient woodland', that is, wooded since at least 1600. Within the wood, however, were areas of open ground and heath used for grazing, whilst estate documents from the 18th and 19th centuries confirm that coppicing took place.

Charcoal-making and coppicing had resulted in the loss of most of the large trees from Yarner Wood. In the 1870s and 1880s there was still active charcoal-making in the wood, but the timber was of poor quality and mainly used for supplying firewood to Yarner House. When production of both of these commodities ended at the end of the 19th century, the woodland was largely neglected for the next 50 years.

The sale documents for the Yarner Estate (December, 1950) state that:

The Forestry Commission has intimated that, subject to an undertaking to replant and under present conditions, felling licences would be favourably considered for a clear fell of Lot 24 (Yarner Wood) with the exception of the conifer plantations...

The documents emphasise that the whole of Lot 24, i.e. Yarner Wood 'including the Moorland, is suitable for SOFTWOOD PLANTING'. This would certainly have led to the felling of much of the oak woodland and replanting with non-native conifers as well as the planting up of the heathland areas.

The oak woodland, however, was not highly valued at the time by either foresters or nature conservationists. Why then did it become a national nature reserve?

The major reason for purchasing Yarner Wood was to set up a large woodland reserve to carry out experimental management without threatening any rare species of plants or animals. It must be remembered that in 1951 much of the countryside (and particularly Devon) was still unspoilt by intensive agriculture and urban expansion, and there was a strong need to study the dynamics of ecosystems as well as protecting special areas. National nature reserves were seen primarily as outdoor laboratories for ecologists.

The woodland management programme that was adopted aimed to transform what was regarded as neglected and, in places, 'moribund' woodland into a 'vigorous and diverse woodland'. On the moorland boundary belts of non-indigenous beech and Japanese larch were planted and, within the woodland, a programme of replanting was initiated using mixed hardwoods such as sessile oak, beech, alder, hazel and wych elm with conifer 'nurse' trees. This was carried out in small clear-felled blocks within the canopy and on existing open ground. The thinking behind this was that the dominance of oak was probably artificial due to it being favoured by the desire to produce charcoal. This approach had several flaws, most notable of which were the destruction of the transitional woodland moorland zone with which several rare species are closely associated, obscuring the historical pattern of vegetation development, the widespread use of non-local planting stock and the felling of some mature trees. Above all, however, it overlooked the value of the site as an example of western oakwood in which oak and birch are dominant species and which is rare in Europe as a whole.

Since the 1970s management policy for Yarner Wood has aimed at building on the natural strengths of the site rather than trying to alter its fundamental nature. The key species groups of western oak woodland are a distinctive avifauna, featuring birds such as pied flycatcher, redstart, wood warbler, ferns, bryophytes and lichens. These all require the presence of oak canopy, whilst other species, such as tree pipit and lesser spotted woodpecker, require the more open conditions associated with the early successional stages. Woodland management is now based on the singling of old coppice stools and gradual light thinning of even aged standard trees in order to diversify the structure and increase the amount of dead wood. The long-term aim is to establish a woodland that is self-perpetuating through natural regeneration rather than planting and to maintain at least 10% of the current woodland as permanent open space.

The woodland management is now supported by the Forestry Commission's Woodland Grant Scheme, completing an interesting process which started with nature conservation management carried out via forestry prescriptions and which has developed into nature-conservation prescriptions being supported by forestry policy. (David Rogers, February 2000, *British Wildlife* Volume 11 Number 3.)

Yarner Wood is also now part of a European Union candidate Special Area of Conservation because of the importance of its western acidic oakwood as well as being a Site of Special Scientific Interest and a national nature reserve. Thus, from being a neglected woodland in Phillpotts' *The Forest on the Hill*, Yarner has become an internationally important site that is afforded the highest possible level of legal protection or, as the closing lines of the novel state, 'Law reigned as ever round her'.

Phil Page is Site Manager of Yarner Wood for English Nature.

❋ ❋ ❋ ❋ ❋

Miscellanea

Inevitably, this chapter, being the last of the book, contains what might appear to be a random set of sections. However, everything included is, or has been, enormously important to Bovey life. Unfortunately, there are aspects of Bovey Tracey which have been excluded through lack of new knowledge, and some of the sections included here are rather sketchy. The Heritage Trust would be very grateful for any extra information on these subjects or other institutions in Bovey.

The Fire Service
by Roy Wills

The fire service in Bovey Tracey today is a professionally-trained team of retained firefighters, part of Devon Fire and Rescue Service, and a far cry from their forebears in the 19th century. Then they were generally employed by insurance companies, and would only extinguish fires in dwellings if their owners subscribed to that particular company. Those who could afford the insurance premiums identified their properties by affixing 'firemarks' - a metal plate bearing the company's emblem - to the front of their buildings. In the event of a fire this enabled the firefighters to see whether that property was entitled to have the fire put out! Two firemarks of the Royal Insurance Company still remain in the town, one on the wall of 'Pixie Corner' in Fore Street and the other at number 75 Mary Street.

Many factories across the country at this time had their own fire pumps, manned by their own employees, and in this Bovey Tracey was no exception. Bovey Pottery had a manually-operated 1898 Shand Mason pump, which was kept in working order at their Pottery Road premises until 1957. It remained there after the pottery closed down and was bought, along with the former pottery buildings, by Wyatt and Bruce when they expanded their corn milling business from their main works at Station Road. To this day it is still owned by Mr Gordon Bruce and, with his kind permission, is currently on display at its original base, now the House of Marbles.

Candy Tiles at Heathfield owned a Shand Mason single horizontal cylinder steam-powered pump to safeguard their factory. This was sold to a private buyer in the 1990s and restored to working order, but is no longer in Devon.

In 1894 the passing of the Local Government Act made parish, rural district and urban district councils responsible for fire-fighting in the areas they each covered. By the dawn of the 20th century Bovey Tracey had been provided with a manually-operated pump, and had a crew of some 20 men which provided an effective fire-fighting capability for the parish. The fire station at this time was at the rear of the town hall, in the room now used as the police office.

Until 1926 the fire engine was horse-drawn and consisted of a large semi rotary manual pump on four wheels with a platform at each side on which the firemen stood. Two horses were needed for local fires, but four were used for calls to country areas. These horses were stabled at the Dolphin Hotel or Railway Hotel, and the engine was kept at the town hall. The manual pump required 24 men to work it at full pressure. Long handles were moved up and down on either side of the appliance to pump the water. The brigade, at this time, consisted of only eight or nine men, so they relied largely on volunteers to assist. In 1925, when Bovey Mill caught fire, everyone available in the town was called on to help. Luckily, the firemen decided to manhandle the pump down through the town for the sake of speed because the horses, apparently frightened by the fire, could not be caught. This was the biggest fire ever seen in Bovey, and the firemen worked from 2.30 a.m. on the Friday until 6 a.m. on the following Monday. The last fire of any size attended by the old horse-drawn fire engine was at Chapple House, where the house was destroyed.

In 1926 the first motor fire engine, a Stanley Ford with hard tyres and incorporating a motor pump and an overhead ladder, was bought. Up until that time the men had been called out by messenger, but then, for daytime calls, the maroon, a kind of rocket, was introduced. Night calls were still made by sending a messenger to the men's houses. Geoffrey Coombes remembers how his father, Albert, on receiving a message that there was a fire, would blow a whistle to wake his sons who would then run round Bovey to wake up the firemen. Firemen's houses had to have their gateposts painted white, so the boys would know which house to call at. The disadvantage with the maroon system was that men often came running to the fire station because they had heard a loud explosion, perhaps blasting, and had mistaken it for the rocket. After the war the maroon system was abandoned, and a remote control system of bells in the firemen's houses was installed. In addition, a siren on the roof of the town hall was sounded for calls between 7 a.m. and 10 p.m. Like the maroon, this had the added benefit of informing people in the town that the fire crew would be making their way to the station, the way often being cleared for them by people heeding this warning. This was superseded in 1977, when bleepers were introduced – quite large devices at the time but, as technology developed, now small enough to be comfortably carried in a pocket. The only disadvantage of the silencing of the siren was that townsfolk were unaware that the fire crew had been called out and no longer took appropriate action to allow the firemen to get to the station without hindrance, whether it be on foot, bicycle, car or works vehicle.

In 1934 it was decided that a new fire engine was needed. Major W.G. Hole organised a subscription list and gave ten guineas to the fund. Dame Violet Wills donated £100, and the rest of the town gave various sums from 2/6d. to £5. In all, £900 was raised to buy it – today a new fire engine costs over £125,000! A competition was held to choose its name, and Dame Violet Wills was asked to christen it the 'Queen Mary'. This engine, a Dennis 'Ace' pump with 'New World'

Bovey fire brigade in 1955. Back row, left to right: Roy Coombes, Jim Howard, Geoff Wills, Reg Bellinger, Leonard Coombes and Bill Harris. Front row, left to right: Frank Phillips, Harold Heale, Les Harris and Geoffrey Coombes (Victor Coombes)

The Dodge fire appliance based at Bovey from 1958 until 1976 (Joe Small)

bodywork, had a 30 feet ladder and carried 50 gallons of water, and was the first in which the men could sit down when going to the fire. It served the town well for more than 20 years, also being called into action in Plymouth during the Blitz. In 1958 it left the town to be used as a reserve engine for Devon County Fire Service. Then, in 1962, it was bought privately and used as a breakdown truck in Lyme Regis, Dorset, where, some years later, it was spotted by a local woman on holiday lying in a field. Geoff Wills, his son, John, and some friends set off to rescue what was left of the engine, and it was brought back to Bovey in pieces in the hope that it could be restored, but, unfortunately, this proved to be impractical.

As international tensions rose, and the likelihood of a second world war seemed inevitable, the government recognised difficulties with the many fire brigades which had been established countrywide. One basic, but serious, problem was the inability of adjacent brigades to work efficiently together due to the wide variety of fire hose and fittings which each had chosen, and which were not compatible. The result was the introduction of The Fire Brigades Act of 1938 which, amongst other things, sought to ensure that all brigades would use the same type of hose fittings. This Act also required the formation of the Auxiliary Fire Service in order that adequate numbers of personnel would be available at times of national emergencies - they were to be well used in the forthcoming years. In 1941 problems still existed and all fire brigades were unified by the creation of the National Fire Service, so that a more efficient response could be guaranteed following the blitzing of many cities in 1940 and 1941, when resources then available could not cope.

In the 1950s the Bovey brigade had a second appliance, a Fordson with a front-mounted pump; this was also provided with a trailer-mounted larger capacity Drysdale pump. These pumps were both housed in the bays beneath the town hall, where the station remained until 1979.

After the Second World War the N.F.S. remained as such until 1947, when the Fire Services Act returned control of fire services to local authorities, but on a much more organised basis than when they were amalgamated in 1941. This resulted in the formation of the Devon County Fire Service, to which the Bovey Tracey Station was attached along with separate brigades in Exeter and Plymouth. In 1973 local government reorganisation saw the amalgamation of the Devon County Fire Service, Exeter City Fire Brigade and Plymouth City Fire Brigade into the Devon Fire Brigade, which, with 58 stations, made it one of the largest 'shire' brigades in the country. A change of name was made to the Devon Fire and Rescue Service in 1987 to more accurately reflect the wide-ranging roles undertaken by the service as the dawn of the 21st century drew near.

Throughout its history the fire service in Bovey Tracey has been loyally served by generations of several families in the town, a tradition upheld to this day. Among the names that regularly feature are the Coombes, with four generations serving, including Albert from 1923 to 1946, his three sons, Roy, Leonard and Geoffrey, who served for 25, 31 and 30 years respectively, and Geoffrey's son, Clifford, who served from 1965 until 1999. In their time, apart from Albert, who was second in command when Leonard Mardon was first officer, they all became officers in charge of the station. The Harris family has seen three generations in the brigade, William joining in 1920, becoming the officer in charge, and serving for 37 years, his son, Les, and, currently, Les's son, Paul, who has thus far served since 1976. The Wills family, too, have served the town well, with Geoff, who retired in 1983 having given over 36 years service, and, currently, his two sons, Roy and Ian: Roy joined in 1974 and has been station commander since 1999 and Ian joined in 1976. John Lavis was from another well-known family. His grandson, Noel, followed in his footsteps and Noel's brother-in-law, Joe Small, served for more than 34 years until 2000. Similarly George Heale gave long service to the town, as did his son, Harold, until his retirement in the early 1970s. Another member of a well-known local family who has been in the service for over 24 years to date is Michael Steer.

Recruitment is becoming more difficult now. In the past most people lived and worked within the locality, but with a more mobile population nationwide there are difficulties in finding volunteers able to commit themselves to the life of a retained firefighter, able to respond from home or work to get the fire appliance on the road in under five minutes at any time of the day or night, every day of the year.

Firefighters have always had to face difficult and demanding conditions with enormous pressure on them to respond quickly to calls, today's five minute response from receipt of a call representing a vast difference from the days of the horse-drawn engine, when it often took up to 30 minutes before the team was ready to leave. At his retirement William Harris told many stories of fires he had dealt with, including one during the war. On that occasion he attended a farm fire at North Bovey when it was so cold that water from the hoses froze on the men's clothes, and when the water was turned off the hoses themselves became frozen solid, making it almost impossible for them to be rolled up. The men's clothes became so stiff with ice that they could barely move. Tragically, Mr Harris had seen his own home destroyed by fire in 1937, when a piece of burning paper from a bonfire had blown onto a thatched roof in the row of terraced cottages where he lived in Mary Street and resulted in four houses, including his, being burnt down.

On 18th September 1979 the fire station moved to Marlborough Terrace from its former site at the town hall, and remains a busy retained station, responding to more than 250 calls each year. Some of these still involve fire-fighting, now fraught with many more hazards than in the past due to the much-increased use of plastics, chemicals and other substances which can result in the release of toxic smoke when burnt. However, there has been a dramatic increase in calls for a variety of other reasons. These include attending the scene of road traffic accidents and leaks and spillages of substances and also providing assistance in the rescue of persons and animals from life-threatening situations, all of which today's firefighters have to be trained and prepared for. Past animal rescues have included recovering a dog from a mine shaft at Hennock, pulling cattle from slurry pits and boggy ground, rescuing horses from swimming pools, and, although not as frequent as one is led to believe, retrieving cats from trees. The area now covered by Bovey's crew extends from Stover on the Newton Abbot road to Lustleigh in a north/south direction and from Liverton/Haytor to Doddiscombsleigh in the Teign Valley and Haldon Hill on the A38 in an east/west direction.

Perhaps the worst fire in recent years, and certainly one of Devon's biggest moorland fires, was the blaze on Trendlebere Down. Here, because of the dry conditions and a changing wind direction, the fire moved at a frightening speed, with flames reaching 30 feet high, and, despite the attendance of more than 30 appliances from across the county, some 325 acres of heathland were lost.

Training and equipment continues to be regularly upgraded, and in May 2003 Bovey Tracey acquired a new Ford Ranger-based lightweight 4 x 4 fire appliance which carries enough equipment

220

and water to enable firefighters to tackle a fire until extra resources arrive, and was specially commissioned for use in Devon's narrow lanes. Access to properties along such lanes had been the cause of much concern to personnel in the past, and the value of the new appliance was realised only a day after coming into service when it was used to put out a car fire on a farm track in Ilsington.

Bovey Tracey Hospital
Information from The Bovey Tracey and District Hospital, published by
Morgan Laird & Co, and kindly lent by Hester Pickles

Bovey Tracey cottage hospital 'nobly projected and sustained' by Adela Divett, who lived at St Mary's, was originally sited in a property in Heathfield Terrace. In 1910, under the supervision of Miss Hoare, who remained as matron until the end of 1914, the hospital moved to Marlborough Terrace. It was only there a year when the landlord gave notice, so in 1911 it moved to Revelstoke in Mary Street. This site was not very satisfactory as the hospital only had six beds, and was situated on a noisy hill where vehicles changed gear and sounded their horns. A newspaper report at the time said, 'the need for a new hospital becomes increasingly urgent, largely due to the number of road traffic accidents'.

In the late 1920s a committee was formed to plan the building of a brand new purpose-built hospital, and set into motion the necessary fund-raising activities. Mrs Trelawney gave the building site, Mr A.A. Manning gave the land for widening the approach to the hospital, the Misses

Violet Wills laying the foundation stone of the new hospital in 1931, with Mrs Trelawney, Albert Coombes (the builder) behind and Mr S. Higgott (the architect) to the right (Herbert Norris & Son, courtesy of Victor Coombes)

Mackinnon held a fete at Colehayes, and generous donations were given by Dame Violet Wills, Mr and Mrs Dahl of Three Corners and many of the tradespeople of Bovey. A brick-buying scheme was also inaugurated. On 22nd October 1931 Dame Violet Wills laid the foundation stone for the single-storey building, and in May 1932 the doors were opened to patients.

Bovey Tracey's new hospital in 1932 (Steer & Ellis, courtesy of Hester Pickles)

The hospital, which cost just over £4,000, all raised by public subscription, was built by Coombes and Steer. The new building had a men's and women's ward, each with four beds 'with ample space for additional beds or cots in an emergency', two private wards, 'adequate accommodation for Matron and Staff', a kitchen, a scullery and a larder. The operating theatre was well equipped with the latest type of operating table, non-shadow electric lamp and sterilising apparatus, and there was an adjoining anaesthetising room. The surgeons were Dr Frank Arnott and Dr Jack Harrisson, and Miss Wakeford was the first matron.

The building was designed to give the maximum amount of air and light, with the wards on the sunny side, and with an outlook over the valley and moors which could 'not fail to be beneficial' to the patients.

Jane Arnott (now Lady Jane Hampton) remembers a summer just after she left school when she worked as a cook at the hospital. Often Miss Gunthorpe, the then matron and a woman with a big personality, came into the kitchen and helped her cook. It is difficult to imagine such a thing happening now.

Although the committee had raised enough money for the hospital to be built without debt, running it in pre-National Health days was always a problem, and it remained largely dependent on subscriptions and donations. From the early 1900s the hospital was supported by the annual hospital carnival and then, in the 1930s, Bill Blackmore of Dartmoor Dairy started the Spion Kop carnival, which was held in November. Joe Bezley, the local bank manager, was the honorary treasurer for many years and somehow, with his committee, managed to keep the hospital going.

In the early 1960s there was a threat to close the hospital, so in 1963 a special meeting was called, which drew one of the largest attendances ever to a meeting in Bovey. As a result, a strong Save the Hospital committee was set up. In 1964 the parish council reported that their efforts had been successful, and that the hospital had been saved for at least ten years. The committee was then wound up to be replaced by a League of Friends, who, every year since, has raised large sums of money to buy expensive pieces of equipment and other items to make the patients more comfortable. In 1990 they were able to contribute £20,000 to up-grade the hospital when storm damage to the building meant that much-needed improvements were brought forward.

Gas and Electricity

Early street lighting was first by gas, and then by a combination of gas and electricity. In 1881 a public meeting was called to discuss lighting the town by gas. A private company was formed and, by 1884, gas had been brought to Bovey, the gasworks being sited on the turning into the old Heathfield Road.

In 1910 the Dartmoor Electric Supply Company was formed with capital of £3,000, and the main generating station was sited at Mrs Hellier's mill, behind what is now the Dartmoor Garage. This new supply was not welcomed by everyone; in 1909 Mr Bentinck had requested that light should not be brought to Bovey Tracey by an overhead system. It was eventually agreed that the power wires should be put behind the houses so as not to be visible from the streets. When crossing roads, they were to be put underground.

Dartmoor Electric Supply Company's premises in 1912 (B.T. Heritage Trust)

During 1917 the very important point of lighting the public urinal was raised. The gas company agreed to do this for the sum of £9 as soon as permission had been received from the police. The Chief Constable gave his permission – provided 'rules and regulations as to shading were observed'.

In 1920 the gas company ceased to provide public lighting, and the last remaining gas standards in the town were taken down in 1924.

David Brealey remembers as a child in the 1930s living at the electric works – by now owned by the Teignmouth Electric Light Company – because his father, Bill, was in charge there and was needed 24 hours a day to keep the turbines going. They left in 1938 when Bovey was put onto the national grid.

Water

Long ago most people would have obtained their water supply from the River Bovey. Then the main supply of water came from Ashwell spring, which ran through the main street as an open leat. In the 1870s the first piped water was supplied in the form of standpipes at regular intervals throughout the town rather than to individual houses. In 1897 a resolution from the joint committees of the parishes of Bovey and Lustleigh resolved *to request the District Council to push forward the joint water scheme as soon as possible, looking at the grave need of a pure water supply for both parishes.*

The search was on for a new water source. Messrs Ferguson, Bovey, Bond and Beer walked over Southcott Moors above Becky Falls but came away with the impression that the cost of draining this area was considerable. They also visited Leighon but again decided there were too many owners to deal with, and contamination from various farms would be too great for it to be a viable proposition. Eventually it was agreed that the surveyor should be asked to 'prepare a scheme for a three months water supply for 1500 inhabitants at 20 gallons per head'.

Meanwhile, in the town, the water bailiff was asked to inspect all the taps to prevent water wastage. The owners of St Mary's were asked to disconnect the parochial water supply used for automatic flushing of the house sewers as the connection was made without permission.

After the summer in 1911 several of the houses at the higher levels only had water at intervals, and some had none at all for two days. Supplies were taken from the Pottery Leat, and the watercart went round with slop water from the river. Mr W.M.G. Singer of Leighon was approached again, but was unable to help as he did not have enough for his own needs. However, Sir Harry Eve of Yarner allowed water to be taken from the Pullabrook Leat at a cost of £1 per month to ease the situation.

On 12th January 1913 Sir Harry wrote that he was giving permission to sink trial pits and trenches at Yarner with a view to bolstering the town's water supply. The parish, at that time, had a population of 2,800 and extended to 7,567 acres. In 1915 the sum of £3,100 was sanctioned to carry out the Yarner scheme, but this was held up for the duration of the war 'owing to the state of the finances of the country'. In 1919 the RDC suggested that the Yarner work be put into operation as this would have the extra benefit of providing employment, but the parish council was very concerned about the cost, which was now three times the estimate of 1915. But then, in June of that year, the Trough Lane reservoir ran dry: the council was forced to give a mandate for the expense.

With the purchase of the permanent rights of the Pullabrook Stream and 9 acres of land, the council felt a 'most satisfactory result and quantity of water' had been achieved. The whole scheme ended with Bovey Tracey being 'as well supplied with water as any town of its size in the County'. There were still complaints, of course. One resident wrote complaining that he only had an intermittent supply, with sometimes no water all day, in spite of paying his water rents in advance. His only recourse was to take water from the Pottery Leat, 'which I should only do under the direst necessity'.

In 1925 the thorny problem of water rents was considered. Bovey Tracey Parish Council received a letter from Newton Abbot Rural District Council clearing up a specific point about the legality of a separate charge for water used for domestic baths.

… under the Waterworks Clauses Acts it has been held that the use of water for a bath is use of water for 'domestic purposes' and that therefore the Council are not entitled to make a separate charge for domestic baths. The charges for these baths should therefore be omitted from future Water Rents …

Once the reservoirs of Tottiford, Trenchford and Kennick had been opened water shortages were not a great problem until the drought of 1976, which was believed to be an exceptional event!

Brimley Post Office
by Stephanie Wills

Brimley Sub-Post Office was first established at 1 Shaptor View in 1931, in a lean-to built on the side of the house and with an entrance from the granite tramway. The sub-postmistress was Mrs Lamble, who was assisted by her daughter, Joan. It closed in 1939 when Joan became Mrs Chambers and moved away to Hampshire.

The post office then transferred to a purpose-built shed in the grounds of Hemerdon, in Brimley

The Bovey Tracey Post Office staff in 1905, when the post office was in Union Square. Louis Steer is on the right-hand end of the back row (Norah Davis)

Brimley Post Office in 1956 (Stephanie Wills)

Road, where it also sold, as the Shaptor View premises had, groceries, confectionery and tobacco. The sub-postmistress was Phyllis Blackmore until her marriage to Harold Dover in 1945.

Dorothy McKenney, who had fled from the clutches of the Germans in the Channel Islands with her daughter, Stephanie, became postmistress in January 1946. She stayed at this small office until 1954, when the present post office was constructed in Ashburton Road, near Ashburton Bridge, and opened on 20th September.

Stephanie married Geoffrey Wills in 1949 and took over from her mother in 1966 – at the same time as bringing up three sons – John, Roy and Ian. An extension was built on the front of the existing shop in 1987. With lots of support and help from Geoffrey, who also worked for Coombes and played an important part in the fire service, Stephanie continued as sub-postmistress until she retired in January 1994. Her son, Ian, has continued as sub-postmaster, with his wife, Marion, running the general store section of the business.

Tracey Almshouses

In 1910 the Tracey family donated five almshouses, four acres of land and some war stock in memory of Mrs A.M. Tracey, who had died in 1902, and her son, P.W. Tracey. The income from the land and the stock was to buy coal for the residents and carry out any maintenance necessary to the buildings. As the years went by this income became far too little to cope with rising costs, and by 1984 it became obvious that the condition of the buildings was a matter for serious concern. The five houses had become sub-standard accommodation, with no bathrooms and only a small, open-hearth fireplace to provide heating for the elderly residents.

In July 1989 the trustees sold Mannings Meadow to a consortium of builders who had planning permission for a housing estate. This provided sufficient money to refurbish the existing houses, which had already been listed for preservation, and to build three new dwellings. All were completed to a high standard. The income from the invested money, as well as providing free accommodation for Bovey residents, is also able to provide help for many local charities.

The Bovey Tracey Town Trust
by David Wedden

In 1883 the property of the 'Mayor and Freeholders of Bovey Tracey' was dissolved by the Municipal Corporation Act 1883, and in 1891 the Charity Commissioners put the Bovey Tracey Town Trust in charge of this property.

Minutes show that certain fields, namely Starpark (or Pound Field), Great Portrieve Park and Little Portrieve Park, in the parish provided part of the income from which the trust donated various amounts to the district council and to Bovey Tracey Parish Council towards the upkeep of the roads and pavements.

In 1894 it was resolved, in accordance with the Charity Commissioners, that the Bovey Tracey Town Trust be managed by the trustees and not by the parish council, that ' all chattels of the Town Trust be put up in the town hall for their preservation and protection', and that 'a donation of £20 towards equipping the fire brigade with new uniforms and appliances' was to be given.

In 1925 the Town Trust received a bequest under the Samuel Croker Will Trust to administer a sum of £1,600, of which £1,000 had to be used for the provision of almshouses. After consideration by the Charity Commissioners, permission was given to the proposal for the building of two almshouses; the trustees argued for three, and with the selling of Straypark (£765) raised sufficient funds for another house. Unity Builders submitted the lowest tender for the development of £1,000. The opening ceremony of Samuel Croker Almshouses was performed by Major Hole and took place on 7th July 1929. The first residents were Thomas Long, Samuel Prowse and George Pinsent.

Over the ensuing years the trustees continued to manage the affairs of the charities and supported the town with many donations towards its upkeep, including donations towards the firemen's uniforms and fire wagon/engine.

In 1987 the trustees received a letter from the Independent Broadcasting Company seeking permission to site an aerial on Little Portrieve Park, Trough Lane. This, along with the rental figure, was agreed unanimously. The mast was erected in 1989 and greatly improved the quality of television reception. Three years ago two more users were added, namely Vodafone and Airwaves, to the benefit of the trust.

The early 1990s saw the trust drawing on investments for the continuing heavy maintenance costs with, unfortunately, insufficient money available for

Samuel Croker Almshouses (Dave Wedden)

refurbishment. After much discussion the trustees decided to approach the Tracey Almshouse Trust to ask if they could help financially and, fortunately, the Charity Commissioners agreed that funds could be transferred to a like-for-like charity. The Tracey Almshouse Trust then granted them, in 1996, a considerable sum towards refurbishment. This enabled the almshouses to be modernised, with the fitting of double glazing throughout, the installation of gas central heating, the repainting of the exterior and the construction of a new footpath.

The Bovey Tracey Town Trust hopes that, from the renegotiated rent from the transmitter site, they can continue to support charitable organisations in the town.

Bovey Tracey Chamber of Trade
by Pat Tregoning

The Bovey Tracey Chamber of Trade was formed in 1967 after the demise of the 'come to South Devon Movement'. The first chairman was James Stagg, a local author who ran a small business with his wife in Fore Street. The membership was about 60 and consisted mainly of small shopkeepers, although there were some larger concerns such as Wyatt and Bruce, E. Bowden and Sons, Heltor Ltd, all three banks and most of the hotels. The annual subscription for firms with fewer than five employees was one guinea, for those with more than five and less than twenty-five two guineas, and for larger concerns five guineas. The main objective of the chamber was the promotion of the town for trade and as a tourist centre.

The first members' annual dinner was held at the Moorland Hotel, Haytor, on 27th November 1968, with dancing to the Sid Weeks Trio. The tickets cost £1 10s. each, but the event made a loss of £5.

The chamber produced the town guide and, in 1970, opened the information centre in the new car park. Elizabeth Hebditch offered her summerhouse as a temporary base, so Norman Broom had the task of dismantling this from the garden at Coombe Cross, transporting it through the town, and re-erecting it in the car park. The centre, run entirely by volunteers, sold books, guides and maps, and provided accommodation lists.

In 1971, with the town council's blessing, the chamber entered the Britain in Bloom competition and won a silver rose bowl for first in its class. Members also assisted the annual Bovey Tracey carnival by hanging the street bunting and organising the carnival fancy-dress dance, the shop window dressing and the misplaced article competitions. For many years, at Christmas, the chamber supplied, erected and fitted the lighting for the town Christmas tree, which was sited, first of all, at Parke View meadow and then, later, in Union Square.

In March 2001 the chamber was renamed Bovey Tracey and District Business Federation but, sadly, this did not save it, and in November of that year an extraordinary meeting was called and the federation was wound up.

The Ambulance Service
Information from George Harvey and Stephanie Wills

Bovey Tracey receiving its first ambulance on 6th March 1948. In the top right-hand corner the old town morgue can be seen (Stephanie Wills)

The money for Bovey's first ambulance was donated by Dame Violet Wills, and the service appears to have been run jointly by St John's and the Red Cross. Renee Clouting, of the Red Cross, was in charge of the nurses, and she asked Stephanie Wills to join the ambulance service as a volunteer. Stephanie had joined the Red Cross when she was aged 16 and learnt first aid and home nursing.

Stephanie remained with the service for 23 years, being paid 3/- an hour when she joined and the same sum when she left in the mid-1970s. The ambulance was kept in Moir and Davey's garage and volunteers drove it, organised by Jack Webber of the St John's Brigade. Amongst the drivers were Les Wyatt, Walt Kendal, Arthur Pritchard, Tom Donegan, Ron Brimblecombe, George Harvey and Edna Young.

The drivers and nurses had to do courses to keep them up-to-date, but there were still surprises when they were called out. During her time Stephanie remembers helping to deliver two babies in the ambulance. George Harvey remembers being called to Widecombe, where a landlord was trying to evict a tenant who had become mentally disturbed. The doctor and police were already there, but George was the one to coax the man to open the door. He was the first in, to be greeted with a shotgun pointed at him. In the mêlée that ensued to remove the shotgun, the doctor caught hold of George's leg to deliver a sedative, thinking he was the patient. Luckily, George stopped him in time! On another occasion a young man in Moretonhampstead had taken LSD and, thinking he could fly, had jumped out of an upstairs window. Amazingly, he fell into the back of a small pick-up truck below and was barely hurt, but he had to be tied to the stretcher to be taken to hospital. George did the shift between 6 p.m. and 6 a.m., and then went to work at Wyatt and Bruce's the next day.

In the mid-1970s the service was 'professionalised' and centred in Newton Abbot.

Some Events and Celebrations

Above: The hunt meeting outside The Dolphin in 1906 (Chapman & Son, courtesy of Dave Lewis)

Below: Bill Blackmore (dairyman) with Doris Martin (now Archer) in the early 1930s (Arthur Weeks)

People dressed for the carnival outside the Union Hotel in the 1930s (Dave Lewis)

Bovey carnival in the mid-1930s. Geoff Wills is the second child on the left (Geoff Wills)

Members of the carnival outside Brimicombe's shop (now The Fruit Shop) in the 1940s. Flo Netley and Kathleen Wills are in the centre of the photograph (Dave Lewis)

Every year from 1947 until the late 1950s Marie Goss wrote and produced pantomimes which were put on at Wickham Hall and in the outlying villages around Bovey. Cinderella was the first production. Back row, left to right: Betty Bates, Ursula Ellis, Stephanie McKenney (Wills), Audrey Lowry, Jean Carpenter (Luxton), Kathleen Brealey (Stone), Ena Vaudrey, Daphne Nevard, Marie Goss, Mary Godfrey, Pat Gardener (Coombes), Molly Bent, Margaret Cox and Brenda Gardener. Front row, left to right: Theresa Wyatt (Mann), Julienne Schneider, ?, ?, Doreen May (Radford), Jean Mellor (Cartwright) and Doris Kitkat (Stephanie Wills)

Mrs Daymond crowning Hester Waldron and Peter Caunter as carnival queen and prince in 1948 (or, possibly, 1949) in Wickham Hall. Jill Cox and Lionel Treeby are their attendants (Andy Waldron)

231

Bovey Band outing to Princetown in 1948 (Andy Waldron)

First-prize winners in the carnival of 1952. From left to right: Bert Maunder, Les Harris, Alec Small, John Small and Fred Coniam (Les Harris)

Coronation procession of children in 1953 (Dave Lewis)

Charlie Drake crowning the carnival queen, Valerie Doneghan, in 1962. Also in the photograph, from the left: Derek Hart, Diane Miller, Jackie Rae and Sylvia Morgan (Dave Lewis)

Church fete at Grey Gables in 1966. Standing, left to right: Mr Wallace, Brian Womble, Clive Ralph, Mike Steer, Mrs Hole, Les Smith and Major Hole (of Parke). Seated, left to right: Mr Johnson, Billy Endacott and ? (Courtesy of Judy Diss)

Above: The football club entry for the carnival of 1970. Back row, left to right: Ken Phillips, Les Westlake, Barry Coombes, Clifford Paddon, Alfie Harrison and Ted Butt. Front row, left to right: John Small, John Smith, Chris Carpenter, Derek Hart and Peter Reece (Joan & Derek Hart)

Below: 'Mod Cons'. Catering students from Coombe Cross Hotel win first prize in the 1970s (Elizabeth Hebditch)

Above left: A first-prize winning tableau in 1970. From the left: Christine Pedrick, Claire Pedrick and Kay Thompson (Christine Pedrick)

Above right: Violet Lewis wins first prize as Cleopatra in 1976 (Dave Lewis)

Above: The marriage of Prince Charles and Lady Diana Spencer being celebrated in Brimley in 1981 (Stephanie Wills)

Left: Princess Diana visited Bovey Tracey on 11th March 1983. Here Faye and George Gribble are being presented to her by Joan Rooke (chairman of Teignbridge District Council (Faye Gribble)

Adverse Weather

Bovey Tracey was particularly prone to flooding until the flood defence schemes were put in place. Although heavy snowfalls were less common, there were occasions when life was disrupted by snow. Nowadays, perhaps as a result of climate change, high winds are more of a hazard.

Floods in 1930 (Pat Tregoning)

Snow in Dolphin Square in the early part of the 20th century (Dave Lewis)

High winds blow trees over in St John's churchyard in 1987 (Mike Steer)

A Glimpse of Bovey in 2003/4
photography by Karen Lang

Index

Compiled by John Parnell

Black, James 191
Black, James Loveys 87, 191
Black, John 191
Black, John & Dinah 191
Black, Les 178
Blackmore, Mrs 124
Blackmore, Bill 222
Blackmore, Phyllis 226
Blackmore, Stan 130
Blake, Charles Davey 47
Blandford, R.S. (Captain) 168, 171
Bloomfield, Reverend 91
Bodkin, Miss 102
Bolland, Bim 185
Bolt, William 33
Bond, Mr 224
Bond, Frank 50
Bond, Peter 11
Bond, William 50
Booker, Tom & Joan 173
Bouck, Baron & Baroness 34, 98, 110
Bovey, Mr 224
Bowden, Arthur (Private) 31
Bowden, Bert 58
Bowden, Betty 58
Bowden, C. (Mr & Mrs) 32
Bowden, Derek 58
Bowden, Edwin 58
Bowden, Emmanuel 56, 58
Bowden, Flossie 58
Bowden, Henry 32, 58
Bowden, Herbert 58
Bowden, Louie 58
Bowden, Wilfred 30
Bowden, William 32, 58
Bowden, Yvonne 58
Boyce (family) 11
Boyce, William 29
Brealey, A. 124
Brealey, Betty 158
Brealey, Bill 223
Brealey, C. 12
Brealey, David 223
Brealey, Les 132
Brealey, Martin 158
Brealey, William 36, 159
Brett, Brian 177
Brimblecombe, Ron 228
Brooks, Richard 196
Broom, Anne 184, 185, 197
Broom, Norman 227
Brown (family) 193

Brown, Mr 104
Brown, Private 35
Brown, I. 157, 158, 184
Brown, James 157, 158, 183, 184
Browning, Angela 184
Bruce, Gordon 217
Bruce, James Scott 60
Bruce, Keith 60
Brunel 67
Budd, Christopher (Reverend) 83
Buller, Henrietta 171
Buller, Thomas Wentworth (Captain)
   47, 171
Buller, Wentworth William 47
Bunclarke, C. 126
Burgess, Roy
Burnett, Frank (Private) 28
Burnett, John 28
Butler, Frank 168
Butler, Joseph 173
Butt, Ted 165

C

Calchie, Delarose 131
Cambell, Misses 101
Cann, Mrs 158
Cann, John 25
Carpenter (family) 193
Carpenter, Mr 147, 148
Carpenter, Barbara (née Netley) 174
Carpenter, David 92
Carpenter, Robert 11
Carpenter, S. 89
Carroll, Stephen 214
Carter, John 167
Cartwright, Benjamin 183, 184
Carveth, Ian 177
Caunter (family) 193
Caunter, C. 126
Caunter, Michael 64, 171
Chadwick, Alan 114
Chadwick, Henry 114
Chadwick, Percival S. (Reverend) 114
Chamberlain, Mrs 82
Chambers, Joan (née Lamble) 224
Chapman, Chris 51
Chapman, J.C. (Dr) 135
Charles I 80
Christopher (family) 193
Chudleigh, Mr 15
Chudley, Francis 56, 62, 63

Devonport, Angela 83
Dewhurst, Peter & Tina 173
Diamond, Mr 30
Diana, Princess of Wales 203
Divett (family) 191
Divett, Miss 12
Divett, Adela 116, 221
Divett, Edward MP 87 116
Divett, John 47, 66, 116, 171
Donegan, Tom 228
Dover, Harold 226
Drake, Mr 89
Drake, Charlie 165
Duff, Sean & Meryl 168
Durston, Thomas 93
Duxbury, Reverend 11
Dymond (census) 15

E

Eden, Anthony 125
Edgecombe, Fred 107, 108
Edmonds, Grace 15
Edric 10
Edward VI 80, 215
Edward VII 148
Edward VIII 148, 150
Ehlers, Lily 195
Eisenhower, General 134
Elliot, Walter 136
Ellis (census) 15
Ellis, John 111
Ellis, William 24, 25, 46, 107
Elphick, Ronnie 177
Endacott, E. (Private) 35
Endacott, George 174
Evans, Mr 27
Evans, Jack 214
Evans, Leonard 214, 215
Evans, Mabel (née Ridgway) 214, 215
Evans, Nick 174
Eve, Harry Trelawney (Sir) 114, 214, 224
Eveleigh, Mrs 107
Eveleigh, Alice 109
Eveleigh, Nicholas 109

F

Fairfax, Thomas (Sir) 24
Fanshawe, Charles (Reverend) 105
Farnes, Florentina 201
Farnes, Kate 201

Farquarson, Catherine 196
Ferguson, Mr 224
Ferguson, Beatrice 113
Ferguson, G.W. (Second Lieutenant) 35
Ferguson, Henry Tanner 113
Ferguson, Mary 36
Fiddes, John 96
Findlay, Wallace 48
Fisher, Billy 11
Flood, Noah 13, 84
Foley, Charles (Father) 83
Forbes, James (Reverend) 80
Fortescue, Lord 145
Fowler, Charles 116
Fox, (family) 50
Fox, Frances 90
Fragel, Elizabeth 122
Frances Constance (Sister) 124
Freeman, P.D. 105
French (family) 193
French, Frank 163
French, Fred (Private) 31
Frenche, John 192
Frost (family) 193
Fry, Sydney 30

G

Gale (census) 15
Gale, Alfred & Stella 131
Gale, Bill 160
Gale, Christine 160
Gate, James 11
Gaton, Tony 155
Gay, Mrs 130
George V 148, 150, 155
George VI 126, 148, 155
George, Bishop of Coutance 108
Gibbs, Lewis 154
Gilberte, Edward 13
Gilberte, William 13
Gilley, Cyril 52
Gilley, Glenda 52
Gilley, J. (Mr & Mrs) 37
Gilley, John 37, 52
Gilley, William 52
Gilpin, Jean (née Harris) 160
Glanville, Betty 58
Glanville, Randolph 58
Godsland, Mr 148
Gooding, Mel 205
Goodwyn, Dr 27

Y

✳ ✳ ✳ ✳ ✳

List of Subscribers

Mr & Mrs M. Bailey	Orchard House, East Street, Bovey Tracey, Devon.
Mr & Mrs George C. Barclay	Whitstone House, Bovey Tracey, Devon.
Anthony E. Beard	Bittleford Parks, Widecombe-in-the-Moor, Devon.
Andy Billington	Bristol.
Anita Billington	Travanna, Bovey Tracey, Devon.
Jon Billington	Los Angeles, California, USA.
Bert & Betty Bowden	'Bywaters', Avenue Road, Bovey Tracey, Devon (*3 copies*).
Mr H. & Mrs Y. Bowden	'Erika', 2 Heatherdene, Bovey Tracey, Devon.
Mrs D. J. Brealey	33 Fore Street, Bovey Tracey, Devon.
Mr L. C. Brealey	Trevone, Newton Road, Bovey Tracey, Devon.
Brian E. Brett	3 Forge Place, Bovey Tracey, Devon.
Norman & Anne Broom	Xanadu, Bovey Tracey, Devon.
Jonathan & Holly Brown	39 Lahn Drive, Droitwich Spa, Worcs.
Mrs S. Caterer (née Stevens)	8 Eliot Road, The Chells, Stevenage, Herts.
Peter Caunter	Brahmbuschweg 1, 30900 Wedemark, Germany.
Eric William Clutton	Church Hill House, East Street, Bovey Tracey, Devon.
Geoff & Anne Coish	11 Kiln Road, Bovey Tracey, Devon.
Doris I. Collins	Bovey Tracey, Devon.
Patricia Collins	1 St John's Close, Bovey Tracey, Devon.
Mary Katarina Colver	32 Rendells Meadow, Bovey Tracey, Devon.
Mrs Audrey Conibear	Marwood House, Leyburn, N. Yorks.
Mr & Mrs F. M. Connor	Meadow Hayes, Avenue Road, Bovey Tracey, Devon.
Mr V. L. Coombes	8 Indio Road, Bovey Tracey, Devon.
John Courtiour	Bovey Tracey, Devon.
Sue & Barry Cross	
Steve & Jan Curd	6 Storrs Close, Bovey Tracey, Devon.
Mrs Norah Davis (née Steer)	Bovey Tracey, Devon.
Charles Dixon	Greenhill, Hennock, Bovey Tracey, Devon.
Margaret Drake	The Mews, South View, Bovey Tracey, Devon.
Tim & Kathy Dunce	Bucks Cottage, Bucks Lane, Bovey Tracey, Devon.
Mrs Sylvia Ellis	Summerleigh, Mary Street, Bovey Tracey, Devon.
Mr Graham Fice	19 Rosebank Crescent, Exeter, Devon.
John & Felicity Foulkes	Orchard Meadow House, Coombe Cross, Bovey Tracey, Devon.
Todd & Jim Fredericks	14 Mannings Meadow, Bovey Tracey, Devon.
Mrs C. Gale	April Cottage, 23 Coombe Close, Bovey Tracey, Devon.
Jennifer Garnsey (née Wyatt)	49 Lane Field Road, Bideford, Devon.
Dr P. G. Gill	Bovey Tracey, Devon.
Nigel & Ann Gillingham	Cranbrook, Moretonhampstead Road, Bovey Tracey, Devon.
Mr & Mrs H. Gilpin	Greystones, Burton Row, Brent Knoll, Highbridge, Somerset.
Felicity Guest	
Gordon Haigh	23 Wallfield Road, Bovey Tracey, Devon.

Stuart & Margery Hands	Bickington, Newton Abbot, Devon.
Mrs Brenda Harper	9 Mannings Meadow, Bovey Tracey, Devon.
Chris & Annie Harper	Brimley Lodge, Bovey Tracey, Devon.
Les Harris	14 Staddons View, Bovey Tracey, Devon.
Jean & Maurice Hart	11 Bullands Close, Bovey Tracey, Devon.
George & Eileen Harvey	Liverton, Devon.
Mr George Heale	4 Heath Hill, Heathfield, Newton Abbot, Devon.
Mr & Mrs S. Heale	Rainbows End, Pottery Close, Bovey Tracey, Devon.
Sherryl Healey	Bovey Tracey, Devon.
Susie Healey	Bovey Tracey, Devon.
Mr Francis Heath	22 Cromwell's Way, Bovey Tracey, Devon.
Dr Barry G. M. Helme	Wrafton House, Old Road, Liskeard, Cornwall (2 copies).
Andrea Herat	Bovey Tracey, Devon.
Mr & Mrs R. Heyward	9 Walnut Close, Exminster, Devon.
Guy & Frances Holding	Bovey Tracey, Devon.
Mr & Mrs R. W. Hubbard	23 Sett Close, Bovey Tracey, Devon.
Valerie Huish	Bovey Tracey, Devon.
David & Sheila Iley	41 Ashburton Road, Bovey Tracey, Devon.
K. J. Irving	Brooklands, Sigford, Devon.
Roy & Diane Jeeves	Bovey Tracey, Devon.
Tim & Ann Jenkinson	Liverton, Devon.
David R. W. Jervois	Lower Close, Chapple Road, Bovey Tracey, Devon.
Monica E. Jewson	4 Newbury Drive, Bovey Tracey, Devon.
Hannah L. Juniper	Bovey Tracey, Devon.
Mr & Mrs L. C. Knight	150 North Road, Invercargill, New Zealand.
Mike & Karen Lang	Woodstock, Liverton, Devon.
Louie & Noel Lavis	Newlands, Bovey Tracey, Devon.
Miss Sarah Anne Laws	Heathlands, Heatree Cross, Manaton, Devon.
Nick & Janie Lee	Uppincott Farm, Shobrooke, Crediton, Devon.
Dot & Chris Leete	New Park, Bovey Tracey, Devon.
John F. Lockley	
Mr & Mrs Richard Mann	
John & Anne Massey	Brynteg, Higher Bibbery, Bovey Tracey, Devon.
Mrs J. Miller (née Stevens)	11 Rosehill Gardens, Kingskerswell, Newton Abbot, Devon.
Mr David J. Moir	3 Blenheim Terrace, Bovey Tracey, Devon.
Mr John R. Moir	3 Blenheim Terrace, Bovey Tracey, Devon.
Mrs May Moir	3 Blenheim Terrace, Bovey Tracey, Devon.
Lilian Moore	Laurels Cottage, Hind Street, Bovey Tracey, Devon.
Vernon & Button Morgan	St Mary's Manor, Bovey Tracey, Devon.
J. Morris & P. Wright	Southbrook Court, Bovey Tracey, Devon.
Mrs B. Motz	7 Abbey Close, Bovey Tracey, Devon.
Walter Edward Mountford M.C.I.B.	Church Meadow, Coombe Cross, Bovey Tracey, Devon (2 copies).
Jacqueline & John Osmond	81 Churchfields Drive, Bovey Tracey, Devon.
Pearl Page (née Saunders)	60 De Lucy Avenue, Alresford, Hants.
John & Adina Parnell	Bovey Tracey, Devon.

Dr Laurence & Mrs Frances Pearce   Brookfield House, Challabrook Lane, Bovey Tracey, Devon.
Mrs Sheila Perigal
Mr & Mrs R. Pickford   Wyzes Patch, Bovey Tracey, Devon.
Mr J. D. Pike   Heathercombe, Manaton, Devon.
Professor John Porter
Kevin, Dawn, George &
  Anna Presland   Hind Street House, Bovey Tracey, Devon.

Greg Ramstedt   Utah, USA.
Rosemary Rawlins   Bovey Tracey, Devon.
Robert Rhys   Bovey Tracey, Devon.
Mrs Anne Roberts   23 Lakeside Close, New Park, Bovey Tracey, Devon.
Elayne Rowed (née Yendall)   Longways, Mary Street, Bovey Tracey, Devon.

Mr & Mrs J. Small   9 Storrs Close, Bovey Tracey, Devon.
Sylvia & Les Smith   Formerly of 'The Smithy', Brimley Road, Bovey Tracey, Devon.
David, Camilla & Emily Stanley
Jennifer Stanley
Dr & Mrs P. Stanley
Jo & Brian Steer   17 Brimley Park, Bovey Tracey, Devon.
Dr Michael Steer   Royal Institute for Deaf & Blind Children, Private Bag 29,
  Parramatta, NSW, Australia.
Lorraine & Bill Stocking   17 Rendells Meadow, Bovey Tracey, Devon.
Ann & Geoffrey Stone   Devon View, Higher Brimley, Bovey Tracey, Devon.

Peter Taylor   Bovey Tracey, Devon.
Mrs Glenda Thomson   3 Marlborough Terrace, Bovey Tracey, Devon.
Jackie, Abbie & Richard Tomlinson   4 Haymans Cottages, Liverton, Devon.
Joan & Derrick Towell   2 Haymans Cottages, Liverton, Devon.
Patrick Tregoning   6 Blenheim Terrace, Bovey Tracey, Devon.
Rev. Raymond C. Tucker   34 Hawker Close, Merley, Wimborne, Dorset.

Charles Upham   Langaller Farm, Bovey Tracey, Devon.
Hedley & Marion Upham   Gratner, Langaller Lane, Bovey Tracey, Devon.
Stewart & Gail Upham   Langaller Farm, Bovey Tracey, Devon.

Mrs Olive Vinnicombe   Newton Abbot, Devon.

Mr & Mrs K. Wakefield   Thomas' of Bovey, Bakers & Confectioners (2 copies).
Janice Wallace   Beal Farm House, Chudleigh Knighton, Devon.
Nick Walter   Chudleigh, Devon.
Mrs Carol Walters   18 Pottery Road, Bovey Tracey, Devon.
Mr & Mrs Aubrey Warren   Ingsdon View, Old Liverton Village, Newton Abbot, Devon.
Mrs D. Wearing (née Heale)   38 Priorslee Village, Telford, Shropshire.
Mr & Mrs John Westcott   12 Newlands Drive, Bovey Tracey, Devon.
Geoff & Steph Wills   'St Helier', Ashburton Road, Bovey Tracey, Devon (2 copies).
Ian, Marion, Shaun, Anthony &
  Stuart Wills   The Flat, Brimley Post Office, Bovey Tracey, Devon.
John Wills   3 Station Road, Bovey Tracey, Devon.
Mrs Patricia Wills (née Brealey)   63 Fore Street, Bovey Tracey, Devon.
Roy, Carole, Helen & Julie Wills   14 Storrs Close, Bovey Tracey, Devon.
Ms R. Wurtzburg   Old Whitstone, Bovey Tracey, Devon.